Colonel John Mann, Jr.

His Kith

His Kin

His Ancestors

His Descendants

Timothy A. Mann

HERITAGE BOOKS
2011

HERITAGE BOOKS

AN IMPRINT OF HERITAGE BOOKS, INC.

Books, CDs, and more—Worldwide

For our listing of thousands of titles see our website
at
www.HeritageBooks.com

Published 2011 by
HERITAGE BOOKS, INC.
Publishing Division
100 Railroad Ave. #104
Westminster, Maryland 21157

International Standard Book Numbers
Paperbound: 978-0-7884-5162-1
Clothbound: 978-0-7884-8748-4

Colonel John Mann Jr.

His kith, his kin,
his ancestors and descendants.

Timothy A. Mann

©1999, 2011

Preface

This book begins with what is known about our German ancestor. His is the first chapter, his son, the emigrant, is the second. Information compiled on the emigrant's children make the remaining chapters.

There is a complete index in the back of this book. Not all information in this book has been sourced, but unsourced information has been included for use as a possible research lead.

When researching the Virginia Mann families, take note that some researchers and local historians inadvertently mixed the English and German Mann families who lived within five miles of each other. The research in this book attempts to maintain the separation and is focused on the German Mann family.

Colonel John Mann Jr.   His kith and kin, his ancestors, his descendants.

Acknowledgments

This book represents not only my research, but is also a compilation of data from John and Rose Mann. Other researchers that generously shared their research include:

Phyllis Crick, Wally Garchow, Lucille Hartman, Phyllis Knouff, Pete Mann, Frank Oglesby, Larry Ross, and Nancy Stump.

Colonel John Mann Jr.   His kith and kin, his ancestors, his descendants.

Table of Contents

Colonel John Mann Jr.   His kith and kin, his ancestors, his descendants.

Dorsey Virgil Mann

Mary Jane Moyer Mann

Colonel John Mann served and trained under two of the nation's most famous "Indian fighters", Simon Kenton, and Benjamin Whiteman. He and his brother, Major Jacob Mann, were active in the Ohio Militia. They both served with distinction during the War of 1812. The Major led groups of sharpshooters on the frontier and remained in government service after the state had dismissed most men from duty. The Colonel led the Miami County Militia until he was appointed to higher command within the Ohio Militia.

The following is a timeline for the Mann brothers........

<u>1767</u>- John Mann Jr. is born to John and Susannah Mann.

<u>1791</u>- John Mann Sr. gives his consent for John Jr. to marry Fanny Williams.

<u>1791</u>- Isaac is born to John Jr. and Fanny.

<u>1793</u>- John marries Barbara Williams, Fanny's cousin.

<u>1794</u>- A son, George, is born to John and Barbara.

<u>1797</u>- John and Barbara's daughter Fanny is born in Virginia. John comes to Ohio with George Williams to locate a claim and plant corn for John's father-in-law, Michael Williams. They locate a claim on Mad River near Dayton. After this is achieved they return to bring their families back.

<u>1798</u>- They return in Autumn. They live near Dayton for a year, then move to Honey Creek in Elizabeth Township, Miami County, Ohio.

<u>1799</u>- Sergeant John Mann is listed in Virginia Militia records as "having removed to the Miami's." John and Jacob have now established themselves as early settlers in Elizabeth Township, in Miami County, Ohio.

<u>1801</u>- Their sister-in-law, Betsy Moyer Mann Harman, settles near by in Staunton Township.

<u>1801</u>- For much of his life Jacob is noted in Miami county as one of the highest class of hunters. According to Asa Coleman's reminisces, Jacob often made hunting his principal business.

<u>1801/09</u>- Jacob Mann surveys and maps out early roads in Miami County, Ohio.

<u>1803</u>- By April, their parents, John Sr. and Susannah, are living here with them, and have put their 500 acre farm in Virginia up for sale. John's sister, Elizabeth Battrell and her husband John, also come to live with them.

<u>1804</u>- John and Barbara return to Virginia to manage the sales of their families' lands. While they are in Virginia, their son Charles is born.

<u>1805</u>- In December, John Mann Sr. enters land in Cincinnati. The plot was Range 10, Township 2, Section 25, Part section 307.20 acres. His residence at time of entry is listed as Montgomery County, Ohio (now Miami County, Elizabeth Township). The land entry for John Mann Jr. was Range 9, Township 1. Section 6, Part section: North 1/2 and the South 1/2 fraction 216.16 acres. His residence at time of entry is listed as Montgomery County, Ohio (now Miami County, Bethel Township).

<u>1806</u>- John Mann becomes an Ensign in the Ohio Militia under General James Findlay. Later that year, he is promoted to the rank of Captain.

<u>1807</u>- Jacob serves as a Lieutenant in the Ohio Militia, in Miami County, Ohio.

<u>1808</u>- John Mann and his brother-in-law, John Battrell, are appointed guardians of John and Molly Mann, children of George and Betsy Moyer Mann Harman. (Probate Court Case #15.) The children stay originally with the Battrells, then later stay with John and Barbara Mann.

<u>1809</u>- John Mann is serving as a Major in the Montgomery County, Ohio Militia.

<u>1811</u>- John Mann is serving as a Major for the 2nd Regiment, 5th Brigade, 1st Division of the Ohio Militia.   Later that year, John Mann and Alexander Ewing are both promoted to the rank of Colonel for acts of valor.

<u>1812</u>- John Mann is Colonel over the Miami County Militia when the War of 1812 begins.

<u>1812/13</u>- Several companies of volunteers are organized, of which Jacob Mann was a Captain in the Miami County, Ohio Militia. Records show him as an Ensign, Captain, then Major, serving under his brother. It is recorded that during the war he participated in Harrison's campaign to free Fort Wayne. While spying out the land with Captain Logan, another scout, they came upon an ambush planned for Harrison, and when exchanging fire Jacob shoots the noted Pottawatomie chief, Metea, in the arm as he was attempting to hide behind a tree, rendering the arm useless for life.

<u>1813</u>- Later during the war, John becomes Colonel over the 1st Regiment, 2nd Brigade, 5th Division. His assigned rank is Field Colonel, which means he will lead troops in battle. The counties in this regiment are Montgomery, Preble, Miami, and Darke. Jacob becomes a Major and also serves in the 5th division.

<u>1814</u>- Jacob Mann marries Elizabeth Shell.

<u>1815</u>- Jacob becomes a Mason and charter member of Franklin Masonic Lodge in Miami County, Ohio. A son, James, is born to Jacob and Elizabeth.

<u>1816</u>- Major Jacob Mann is the Battalion Commander for Miami County. At this time, Miami County belongs to the 2nd Regiment, 2nd Brigade, 5th Division of the Ohio Militia.

<u>1817</u>- A daughter, Priscilla, is born to Jacob and Elizabeth.

<u>1818</u>- John and Elizabeth Battrell move to Delaware County, Indiana.

<u>1826</u>- George Mann, John and Barbara's son, dies leaving his widow, Margaret Pearson Mann, to raise their children Abel and Ruth.

<u>1826</u>- A daughter, Mary, is born to Jacob and Elizabeth.

<u>1827</u>- A son, Isaac, is born to Jacob and Elizabeth.

<u>1828</u>- Jacob Jr. is born to Jacob and Elizabeth.

<u>1828</u>- John Mann Jr. and Barbara Mann sell their farm in Miami County, Ohio and move to Loramie Township, in Shelby County, Ohio.   John becomes Director of School District #2 in Loramie Township, Shelby County, Ohio.

<u>1829</u>- Jacob Mann erects the first distillery of any magnitude in Miami County.

<u>1830</u>- A son, John, is born to Jacob and Elizabeth.

<u>1831</u>- Barbara, John's second wife dies.

<u>1832</u>- John Mann Jr. marries Rachael Berry.

<u>1833</u>- Henry, Jacob and Elizabeth's 5th son is born.

<u>1833</u>- John Mann Jr. dies in the latter part of May.   The Executors notice of Col. John Mann's death was placed in the Piqua Gazette, dated 13 July.

<u>1833</u>- After his death, his youngest daughter, Cynthiana, is born to his widow Rachael.

<u>1833</u>- Probate Court, Shelby County, Ohio. Estate package A78 is filed for John Mann. These records show no mention of his deceased son George. All other children are mentioned.

<u>1834</u>- The Estate Executor of Col. John Mann's estate files suit against John's widow, Rachael Berry Mann, seeking land to be sold to satisfy debts.

<u>1835</u>- Ruth and Abel Mann file suit against John and Barbara's youngest son, Charles. Charles had been entrusted by John Mann with provision for their father's share of inheritance.

<u>1836</u>- A daughter, Caroline, is born to Jacob and Elizabeth.

<u>1857</u>- On March 14, Jacob Mann dies.

<u>1858</u>- On March 15, Elizabeth, Jacob's wife dies.

Chapter 1

Hans Mann
our German Father

Colonel John Mann Jr. His kith, his kin, his ancestors, his descendants.

Our German Father

1. HANS[1] MANN. He was listed as a citizen of Siegelspach, Germany.

Children of HANS MANN are:

2.   i. GEORGE BERNARD (JERG BERNHART MOHN)[2] MANN, b. 1701, GERMANY; d. Aft. March 15, 1769, VIRGINIA.
     ii. CATRIN MANN.

Sources for this information are:
1. 1982 Yearbook of the Pennsylvania German Society, Box 97, Breinigsville, Pa. 18031
2. Eighteenth Century Emigrants from German-Speaking Lands to North America, Volume 1. The Northern Kraichgau, by Annette Kunselman Burgert. 1983.

Chapter 2

George Bernard Mann
our emigrant ancestor

Our Immigrant Ancestor

2. GEORGE BERNARD (JERG BERNHART MOHN)² MANN (HANS¹) was born 1701 in GERMANY, and died Aft. March 15, 1769 in VIRGINIA.

"September 21, 1732, George, his 2nd wife, Jacob, and George's sister Catrin arrived in Philadelphia Pa. on the Pink Plaisance, John Paret, Master. They came from Rotterdam, last from Cowes."

"May 1, 1744 George sold his land in Lancaster County Pa, and went to Virginia."

"April 17, 1749, Barnet Man purchased 320 acres lying between Shanadoah and the Peaked Mountain on Stony Run."

Other spellings of his name are George Barnet Man, George Bernhart Mohr, Jerg Bernhart Mohn, and Gorg Bernhart Mann.

He married (1) ANNA MARGRETHA GEISSER, daughter of Herr Christian Geisser, ("des Gerichts") September 14, 1723 in REIHEN, GERMANY. She died October 29ᵗʰ, 1730, aged 27years, nine months, 14 days. He married (2) MARIA ANNA MARGRETHA, 1731, in GERMANY. Maria died after 1768.

   Children of GEORGE MANN and ANNA GEISSER are:
3.   i.   (JOHN)JACOB³ MANN, b. December 03, 1724, GERMANY; d. Aft.
            1788, VIRGINIA.
     ii.   GEORGE BERNARD MANN, b. November 25, 1726, GERMANY; he did
            not come with his father to America, so we assume he died in
            Germany.
    iii.   MARIA MARGRETHA MANN, b. December 18, 1729, SINSHEIM,
            GERMANY; she did not come with her father to America, so we
            assume she died in Germany.

   Children of GEORGE MANN and MARIA are:
     iv.   ANNA MARIA³ MANN, b. February 09, 1732, SINSHEIM, GERMANY; she
            did not come to America with her father, so we assume she
            died in Germany.
4.   v.   GEORGE ADAM MANN, b. May 1, 1734, NEW HOLLAND, PENNSYLVANIA;
            Baptized May 5, 1734. d. 1821, GREENE COUNTY, OHIO.
5.   vi. CHARLES (GEORG CARL) MANN, b. August 06, 1735, NEW HOLLAND,
            PENNSYLVANIA; Baptized September 11, 1735.

Colonel John Mann Jr. His kith, his kin, his ancestors, his descendants.

6.   vii. GEORGE (CUNRADT) MANN, b. April 25, 1737, NEW HOLLAND,
           PENNSYLVANIA. Baptized May 29, 1737.
     viii. CATARINA MANN, b. May 06, 1739, NEW HOLLAND, PENNSYLVANIA.
           Baptized November 6, 1739.
7.   ix. CATARINA MANN, b. May 24, 1741, NEW HOLLAND, PENNSYLVANIA;
           Baptized June 21, 1741.
8.   x. JOHN SR. MANN, b. 1745, NEW HOLLAND, LANCASTER COUNTY,
           PENNSYLVANIA.

Sources for Chapter 2 are:

1. 1982 Yearbook of the Pennsylvania German Society Box97,
   Breinigsville, Pa. 18031.
2. Eighteenth Century Emigrants from German-Speaking Lands to North America,
   Volume 1. The Northern Kraichgau, by Annette Kunselman Burgert. 1983.
3. A Collection of Upwards of Thirty-Thousand Names of German, Swiss, Dutch,
   French, and other Emigrants in Pennsylvania from 1727 to 1776. By
   Professor I. D. Rupp. Reprinted 1975.
4. Records of Pastoral Acts at Trinity Evangelical Lutheran Church, New
   Holland, Lancaster County, Pennsylvania.
5. George Adam Mann 1734-1821, A Family on Four Frontiers. By Dorothy
   Knoff.
6. International Genealogical Society (IGS) Surname Index, 1992. By The
   Church of Jesus Christ Latter-Day Saints.

Chapter 3

Jacob Mann
and his descendants

Jacob Mann and his Descendants

1. (JOHN) JACOB[3] MANN *(GEORGE BERNARD (JERG BERNHART MOHN)[2], HANS[1])*
was born December 03, 1724 in GERMANY, and died Aft. 1788 in VIRGINIA.
He married BARBARA MILLER 1756 in AUGUSTA COUNTY, VIRGINIA, daughter of
JACOB MILLER and C. MUELLER.
"September 21, 1732, Jacob and his parents arrived in Philadelphia Pa.
on the Pink Plaisance, John Paret, Master. They came from Rotterdam,
last from Cowes."

   Children of JACOB MANN and BARBARA MILLER are:

2.   i.   JACOB[4] MANN, d. 1815.
3.   ii.   ADAM MANN, b. 1761.
        iii.   ELIZABETH MANN, b. 1762, AUGUSTA COUNTY, VIRGINIA; m.
               WILLIAM MADDRY, February 25, 1783, ROCKINGHAM/GREENBRIER
               COUNTY, VIRGINIA.
         iv.   MARY MANN, b. 1763; m. JAMES STEPHENS, December 16, 1784,
               ROCKINGHAM/GREENBRIER COUNTY, VIRGINIA.
          v.   PRISCILLA MANN, b. 1768; m. UNKNOWN, June 18, 1787.

Generation No. 2 of Jacob Mann

2.   JACOB⁴ MANN *(JACOB³, GEORGE BERNARD², HANS¹)* died 1815. He married MARY KESSINGER August 24, 1779 in GREENBRIER COUNTY, VIRGINIA, daughter of M. KESSINGER and C. TASSENS.

Children of JACOB MANN and MARY KESSINGER are:

4.   i.   MOSES⁵ MANN.
5.   ii.   JOHN MANN, b. 1770.
6.   iii.   ADAM MANN, b. 1771.
7.   iv.   JACOB MANN, b. 1780, MONROE COUNTY, VIRGINIA.
8.   v.   JAMES MANN, b. 1785, MONROE COUNTY, VIRGINIA; d. 1855.
9.   vi.   ISAAC MANN, b. 1787, MONROE COUNTY, VIRGINIA.
        vii.   MICHAEL MANN, b. 1793; m. CYNTHIA WALKER.
       viii.   SUSAN MANN, b. 1795, MONROE COUNTY, VIRGINIA; m. JOHN C. MADDY, 1828.

3.   ADAM⁴ MANN *(JACOB³, GEORGE BERNARD², HANS¹)* was born 1761. He married (1) MARY MADDY December 09, 1783 in ROCKINGHAM/GREENBRIER COUNTY, VIRGINIA. He married (2) POLLY FLINN May 03, 1790 in ROCKINGHAM/GREENBRIER COUNTY, VIRGINIA.

Children of ADAM MANN and MARY MADDY are:
         i.   WILLIAM⁵ MANN.
        ii.   ELIZABETH MANN, b. 1784; m. JOHN HALSTEAD, 1799.

Children of ADAM MANN and POLLY FLINN are:
10.   iii.   ADAM⁵ MANN.
        iv.   SARAH MANN, m. WILLIAM CUMMINGS, 1811.
11.   v.   HENRY MANN.
12.   vi.   JAMES MANN, d. 1835.
        vii.   JANE MANN, m. MR. HARVEY.
       viii.   JOSEPH MANN.
         ix.   CHLOE MANN, m. MR. GIBSON.
          x.   JOHN MANN.

Generation No. 3 of Jacob Mann

4. MOSES⁵ MANN *(JACOB⁴, JACOB³, GEORGE BERNARD², HANS¹)*. He married SARAH SWINNEY (2ND WIFE).

Children of MOSES MANN and SARAH SWINNEY are:
- i. ELIAS⁶ MANN, m. HARRIET BALLARD.
- ii. MALINDA MANN, m. HENRY HARVEY.
- iii. MARTHA MANN, m. WILSON GIBSON, 1845.
- iv. MARY J. MANN, m. ADAM GIBSON.
- v. DELILAH MANN, m. JOHN MCCORKLE.

5. JOHN⁵ MANN *(JACOB⁴, JACOB³, GEORGE BERNARD², HANS¹)* was born 1770. He married MILLIE HARVEY 1801.

Children of JOHN MANN and MILLIE HARVEY are:
- i. ALEXANDER⁶ MANN, m. (1) POLLY MILLER, 1810; m. (2) ISABELLA STEPHENSON, 1811.
- 13. ii. POLLY MANN.
- iii. WILLIAM MANN, b. 1805; m. SARAH HALSTEAD.
- iv. BLUFORD MANN, b. 1809; m. ELIZABETH MANN.

6. ADAM⁵ MANN *(JACOB⁴, JACOB³, GEORGE BERNARD², HANS¹)* was born 1771. He married (1) ELIZABETH YOUNG 1808. He married (2) NANCY HARVEY 1812.

Children of ADAM MANN and NANCY HARVEY are:
- i. SUSAN⁶ MANN, m. SAMUEL G. ELLISON, 1845.
- ii. JACOB MANN, m. SARAH DUNBAR.
- iii. ARCHIBALD MANN, m. ELIZABETH STEPHENSON, 1838.
- iv. JACK MANN.
- v. LUCY MANN, m. JOHN MILLER, 1844.
- vi. MILLIE MANN, m. JOHN CUMMINGS.
- vii. MARINDA MANN, m. MICHAEL HALE.
- viii. SARAH MANN, m. LORENZO HARVEY.
- ix. CYNTHIA MANN, m. GEORGE MILLER.
- x. AUSTIN MANN, m. SUSAN ELLISON, January 03, 1856.
- xi. LETHA MANN, m. HENRY SMITH.

7. JACOB⁵ MANN *(JACOB⁴, JACOB³, GEORGE BERNARD², HANS¹)* was born 1780 in MONROE COUNTY, VIRGINIA.   He married MILLIE BALLARD 1804.

Children of JACOB MANN and MILLIE BALLARD are:
    i.   ANNIE⁶ MANN, m. WILLIAM WISEMAN.
    ii. ELIZABETH MANN.
    iii. RHODA MANN.
    iv. MORRIS MANN, m. JANE STEPHENSON.
    v.   ELIZA MANN, m. ERVIN MILLER.
    vi. CELIA MANN, b. 1805; m. JOHN HOUCHINS.
    vii. SUSAN MANN, b. 1819; m. JAMES BALLARD.
    viii. GEORGE A. MANN, b. 1823; m. (1) LIZZIE CRINER; m. (2) EMILY A. HALSTEAD, 1845.

8. JAMES⁵ MANN *(JACOB⁴, JACOB³, GEORGE BERNARD², HANS¹)* was born 1785 in MONROE COUNTY, VIRGINIA, and died 1855.   He married (1) PARTHENA. He married (2) LUCY KEATON 1808.

Children of JAMES MANN and LUCY KEATON are:
    i.   WILLIAM⁶ MANN, m. JANE KEATON, 1840.
    ii. MARY MANN, m. JACKSON MANN.
    iii. FLOYD MANN, m. ELIZABETH WISEMAN, 1843.
    iv. EMILY MANN, m. THOMAS H. ALDERSON, 1840.
    v.   CYNTHIA MANN, b. 1809; m. JACKSON MADDY.
14. vi. HENDLEY MANN, b. 1810.
    vii. SQUIRE MANN, b. 1816; m. POLLY MANN.
    viii. ELI MANN, b. 1822; d. 1895; m. NANCY BALLARD.
    ix. MICHAEL MANN, b. 1824; d. 1864; m. CATHERINE RIFFE, 1845.
    x.   ANDREW MANN, b. 1826; d. 1899; m. RHODA HALSTEAD, 1851, MONROE COUNTY, WEST VIRGINIA.
    xi. WOODSON MANN, b. 1833; m. (1) NANCY MITCHELL; m. (2) MARY RAINES.

9. ISAAC[5] MANN (JACOB[4], JACOB[3], GEORGE BERNARD[2], HANS[1]) was born 1787 in MONROE COUNTY, VIRGINIA. He married LUCY STEPHENSON 1825.

 Children of ISAAC MANN and LUCY STEPHENSON are:
   i.   WARD[6] MANN.
15. *ii.*   HENRY GEORGE MANN.
16. *iii.*   BENJAMIN F. MANN.
   iv.   JOHN MANN, b. 1833; d. 1904; m. CYNTHIA KEATON.
   v.   MARY A. MANN, b. 1836; d. 1887; m. JAMES MOHLER.
   vi.   LEAH MANN, b. 1837; d. 1915; m. BALDWIN BALLARD.
   vii.   RACHAEL MANN, b. 1841; d. 1879; m. HUGH BALLARD.

10. ADAM[5] MANN (ADAM[4], JACOB[3], GEORGE BERNARD[2], HANS[1]). He married (1) POLLY MANN, daughter of JOHN MANN and MILLIE HARVEY. He married (2) ELIZABETH BARTON 1845.

 Children of ADAM MANN and POLLY MANN are:
   i.   JOHN[6] MANN.
   ii.   SAMSON MANN.
   iii.   RICIE MANN.
   iv.   RENIE MANN.

 Children of ADAM MANN and ELIZABETH BARTON are:
   v.   OVERTON[6] MANN.
   vi.   AMANDA MANN.
   vii.   ELIZA J. MANN.

11. HENRY[5] MANN (ADAM[4], JACOB[3], GEORGE BERNARD[2], HANS[1]). He married MALINDA SWINNEY 1829.

 Children of HENRY MANN and MALINDA SWINNEY are:
   i.   CHRISTOPHER[6] MANN.
   ii.   MARY A. MANN.

12. JAMES[5] MANN *(ADAM[4], JACOB[3], GEORGE BERNARD[2], HANS[1])* died 1835. He married NANCY W. HUMPHREYS.

Children of JAMES MANN and NANCY HUMPHREYS are:
     i.   ELIZABETH[6] MANN.
    ii.   POLLY MANN.
   iii.   CLARA MANN.
    iv.   MAHALA MANN.
     v.   CLEMENTINA MANN.
    vi.   JULIA A. MANN.
   vii.   LEWIS MANN.
  viii.   ALBERT MANN.
    ix.   GRANVILLE MANN.

Generation No. 4 of Jacob Mann

13. POLLY[6] MANN (JOHN[5], JACOB[4], JACOB[3], GEORGE BERNARD[2], HANS[1]). She married ADAM MANN, son of ADAM MANN and POLLY FLINN.

Children of POLLY MANN and ADAM MANN are:
- i. JOHN[7] MANN.
- ii. SAMSON MANN.
- iii. RICIE MANN.
- iv. RENIE MANN.

14. HENDLEY[6] MANN (JAMES[5], JACOB[4], JACOB[3], GEORGE BERNARD[2], HANS[1]) was born 1810. He married ELIZABETH BALLARD.

Child of HENDLEY MANN and ELIZABETH BALLARD is:
- i. ADDISON[7] MANN, b. 1846.

15. HENRY GEORGE[6] MANN (ISAAC[5], JACOB[4], JACOB[3], GEORGE BERNARD[2], HANS[1]). He married SARAH HARVEY.

Child of HENRY MANN and SARAH HARVEY is:
- i. ANNIE H.[7] MANN, b. 1878.

16. BENJAMIN F.[6] MANN (ISAAC[5], JACOB[4], JACOB[3], GEORGE BERNARD[2], HANS[1]). He married BELLE (ISABELLE) TOLBERT September 29, 1870.

Child of BENJAMIN MANN and BELLE TOLBERT is:
- i. ANNIE[7] MANN, b. 1874.

Colonel John Mann Jr. His kith, his kin, his ancestors, his descendants.

Sources for Chapter 3 are:

1. *1982 Yearbook of the Pennsylvania German Society*, Box 97, Breinigsville, Pa. 18031.
2. *Eighteenth Century Emigrants from German-Speaking Lands to North America, Volume 1. The Northern Kraichgau*, by Annette Kunselman Burgert. 1983.
3. *A Collection of Upwards of Thirty-Thousand Names of German, Swiss, Dutch, French, and other Emigrants in Pennsylvania from 1727 to 1776.* By Professor I.D. Rupp. Reprinted 1975.
4. *George Adam Mann 1734-1821, A Family on Four Frontiers.* By Dorothy Knoff.
5. *International Genealogical Society (IGS) Surname Index, 1992.* By The Church of Jesus Christ Latter-Day Saints.
6. *The History of Monroe County, West Virginia.* By Oren Morton-McClure Co. Inc.
7. *DAR Patriot Index, Centennial Edition Part 2.* Published by the National Society of the Daughters of the American Revolution Centennial Administration.
8. *Virginia Valley Records*, Wayland-Marriages performed by Rev. John Alderson Jr.
9. *Virginia Marriage Records.* By Genealogical Publishing Company.
10. *August 1993 Ancestor File* by the Church of Jesus Christ of Latter-Day Saints.

Chapter 4

George Adam Mann
and his descendants

Descendants of George Adam Mann

1. GEORGE ADAM[3] MANN *(GEORGE BERNARD (JERG BERNHART MOHN)[2], HANS[1])* was born May 1, 1734 in NEW HOLLAND, PENNSYLVANIA. He was baptized May 5, 1734. He died on May 4, 1821 in GREENE COUNTY, OHIO. His wife was MARIA ELIZABETH HERMAN, daughter of JACOB HARMON and CATHERINA. who was born October 22, 1742, in Lancaster County Pennsylvania. They married on December 07, 1762 in PEAKED MOIUNTAIN, VIRGINIA. She died on January 17, 1830. They are both buried in the New Burlington Cemetery, 5 miles south of Xenia, in Greene County, Ohio. When their son George was killed by British sympathizer, George Adam went back to Lancaster County, Pennsylvania and enlisted in the Militia.

Children of GEORGE MANN and MARIA HERMAN are:
- i. GEORGE[4] MANN, b. October 09, 1763, PEAKED MOUNTAIN, VIRGINIA; baptized December 5, 1763. d. 1781, THE REVOLUTIONARY WAR, killed by guerrilla fighters of British sympathy.
2. ii. JACOB MANN, b. March 11, 1764, PEAKED MOUNTAIN, VIRGINIA; d. October 1840, CLINTON COUNTY, OHIO.
- iii. MAGDALENE MANN, b. March 11, 1765, PEAKED MOUNTAIN, VIRGINIA. Baptized June 18, 1765.
3. iv. ELIZABETH MANN, b. 1769, PEAKED MOUNTAIN, VIRGINIA; d. 1819, GREENE COUNTY, OHIO.
4. v. JOHN SR. MANN, b. July 20, 1771, PEAKED MOUNTAIN, VIRGINIA; d. October 17, 1846.
5. vi. PETER MANN, b. 1773, PEAKED MOUNTAIN, VIRGINIA; d. February 06, 1852.
6. vii. HENRY MANN, b. February 04, 1779, PEAKED MOUNTAIN, VIRGINIA; d. February 04, 1858, CLINTON COUNTY, OHIO.
- viii. CHARLES MANN, b. March 01, 1782, PEAKED MOUNTAIN, VIRGINIA; d. December 24, 1865, GREENE COUNTY, OHIO; m. (1) LYDIA JENKINS, b 1786, d. April 5, 1838 in Greene County, Ohio; m. (2) ELIZABETH who was born in Maryland, in 1849.
7. ix. DAVID MANN, b. March 10, 1784, PEAKED MOUNTAIN, VIRGINIA; d. July 29, 1856, GREENE COUNTY, OHIO.

Generation No. 2 of George Adam Mann

2. JACOB⁴ MANN *(GEORGE ADAM³, GEORGE BERNARD (JERG BERNHART MOHN)²,* *HANS¹)* was born March 11, 1764 in PEAKED MOUNTAIN, VIRGINIA, and died October 1840 in CLINTON COUNTY, OHIO. He married CATHERINE MCDANIEL. CATHERINE was born in PITTSYLVANIA COUNTY, VIRGINIA. She died on FEBRUARY 8, 1837 in CLINTON COUNTY, OHIO. They are buried on their farm.

Children of JACOB MANN and CATHERINE MCDANIEL are:

   i.   GEORGE⁵ MANN, b. May 09, 1797, NICHOLAS COUNTY, KENTUCKY.
   ii. HENRY MANN, b. 1799, NICHOLAS COUNTY, KENTUCKY.
   iii. ELIZABETH MANN, b. 1801, NICHOLAS COUNTY, KENTUCKY.
   iv. JOHN MANN, b. 1803, NICHOLAS COUNTY, KENTUCKY.
   v.   MARY MANN, b. 1806, NICHOLAS COUNTY, KENTUCKY.
   vi. MARGARET MANN, b. 1808, NICHOLAS COUNTY, KENTUCKY.
   vii. RHODA MANN, b. 1810, NICHOLAS COUNTY, KENTUCKY; d. March 1882, OHIO.
   viii. MALINDA MANN, b. 1816, CLINTON COUNTY, OHIO.

3. ELIZABETH⁴ MANN *(GEORGE ADAM³, GEORGE BERNARD (JERG BERNHART MOHN)²,* *HANS¹)* was born 1769 in PEAKED MOUNTAIN, VIRGINIA, and died 1819 in GREENE COUNTY, OHIO. She married ADAM SHILLINGER 1786 in ROCKINGHAM COUNTY, VIRGINIA. He was born about 1763, and died August, 1825 in Greene County, Ohio. They are both buried in the New Burlington Cemetery, five miles south of XENIA, in GREENE COUNTY, OHIO.

Children of ELIZABETH MANN and ADAM SHILLINGER are:

   i.   ELIZABETH⁵ SHILLINGER, b. 1789; d. 1871; m. JOEL ELLIS, 1811, OHIO. JOEL was born 1788 and died in 1865.
   ii. JOHN GEORGE SHILLINGER, b. February 07, 1791, PEAKED MOUNTAIN, VIRGINIA, baptized June 7, 1792; d. September 26, 1813, OHIO.
   iii. REBECCA SHILLINGER, b. Abt. 1800, NICHOLAS COUNTY, KENTUCKY.

4. JOHN SR.⁴ MANN *(GEORGE ADAM³, GEORGE BERNARD (JERG BERNHART MOHN)²,* *HANS¹)* was born July 20, 1771 in PEAKED MOUNTAIN, VIRGINIA, baptized July 30, 1771, and died October 17, 1846. He married ELIZABETH JONES,

daughter of JOHN JONES and SARAH.   Elizabeth was born in 1793, and died
May 16, 1864.

Children of JOHN MANN and ELIZABETH JONES are:
- i.   ANNY[5] MANN, m. REUBEN HALL, June 19, 1821.
- ii.   LYDIA MANN, m. BENJAMIN TAYLOR, June 07, 1832, KENTUCKY.
- iii.   NANCY MANN, b. 1808, in NICHOLAS COUNTY, KENTUCKY; m.
        JAMES SHAW, b. 1811.
- iv.   POLLY MANN, b. Abt. 1795, NICHOLAS COUNTY, KENTUCKY; m.
        JACOB DEWITT, July 24, 1811, NICHOLAS COUNTY, KENTUCKY.
- 8.   v.   JACOB MANN, b. October 11, 1796, NICHOLAS COUNTY,
        KENTUCKY; d. December 02, 1871, CLINTON COUNTY, INDIANA.
- 9.   vi.   JOHN JR. MANN, b. Abt. 1804, NICHOLAS COUNTY, KENTUCKY.
- 10.   vii.   CHARLES MANN, b. March 25, 1808, NICHOLAS COUNTY,
        KENTUCKY; d. August 07, 1905.
- 11.   viii.   SARAH (SALLY) MANN, b. 1809, NICHOLAS COUNTY, KENTUCKY; d.
        1850.
- 12.   ix.   DAVID LEWIS MANN, b. February 12, 1811, NICHOLAS COUNTY,
        KENTUCKY; d. July 14, 1881.
- x.   SAMUEL MANN, b. 1816, NICHOLAS COUNTY, KENTUCKY.
- 13.   xi.   CATHERINE MANN, b. 1816, NICHOLAS COUNTY, KENTUCKY.

5.   PETER[4] MANN *(GEORGE ADAM[3], GEORGE BERNARD (JERG BERNHART MOHN)[2],*
HANS[1]) was born 1773 in PEAKED MOUNTAIN, VIRGINIA, and died February
06, 1852.   He married BARBERRY JONES 1800 in NICHOLAS COUNTY, KENTUCKY,
daughter of JACOB JONES and SUSIE EARLYWINE.

Children of PETER MANN and BARBERRY JONES are:
- 14.   i.   JACOB[5] MANN, b. NICHOLAS COUNTY, KENTUCKY.
- ii.   ELIZABETH MANN, b. NICHOLAS COUNTY, KENTUCKY; m. DAVID
        TRIMBLE, June 11, 1829.

- 15.   iii.   WILLIAM MANN, b. 1806.
- 16.   iv.   DAVID MANN, b. March 14, 1809, NICHOLAS COUNTY, KENTUCKY;
        d. August 09, 1888, NICHOLAS COUNTY, KENTUCKY.
- 17.   v.   AMOS MANN, b. March 05, 1811, NICHOLAS COUNTY, KENTUCKY;
        d. August 10, 1897, NICHOLAS COUNTY, KENTUCKY.
- 18.   vi.   EMANUEL MANN, b. 1815, NICHOLAS COUNTY, KENTUCKY.

6. HENRY[4] MANN *(GEORGE ADAM[3], GEORGE BERNARD (JERG BERNHART MOHN)[2],*
HANS[1]) was born February 04, 1779 in PEAKED MOUNTAIN, VIRGINIA, and

died February 04, 1858 in CLINTON COUNTY, OHIO. He married RACHAEL ARENA JOHNS March 14, 1805 in NICHOLAS COUNTY, KENTUCKY. Rachael was born June 17, 1785, and died March 15, 1862, in GREENE COUNTY, OHIO. They are buried in New Burlington Cemetery, in GREENE COUNTY, OHIO.

 Child of HENRY MANN and RACHAEL JOHNS is:
19. i. JOHN[5] MANN, b. 1810, OHIO.

7. *DAVID[4] MANN (GEORGE ADAM[3], GEORGE BERNARD (JERG BERNHART MOHN)[2], HANS[1]) was born March 10, 1784 in PEAKED MOUNTAIN, VIRGINIA, baptized June 6, 1784, and died July 29, 1856 in GREENE COUNTY, OHIO. He married RACHAEL IRVIN. Rachael was born in 1795, in KENTUCKY. She died in 1873, in GREENE COUNTY, OHIO. They are both buried in New Burlington Cemetery, in GREENE COUNTY, OHIO.*

 Children of DAVID MANN and RACHAEL IRVIN are:
  i. DAVID[5] MANN, b. 1818, GREENE COUNTY, OHIO.
  ii. JOHN MANN, b. 1826, GREENE COUNTY, OHIO.
  iii. SARAH MANN, b. 1828, GREENE COUNTY, OHIO.
  iv. HENRY MANN, b. 1831, GREENE COUNTY, OHIO.
  v. JOSEPH MANN, b. 1833, GREENE COUNTY, OHIO.

Generation No. 3 of George Adam Mann

8. JACOB[5] MANN (JOHN SR.[4], GEORGE ADAM[3], GEORGE BERNARD (JERG BERNHART MOHN)[2], HANS[1]) was born October 11, 1796 in NICHOLAS COUNTY, KENTUCKY, and died December 02, 1871 in CLINTON COUNTY, INDIANA. He married ELIZABETH EARLYWINE, who was born in 1803, on October 27, 1818 in NICHOLAS COUNTY, KENTUCKY, daughter of GEORGE EARLYWINE and MARY SNAPP (TRIGG). Jacob is buried in Baker Cemetery, in SCIRCLEVILLE, INDIANA.

Children of JACOB MANN and ELIZABETH EARLYWINE are:

	i.	SARAH A.[6] MANN, b. INDIANA; m. MR. TEVIS.
20.	ii.	GEORGE E. MANN, b. February 15, 1820, NICHOLAS COUNTY, KENTUCKY; d. May 25, 1902, CLINTON COUNTY, INDIANA.
21.	iii.	JOHN W. MANN, b. August 28, 1821, NICHOLAS COUNTY, KENTUCKY; d. August 03, 1896, MINNESOTA.
22.	iv.	EPHRIAM B. MANN, b. 1824, KENTUCKY; d. May 12, 1898, RUSH COUNTY, INDIANA.
23.	v.	WILLIS R. MANN, b. 1825, KENTUCKY; d. September 14, 1905, ROSCOMMON, MICHIGAN.
	vi.	MARY J. MANN, b. 1827, KENTUCKY; m. ALLEN W. BOYCE, March 17, 1850, CLINTON COUNTY, INDIANA.
24.	vii.	WILLAM HENRY MANN, b. January 20, 1830, KENTUCKY; d. June 20, 1908, DENT COUNTY, MISSOURI.
	viii.	ELIZABETH E. MANN, b. 1836, INDIANA; m. GEORGE W. MACHELAN.
	ix.	JACOB MANN, b. 1839, INDIANA; d. 1854, RUSH COUNTY, INDIANA. He is buried in the McCarter Cemetery, in RUSH COUNTY, INDIANA.

9. JOHN JR.[5] MANN (JOHN SR.[4], GEORGE ADAM[3], GEORGE BERNARD (JERG BERNHART MOHN)[2], HANS[1]) was born Abt. 1804 in NICHOLAS COUNTY, KENTUCKY. He married LUCINDA ELLISON (ALLISON) January 09, 1828 in KENTUCKY.

Children of JOHN MANN and LUCINDA ELLISON (ALLISON) are:

	i.	DRUSILA[6] MANN, b. NICHOLAS COUNTY, KENTUCKY.
	ii.	CHARLES MANN, b. NICHOLAS COUNTY, KENTUCKY.
	iii.	MARY A MANN, b. 1830, NICHOLAS COUNTY, KENTUCKY.
	iv.	KILLIAN MANN, b. 1833, NICHOLAS COUNTY, KENTUCKY.
	v.	MAHALA MANN, b. 1835, NICHOLAS COUNTY, KENTUCKY.
	vi.	MARTHA MANN, b. 1839, NICHOLAS COUNTY, KENTUCKY.
	vii.	GEORGE W. MANN, b. 1842, NICHOLAS COUNTY, KENTUCKY.

     viii. HENRY CLAY MANN, b. 1844, NICHOLAS COUNTY, KENTUCKY.
       ix. ELLEN MANN, b. 1846, NICHOLAS COUNTY, KENTUCKY.
        x. RHODA J. MANN, b. 1849, NICHOLAS COUNTY, KENTUCKY.

10. CHARLES⁵ MANN *(JOHN SR.⁴, GEORGE ADAM³, GEORGE BERNARD (JERG BERNHART MOHN)², HANS¹)* was born March 25, 1808 in NICHOLAS COUNTY, KENTUCKY, and died August 07, 1905. He married (1) POLLY AUSTIN 1833 in KENTUCKY. He married (2) KITURAH BUCHANNON (BISHOP) 1856 in NICHOLAS COUNTY, KENTUCKY.

   Children of CHARLES MANN and POLLY AUSTIN are:
       i. AMELIA A.⁶ MANN, b. 1834, NICHOLAS COUNTY, KENTUCKY.
      ii. ELIZA JANE MANN, b. 1835, NICHOLAS COUNTY, KENTUCKY.
     iii. SARAH MANN, b. 1836, NICHOLAS COUNTY, KENTUCKY.
      iv. MINOR MANN, b. 1840, NICHOLAS COUNTY, KENTUCKY.
       v. AUSTIN MANN, b. 1842, NICHOLAS COUNTY, KENTUCKY.
      vi. CHARLES MANN, b. 1844, NICHOLAS COUNTY, KENTUCKY.
     vii. CAROLINE MANN, b. 1846, NICHOLAS COUNTY, KENTUCKY.
    viii. HOLTON MANN, b. 1848, NICHOLAS COUNTY, KENTUCKY.

11. SARAH (SALLY)⁵ MANN *(JOHN SR.⁴, GEORGE ADAM³, GEORGE BERNARD (JERG BERNHART MOHN)², HANS¹)* was born 1809 in NICHOLAS COUNTY, KENTUCKY, and died 1850. She married DAVID GRAY ALLISON 1831.

   Children of SARAH MANN and DAVID ALLISON are:
       i. JOHN⁶ ALLISON, b. 1832, NICHOLAS COUNTY, KENTUCKY.
      ii. ANN E. ALLISON, b. 1834, NICHOLAS COUNTY, KENTUCKY.
     iii. MARGARET ALLISON, b. 1835, NICHOLAS COUNTY, KENTUCKY.
      iv. JACOB ALLISON, b. 1837, NICHOLAS COUNTY, KENTUCKY.
       v. SUSANNA ALLISON, b. 1838, NICHOLAS COUNTY, KENTUCKY.
      vi. ARMILDA ALLISON, b. 1840, NICHOLAS COUNTY, KENTUCKY.
     vii. SALLY A. ALLISON, b. 1842, NICHOLAS COUNTY, KENTUCKY.
    viii. MARY ALLISON, b. 1846, NICHOLAS COUNTY, KENTUCKY.
      ix. RACHAEL F. ALLISON, b. 1847, NICHOLAS COUNTY, KENTUCKY.
       x. LUCRETIA ALLISON, b. 1849, NICHOLAS COUNTY, KENTUCKY.

12. DAVID LEWIS⁵ MANN *(JOHN SR.⁴, GEORGE ADAM³, GEORGE BERNARD (JERG BERNHART MOHN)², HANS¹)* was born February 12, 1811 in NICHOLAS COUNTY, KENTUCKY, and died July 14, 1881. He married ARMILDA ALEXANDER¹ February 25, 1834, daughter of THOMAS ALEXANDER and HARRIET THOMSON.

Children of DAVID MANN and ARMILDA ALEXANDER are:

   i. ELIZABETH ANN[6] MANN, b. February 13, 1835, NICHOLAS COUNTY, KENTUCKY; d. July 31, 1839, NICHOLAS COUNTY, KENTUCKY.

25. ii. JOHN T. MANN, b. April 25, 1837, NICHOLAS COUNTY, KENTUCKY; d. January 24, 1882, DONIPHAN, KANSAS.

   iii. HARRIET JANE MANN, b. March 10, 1839, NICHOLAS COUNTY, KENTUCKY; m. GEORGE M. CAMPBELL, August 16, 1859.

26. iv. MARGARET ELEN MANN, b. December 10, 1840, NICHOLAS COUNTY, KENTUCKY.

27. v. SARAH EVALINE MANN, b. February 20, 1843, NICHOLAS COUNTY, KENTUCKY.

28. vi. MARY ANN MANN, b. March 26, 1845, NICHOLAS COUNTY, KENTUCKY.

29. vii. JAMES OLIVER MANN, b. April 09, 1847, KENTUCKY, NICHOLAS COUNTY, KENTUCKY; d. October 12, 1878, PARISH CHAPEL CEMETERY, NICHOLAS COUNTY, KENTUCKY.

30. viii. DAVID LEWIS JR. MANN, b. May 06, 1849, NICHOLAS COUNTY, KENTUCKY; d. February 15, 1922, ORLANDO, FLORIDA.

   ix. LAURY L. MANN, b. June 28, 1853, NICHOLAS COUNTY, KENTUCKY.

   x. WILLIAM BARTON CUNNINGHAM MANN, b. March 20, 1855, NICHOLAS COUNTY, KENTUCKY; d. October 27, 1860, NICHOLAS COUNTY, KENTUCKY.

   xi. REUBEN D. MANN, b. July 26, 1858, NICHOLAS COUNTY, KENTUCKY; m. MARY A. BARLOW, October 17, 1878.

13. CATHERINE[5] MANN (JOHN SR.[4], GEORGE ADAM[3], GEORGE BERNARD (JERG BERNHART MOHN)[2], HANS[1]) was born 1816 in NICHOLAS COUNTY, KENTUCKY. She married JAMES ALLISON June 10, 1833.

Children of CATHERINE MANN and JAMES ALLISON are:

   i. NATHANIEL[6] ALLISON, b. 1833, NICHOLAS COUNTY, KENTUCKY.

   ii. JOHN A. ALLISON, b. 1835, NICHOLAS COUNTY, KENTUCKY.

   iii. SALLY ALLISON, b. 1839, NICHOLAS COUNTY, KENTUCKY.

   iv. MARION ALLISON, b. 1840, NICHOLAS COUNTY, KENTUCKY.

   v. EMANUEL ALLISON, b. 1842, NICHOLAS COUNTY, KENTUCKY.

   vi. JAMES ALLISON, b. 1844, NICHOLAS COUNTY, KENTUCKY.

   vii. REUBEN ALLISON, b. 1846, NICHOLAS COUNTY, KENTUCKY.

   viii. MARY E. ALLISON, b. 1849, NICHOLAS COUNTY, KENTUCKY.

14. JACOB[5] MANN (PETER[4], GEORGE ADAM[3], GEORGE BERNARD (JERG BERNHART MOHN)[2], HANS[1]) was born in NICHOLAS COUNTY, KENTUCKY. He married (1)

ELIZABETH PEYTON February 09, 1826. He married (2) MARY PEYTON April 22, 1835 in NICHOLAS COUNTY, KENTUCKY.

   Children of JACOB MANN and ELIZABETH PEYTON are:
         i.   MAHATHLIN[6] MANN, m. JOHN BARNETT, August 03, 1841.
31.   ii. ELIAS MANN, b. 1829.

   Children of JACOB MANN and MARY PEYTON are:
         iii. MARY[6] MANN, b. NICHOLAS COUNTY, KENTUCKY; m. JOHN FORD.
         iv. DAVID MANN, b. 1832, NICHOLAS COUNTY, KENTUCKY.
         v.   CATHERINE MANN, b. 1835, NICHOLAS COUNTY, KENTUCKY.
         vi. ANGELINE MANN, b. 1837, NICHOLAS COUNTY, KENTUCKY; m. GEORGE W. HAWYER, 1859.

15.   WILLIAM[5] MANN (PETER[4], GEORGE ADAM[3], GEORGE BERNARD (JERG BERNHART MOHN)[2], HANS[1]) was born 1806. He married RACHAEL SPAHR March 18, 1830.

   Children of WILLIAM MANN and RACHAEL SPAHR are:
         i.   ELIZABETH[6] MANN, b. 1831, NICHOLAS COUNTY, KENTUCKY.
         ii. BARBARA J. MANN, b. 1833, NICHOLAS COUNTY, KENTUCKY.
         iii. WILLIAM H. MANN, b. 1840, NICHOLAS COUNTY, KENTUCKY.
         iv. DANIEL A. MANN, b. 1843, NICHOLAS COUNTY, KENTUCKY.
         v.   MARY E. MANN, b. 1846, NICHOLAS COUNTY, KENTUCKY.
         vi. THOMAS MANN, b. 1851, NICHOLAS COUNTY, KENTUCKY.

16.   DAVID[5] MANN (PETER[4], GEORGE ADAM[3], GEORGE BERNARD (JERG BERNHART MOHN)[2], HANS[1]) was born March 14, 1809 in NICHOLAS COUNTY, KENTUCKY, and died August 09, 1888 in NICHOLAS COUNTY, KENTUCKY. He married OLIVE STOKER January 26, 1832 in NICHOLAS COUNTY, KENTUCKY, daughter of EDWARD STOKER and ELIZABETH CURRANT.

   Children of DAVID MANN and OLIVE STOKER are:
         i.   PRESTON L.[6] MANN, b. 1835, NICHOLAS COUNTY, KENTUCKY.
         ii. MELVINA MANN, b. 1837, NICHOLAS COUNTY, KENTUCKY.
         iii. LUCIEN T. MANN, b. 1839, NICHOLAS COUNTY, KENTUCKY.
         iv. MARY A. MANN, b. 1845, NICHOLAS COUNTY, KENTUCKY.

17.   AMOS[5] MANN (PETER[4], GEORGE ADAM[3], GEORGE BERNARD (JERG BERNHART MOHN)[2], HANS[1]) was born March 05, 1811 in NICHOLAS COUNTY, KENTUCKY, and died August 10, 1897 in NICHOLAS COUNTY, KENTUCKY. He married ELLEN SPARKS.

Children of AMOS MANN and ELLEN SPARKS are:
    i.   ELIZABETH[6] MANN, b. 1833, NICHOLAS COUNTY, KENTUCKY.
   ii.   ELIZA MANN, b. 1835, NICHOLAS COUNTY, KENTUCKY.
  iii.   MADISON MANN, b. 1836, NICHOLAS COUNTY, KENTUCKY.
   iv.   SAMANTHA MANN, b. 1838, NICHOLAS COUNTY, KENTUCKY.
    v.   WILLIAM MANN, b. 1840, NICHOLAS COUNTY, KENTUCKY.
   vi.   EZIEKIEL MANN, b. 1842, NICHOLAS COUNTY, KENTUCKY.
  vii.   MILLY MANN, b. 1844, NICHOLAS COUNTY, KENTUCKY.
 viii.   RACHAEL MANN, b. 1846, NICHOLAS COUNTY, KENTUCKY.
   ix.   JOHN MANN, b. 1848, NICHOLAS COUNTY, KENTUCKY.
    x.   CHARLES MANN, b. 1851, NICHOLAS COUNTY, KENTUCKY.
   xi.   MARY MANN, b. 1853, NICHOLAS COUNTY, KENTUCKY.
  xii.   JEPTHA MANN, b. 1855, NICHOLAS COUNTY, KENTUCKY.
 xiii.   JAMES L. MANN, b. 1859, NICHOLAS COUNTY, KENTUCKY.

18.   EMANUEL[5] MANN (PETER[4], GEORGE ADAM[3], GEORGE BERNARD (JERG BERNHART MOHN)[2], HANS[1]) was born 1815 in NICHOLAS COUNTY, KENTUCKY. He married ELEANOR.

Children of EMANUEL MANN and ELEANOR are:
    i.   GRANVILLE[6] MANN, b. 1838, NICHOLAS COUNTY, KENTUCKY.
   ii.   GARRET MANN, b. 1838, NICHOLAS COUNTY, KENTUCKY.
  iii.   RUSSELL MANN, b. 1840, NICHOLAS COUNTY, KENTUCKY.
   iv.   CLIFTON MANN, b. 1842, NICHOLAS COUNTY, KENTUCKY.
    v.   LOUISA MANN, b. 1844, NICHOLAS COUNTY, KENTUCKY.
   vi.   AMANDA MANN, b. 1846, NICHOLAS COUNTY, KENTUCKY.
  vii.   MARY OLIVE MANN, b. 1848, NICHOLAS COUNTY, KENTUCKY.
 viii.   LUZERNE MANN, b. 1849, NICHOLAS COUNTY, KENTUCKY.

19.   JOHN[5] MANN (HENRY[4], GEORGE ADAM[3], GEORGE BERNARD (JERG BERNHART MOHN)[2], HANS[1]) was born 1810 in OHIO.

Child of JOHN MANN is:
    i.   FRANCIS[6] MANN, b. 1824, OHIO.

Generation No. 4 of George Adam Mann

20. GEORGE E.[6] MANN (JACOB[5], JOHN SR.[4], GEORGE ADAM[3], GEORGE BERNARD (JERG BERNHART MOHN)[2], HANS[1]) was born February 15, 1820 in NICHOLAS COUNTY, KENTUCKY, and died May 25, 1902 in CLINTON COUNTY, INDIANA. He married NANCY CLARK January 20, 1839 in RUSH COUNTY, INDIANA.

   Children of GEORGE MANN and NANCY CLARK are:

32.	i.	JOHN WESLEY[7] MANN, b. January 28, 1840, RUSH COUNTY, INDIANA; d. July 24, 1893, DALLAS COUNTY, MISSOURI.
	ii.	AUSTIN MANN, b. October 11, 1842; d. April 01, 1895.
33.	iii.	JACOB MANN, b. May 12, 1844; d. March 24, 1923.
34.	iv.	WILLIAM MANN, b. March 15, 1846, KENTUCKY; d. 1912, CLINTON COUNTY, INDIANA.
	v.	LYDIA J. MANN, b. May 29, 1848, INDIANA; d. October 22, 1859, INDIANA.
35.	vi.	DAVID MANN, b. August 16, 1850; d. April 15, 1919.
	vii.	MARTHA A. MANN, b. September 22, 1852.
	viii.	NANCY O. MANN, b. June 07, 1857; d. August 06, 1872.
	ix.	GEORGE W. MANN, b. October 05, 1858; d. November 01, 1876.
	x.	CHARLES M. MANN, b. February 14, 1859; d. November 09, 1888.
	xi.	ABRAHAM L. MANN, b. November 06, 1860; d. September 14, 1864.
	xii.	ALLEN M. MANN, b. January 31, 1863; d. April 29, 1938.
	xiii.	ARMILDA MANN, b. January 06, 1868.

21. JOHN W.[6] MANN (JACOB[5], JOHN SR.[4], GEORGE ADAM[3], GEORGE BERNARD (JERG BERNHART MOHN)[2], HANS[1]) was born August 28, 1821 in NICHOLAS COUNTY, KENTUCKY, and died August 03, 1896 in MINNESOTA. He married NANCY P. POWERS February 14, 1841 in CLINTON COUNTY, INDIANA.

   Children of JOHN MANN and NANCY POWERS are:

i.	JAMES M.[7] MANN, b. 1842, INDIANA; d. May 18, 1863, the Civil War..
ii.	JACOB W. MANN, b. 1844, INDIANA.
iii.	ANN E. MANN, b. 1846, INDIANA.
iv.	WILLIS O. MANN, b. 1847, INDIANA.

22. EPHRIAM B.[6] MANN (JACOB[5], JOHN SR.[4], GEORGE ADAM[3], GEORGE BERNARD (JERG BERNHART MOHN)[2], HANS[1]) was born 1824 in KENTUCKY, and died

May 12, 1898 in RUSH COUNTY, INDIANA. He married (1) MATILDA A. MORROW
February 25, 1847 in RUSH COUNTY, INDIANA. He married (2) MARY A.
BROWN November 16, 1852 in INDIANA.

Child of EPHRIAM MANN and MARY BROWN is:
  i. ARMILDA J.[7] MANN, m. MR. ELSTUN.

23. WILLIS R.[6] MANN *(JACOB[5], JOHN SR.[4], GEORGE ADAM[3], GEORGE BERNARD
(JERG BERNHART MOHN)[2], HANS[1])* was born 1825 in KENTUCKY, and died
September 14, 1905 in ROSCOMMON, MICHIGAN. He married ELIZA CONNER
BRISON February 08, 1849 in RUSH COUNTY, INDIANA.

Children of WILLIS MANN and ELIZA BRISON are:
  i. LEWIS A.[7] MANN, b. December 30, 1849, INDIANA.
  ii. CELESTIA A. MANN, b. July 07, 1852, INDIANA; m. MR.
    SHOCKLEY.
  iii. MORTON MANN, b. October 25, 1862, INDIANA.
  iv. EDGAR H. MANN, b. July 25, 1868, RUSH COUNTY, INDIANA.
  v. FRED E. MANN, b. February 29, 1872, INDIANA.

24. WILLAM HENRY[6] MANN *(JACOB[5], JOHN SR.[4], GEORGE ADAM[3], GEORGE BERNARD
(JERG BERNHART MOHN)[2], HANS[1])* was born January 20, 1830 in KENTUCKY,
and died June 20, 1908 in DENT COUNTY, MISSOURI. He married NANCY
ELIZABETH BROCKER February 10, 1851, daughter of ISAAC BROCKER and
MARY.

Children of WILLAM MANN and NANCY BROCKER are:
  i. OSCAR[7] MANN, d. INFANCY.
  ii. EPHRIAM B. MANN, b. July 18, 1852, INDIANA; d. infancy.
36. iii. JOHN WILLIAM MANN, b. July 28, 1854, INDIANA; d. December
    13, 1926, DENT COUNTY, MISSOURI.
37. iv. MARY ELIZABETH MANN, b. February 05, 1857, DENT COUNTY,
    MISSOURI; d. January 26, 1911, SEYMOUR, MISSOURI.
  v. JACOB MARION MANN, b. April 15, 1859, DENT COUNTY,
    MISSOURI; d. May 04, 1949; m. IDA MARIA HESSE, March 07,
    1897.
38. vi. JAMES PRICE MANN, b. October 18, 1861, DENT COUNTY,
    MISSOURI; d. April 30, 1936, LAS VEGAS, NEVADA.
39. vii. ANDREW JACKSON MANN, b. March 29, 1864, DENT COUNTY,
    MISSOURI; d. August 27, 1936, COFFEYVILLE, KANSAS.
  viii. ALONZO LEE MANN, b. September 28, 1867.

ix. LOUIS EDWARD MANN, b. August 18, 1870.

25. JOHN T.[6] MANN *(DAVID LEWIS[5], JOHN SR.[4], GEORGE ADAM[3], GEORGE BERNARD (JERG BERNHART MOHN)[2], HANS[1])* was born April 25, 1837 in NICHOLAS COUNTY, KENTUCKY, and died January 24, 1882 in DONIPHAN, KANSAS. He married MARY F. MILLER June 05, 1860.

Child of JOHN MANN and MARY MILLER is:
 i. GEORGE HENRY HANSON[7] MANN, b. September 16, 1862, DONIPHAN, KANSAS.

26. MARGARET ELEN[6] MANN *(DAVID LEWIS[5], JOHN SR.[4], GEORGE ADAM[3], GEORGE BERNARD (JERG BERNHART MOHN)[2], HANS[1])* was born December 10, 1840 in NICHOLAS COUNTY, KENTUCKY. She married JOHN CASSADAY March 10, 1859.

Children of MARGARET MANN and JOHN CASSADAY are:
 i. SARAH E.[7] CASSADAY, b. 1861, NICHOLAS COUNTY, KENTUCKY.
 ii. DAVID CASSADAY, b. 1863, NICHOLAS COUNTY, KENTUCKY.
 iii. WILLIAM CASSADAY, b. 1865, NICHOLAS COUNTY, KENTUCKY.
 iv. ORA B. CASSADAY, b. 1868, NICHOLAS COUNTY, KENTUCKY.

27. SARAH EVALINE[6] MANN *(DAVID LEWIS[5], JOHN SR.[4], GEORGE ADAM[3], GEORGE BERNARD (JERG BERNHART MOHN)[2], HANS[1])* was born February 20, 1843 in NICHOLAS COUNTY, KENTUCKY. She married BRICE W. HAM November 20, 1862 in KENTUCKY.

Children of SARAH MANN and BRICE HAM are:
 i. CARRIE[7] HAM, b. 1863, NICHOLAS COUNTY, KENTUCKY.
 ii. CHLOE HAM, b. 1864, NICHOLAS COUNTY, KENTUCKY.
 iii. JESSIE B. HAM, b. 1866, NICHOLAS COUNTY, KENTUCKY.
 iv. JAMES L. HAM, b. 1868, NICHOLAS COUNTY, KENTUCKY.

28. MARY ANN[6] MANN *(DAVID LEWIS[5], JOHN SR.[4], GEORGE ADAM[3], GEORGE BERNARD (JERG BERNHART MOHN)[2], HANS[1])* was born March 26, 1845 in NICHOLAS COUNTY, KENTUCKY. She married BENJAMIN L. ISHMAEL March 12, 1864 in BROWN COUNTY, OHIO.

Children of MARY MANN and BENJAMIN ISHMAEL are:
>   i.   OLIVER[7] ISHMAEL, b. April 06, 1865.
>   ii.   MILDRED ISHMAEL, b. May 19, 1867.
> iii.   ARMILDA ISHMAEL, b. May 19, 1867.
>   iv.   JOSEPHUS ISHMAEL, b. 1869.

29.   JAMES OLIVER[6] MANN *(DAVID LEWIS[5], JOHN SR.[4], GEORGE ADAM[3], GEORGE BERNARD (JERG BERNHART MOHN)[2], HANS[1])* was born April 09, 1847 in KENTUCKY, NICHOLAS COUNTY, KENTUCKY, and died October 12, 1878 in PARISH CHAPEL CEMETERY, NICHOLAS COUNTY, KENTUCKY. He married SARAH C..

Child of JAMES MANN and SARAH is:
>   i.   JOHN D.[7] MANN, b. 1868.

30.   DAVID LEWIS JR.[6] MANN *(DAVID LEWIS[5], JOHN SR.[4], GEORGE ADAM[3], GEORGE BERNARD (JERG BERNHART MOHN)[2], HANS[1])* was born May 06, 1849 in NICHOLAS COUNTY, KENTUCKY, and died February 15, 1922 in ORLANDO, FLORIDA. He married ELIZABETH CATHERINE CROSE June 18, 1868, daughter of GEORGE CROSE and REBECCA VAUGHN (WILSON).

Children of DAVID MANN and ELIZABETH CROSE are:
> 40.   i.   MARY (MISSOURI) BELLE[7] MANN, b. June 01, 1869, NICHOLAS COUNTY, KENTUCKY; d. August 02, 1959, PUNTA GORDA, FLORIDA.
>   ii.   VIRGINIA MANN, b. February 03, 1871, KENTUCKY; d. February 20, 1905, WINCHESTER, KENTUCKY; m. (1) ALBERT BLUME, January 31, 1889, BOURBON COUNTY, KENTUCKY; m. (2) W.D. SUTHERLAND, July 05, 1894, CLARK COUNTY, KENTUCKY; m. (3) HORACE LEE GILBERT, January 17, 1900, WINCHESTER, KENTUCKY.

31.   ELIAS[6] MANN *(JACOB[5], PETER[4], GEORGE ADAM[3], GEORGE BERNARD (JERG BERNHART MOHN)[2], HANS[1])* was born 1829. He married MARY BOWIE.

Child of ELIAS MANN and MARY BOWIE is:
>   i.   ROBERT MILTON[7] MANN, b. April 05, 1854, NICHOLAS COUNTY, KENTUCKY; d. August 27, 1938, NICHOLAS COUNTY, KENTUCKY; m. MARIAH WIGGINS.

Generation No. 5 of George Adam Mann

32. JOHN WESLEY[7] MANN (GEORGE E.[6], JACOB[5], JOHN SR.[4], GEORGE ADAM[3], GEORGE BERNARD (JERG BERNHART MOHN)[2], HANS[1]) was born January 28, 1840 in RUSH COUNTY, INDIANA, and died July 24, 1893 in DALLAS COUNTY, MISSOURI. He married MARY ELLEN KING August 16, 1860 in FRONKFORT, INDIANA.

Children of JOHN MANN and MARY KING are:
- i. NANCY J.[8] MANN, b. October 14, 1861, FRANKFORT, INDIANA; d. September 06, 1883; m. MATTHEW GREEN, 1877.
- ii. GEORGE T. MANN, b. February 18, 1866, FRANKFORT, INDIANA; d. July 20, 1956, OKLAHOMA.
- iii. DULCINA MARGARET MANN, b. November 18, 1867, PANAMA, OKLAHOMA; d. Aft. 1927; m. GEORGE ROWAN.
- iv. ORENA B. MANN, b. June 26, 1869, FRANKFORT, INDIANA; d. February 02, 1870.
- v. JACOB S. MANN, b. February 03, 1871; d. 1941, OKLAHOMA.
- vi. WILLIS AUSTIN MANN, b. December 02, 1872, FRANKFORT, INDIANA; d. July 12, 1953, POLK COUNTY, MISSOURI; m. ESTELLA ETHEL STILES, July 19, 1899, BOLIVAR, MISSOURI.
- vii. JOSEPH M. MANN, b. October 12, 1874.
- viii. JOHN LEWIS MANN, b. September 04, 1876, MISSOURI; d. Aft. 1953, ROGERS, ARKANSAS.
- ix. DAVID MANN, b. January 06, 1879, ALDRICH, MISSOURI; d. LEFLORE, OKLAHOMA.
- x. MARY IDA MANN, b. July 18, 1881, ALDRICH, MISSOURI; d. MIAMI, OKLAHOMA; m. MR. SIMMONS.
- xi. BABY BOY MANN, b. November 27, 1883.

33. JACOB[7] MANN (GEORGE E.[6], JACOB[5], JOHN SR.[4], GEORGE ADAM[3], GEORGE BERNARD (JERG BERNHART MOHN)[2], HANS[1]) was born May 12, 1844, and died March 24, 1923. He married HARRIET L. MOORE.

Children of JACOB MANN and HARRIET MOORE are:
- i. MARIA T.[8] MANN, b. 1868, INDIANA.
- ii. LOUISA E. MANN, b. 1871, INDIANA.
- iii. MARY D. MANN, b. 1873, INDIANA.
- iv. NANCY A. MANN, b. 1874, INDIANA.
- v. LOUISA J. MANN, b. 1877, INDIANA.
- vi. ARTHUR A. MANN, b. 1879, INDIANA.

34. WILLIAM[7] MANN *(GEORGE E.[6], JACOB[5], JOHN SR.[4], GEORGE ADAM[3], GEORGE BERNARD (JERG BERNHART MOHN)[2], HANS[1])* was born March 15, 1846 in KENTUCKY, and died 1912 in CLINTON COUNTY, INDIANA.   He married SUSAN.

Children of WILLIAM MANN and SUSAN are:
   i.   ROSA[8] MANN, b. 1871, INDIANA.
   ii.   ROBERT MANN, b. 1875, INDIANA.
   iii.   MINNIE MANN, b. 1879, INDIANA.
   iv.   EMMA MANN, b. 1879, INDIANA.

35. DAVID[7] MANN *(GEORGE E.[6], JACOB[5], JOHN SR.[4], GEORGE ADAM[3], GEORGE BERNARD (JERG BERNHART MOHN)[2], HANS[1])* was born August 16, 1850, and died April 15, 1919.   He married ELIZABETH J.

Children of DAVID MANN and ELIZABETH are:
   i.   SARE IDA O.[8] MANN, b. 1872, INDIANA.
   ii.   PHOEBE C. MANN, b. 1874, INDIANA.
   iii.   GEORGIA MANN, b. 1876, INDIANA.
   iv.   MARY M. MANN, b. 1878, INDIANA.

36. JOHN WILLIAM[7] MANN *(WILLAM HENRY[6], JACOB[5], JOHN SR.[4], GEORGE ADAM[3], GEORGE BERNARD (JERG BERNHART MOHN)[2], HANS[1])* was born July 28, 1854 in INDIANA, and died December 13, 1926 in DENT COUNTY, MISSOURI.   He married (1) JOSIE WARFEL.   He married (2) MATILDA LAVINA CANNON January 20, 1886 in DENT COUNTY, MISSOURI, daughter of ISAAC CANNON and CATHERINE WARD.

Children of JOHN MANN and MATILDA CANNON are:
   i.   BERTHA JAUNITA[8] MANN, b. December 15, 1887, INDIANA.
   ii.   LENOX SULTIER MANN, b. June 21, 1889, INDIANA.
   iii.   ELLA EUNICE MANN, b. October 24, 1892, INDIANA.

37. MARY ELIZABETH[7] MANN *(WILLAM HENRY[6], JACOB[5], JOHN SR.[4], GEORGE ADAM[3], GEORGE BERNARD (JERG BERNHART MOHN)[2], HANS[1])* was born February 05, 1857 in DENT COUNTY, MISSOURI, and died January 26, 1911 in SEYMOUR, MISSOURI.   She married JOSEPH HUNT 1875 in MISSOURI.

Children of MARY MANN and JOSEPH HUNT are:
    i.   CHARLES[8] HUNT.
   ii.   WILLIAM HUNT.
  iii.   MINNIE HUNT.
   iv.   LENOX HUNT.
    v.   JERRY HUNT.
   vi.   ELIZABETH HUNT.
  vii.   JOHN E. HUNT, b. April 03, 1878.

38. JAMES PRICE[7] MANN (WILLAM HENRY[6], JACOB[5], JOHN SR.[4], GEORGE ADAM[3], GEORGE BERNARD (JERG BERNHART MOHN)[2], HANS[1]) was born October 18, 1861 in DENT COUNTY, MISSOURI, and died April 30, 1936 in LAS VEGAS, NEVADA. He married (1) ELLA KNIGHT. He married (2) SALLIE MUNDANIA WELCH January 04, 1885 in SALEM, MISSOURI, daughter of ISOM WELCH and MARTHA HAYES.

Children of JAMES MANN and SALLIE WELCH are:
    i.   BABY[8] MANN.
   ii.   EMMA DAISY MAY MANN, b. November 22, 1885.
  iii.   ESTELLA LEE MANN, b. May 01, 1887.
   iv.   JERRY CLARENCE MANN, b. March 13, 1889.
    v.   LILLIAN TENNESSEE MANN, b. August 05, 1891.
   vi.   LACIE RODENSIA MANN, b. March 03, 1893.
  vii.   JULIA EATHEL MANN, b. April 19, 1894.
 viii.   WILLIAM PERRY MANN, b. August 02, 1895, SALEM, MISSOURI;
         d. November 05, 1918, WWI.

39. ANDREW JACKSON[7] MANN (WILLAM HENRY[6], JACOB[5], JOHN SR.[4], GEORGE ADAM[3], GEORGE BERNARD (JERG BERNHART MOHN)[2], HANS[1]) was born March 29, 1864 in DENT COUNTY, MISSOURI, and died August 27, 1936 in COFFEYVILLE, KANSAS. He married CORA ALICE LEONARD January 02, 1896 in SALEM, MISSOURI, daughter of JEFFERSON LEONARD and SARAH GIBBS.

Children of ANDREW MANN and CORA LEONARD are:
    i.   WILLIAM BRYAN[8] MANN, b. October 05, 1896.
   ii.   FRANK JEFFERSON MANN, b. March 23, 1899.
  iii.   CLIFFORD HERMAN MANN, b. March 24, 1901.
   iv.   ARLA LOGAN MANN, b. June 03, 1904.
    v.   EMIL RAYMOND MANN, b. May 31, 1907.

40.   MARY (MISSOURI) BELLE[7] MANN *(DAVID LEWIS JR.[6], DAVID LEWIS[5], JOHN SR.[4], GEORGE ADAM[3], GEORGE BERNARD (JERG BERNHART MOHN)[2], HANS[1])* was born June 01, 1869 in NICHOLAS COUNTY, KENTUCKY, and died August 02, 1959 in PUNTA GORDA, FLORIDA. She married WILLIAM ANDREW COOPER August 26, 1890 in BEATTYVILLE, KENTUCKY.

     Children of MARY MANN and WILLIAM COOPER are:
41.   i.   WILLIAM MOSS[8] COOPER, b. June 07, 1891, FLOYDSVILLE,
               KENTUCKY; d. July 23, 1930, ST. PETERSBURG, FLORIDA.
          ii. ELIZABETH BLUME COOPER, b. September 27, 1892, FORT
               THOMAS, KENTUCKY; m. (1) JOHN ALLEN CRENSHAW, August 09,
               1921, ORLANDO, FLORIDA; m. (2) HARRY COOPER, November 21,
               1930, FLORIDA.
42.   iii. MARY LOUISE COOPER, b. February 05, 1895, COVINGTON,
               KENTUCKY.
43.   iv. EDWARD DODD COOPER, b. January 22, 1897, CORINTH,
               KENTUCKY; d. October 24, 1970, WAYNESVILLE, NORTH
               CAROLINA.
44.   v.   DOROTHY COOPER, b. December 01, 1903, RICHMOND, VIRGINIA.

Generation No. 6 of George Adam Mann

41. WILLIAM MOSS[8] COOPER (MARY (MISSOURI) BELLE[7] MANN, DAVID LEWIS JR.[6], DAVID LEWIS[5], JOHN SR.[4], GEORGE ADAM[3], GEORGE BERNARD (JERG BERNHART MOHN)[2], HANS[1]) was born June 07, 1891 in FLOYDSVILLE, KENTUCKY, and died July 23, 1930 in ST. PETERSBURG, FLORIDA. He married LOTTIE MAE WALLACE April 05, 1917 in RICHMOND, VIRGINIA, daughter of WILLIAM WALLACE and ALBERTA POWELL (HARRIS).

>   Child of WILLIAM COOPER and LOTTIE WALLACE is:
>   i.   AUDREY ALBERTA[9] COOPER, b. January 23, 1918, RICHMOND, VIRGINIA.

42. MARY LOUISE[8] COOPER (MARY (MISSOURI) BELLE[7] MANN, DAVID LEWIS JR.[6], DAVID LEWIS[5], JOHN SR.[4], GEORGE ADAM[3], GEORGE BERNARD (JERG BERNHART MOHN)[2], HANS[1]) was born February 05, 1895 in COVINGTON, KENTUCKY. She married KELLY SR. BRUCE DAY June 24, 1924 in GAINESVILLE, FLORIDA, son of JOHN DAY and MARGARET MCLIN (DAY).

>   Child of MARY COOPER and KELLY DAY is:
>   i.   KELLY JR. BRUCE[9] DAY, b. September 13, 1926, ORLANDO, FLORIDA.

43. EDWARD DODD[8] COOPER (MARY (MISSOURI) BELLE[7] MANN, DAVID LEWIS JR.[6], DAVID LEWIS[5], JOHN SR.[4], GEORGE ADAM[3], GEORGE BERNARD (JERG BERNHART MOHN)[2], HANS[1]) was born January 22, 1897 in CORINTH, KENTUCKY, and died October 24, 1970 in WAYNESVILLE, NORTH CAROLINA. He married LILLIAN RUTH LEY April 17, 1919 in TAMPA, FLORIDA, daughter of REV. LEY and MARY ROUX.

>   Children of EDWARD COOPER and LILLIAN LEY are:
>   i.   RUTH LEY[9] COOPER, b. May 04, 1920, TAMPA, FLORIDA.
>   ii. MARY BELL COOPER, b. May 04, 1920, TAMPA, FLORIDA; d. May 08, 1920, TAMPA, FLORIDA.
>   iii. MARY VIRGINIA COOPER, b. July 04, 1921, TAMPA, FLORIDA.

44. DOROTHY[8] COOPER (MARY (MISSOURI) BELLE[7] MANN, DAVID LEWIS JR.[6], DAVID LEWIS[5], JOHN SR.[4], GEORGE ADAM[3], GEORGE BERNARD (JERG BERNHART MOHN)[2], HANS[1]) was born December 01, 1903 in RICHMOND, VIRGINIA. She

married GERALD E. KNOFF September 01, 1931 in WINTER HAVEN, FLORIDA, son of FRANK KNOFF and WINNIE THAYER.

Children of DOROTHY COOPER and GERALD KNOFF are:
    i.   ELIZABETH ANN[9] KNOFF, b. June 21, 1935, MERIDAN, CONNETICUT.
   ii.   WILLIAM COOPER KNOFF, b. February 23, 1940, CEDAR FALLS, IOWA.
  iii.   SARA LOUISE KNOFF, b. February 09, 1942, CEDAR FALLS, IOWA.

Colonel John Mann Jr. His kith, his kin, his ancestors, his descendants.

Sources for chapter 4 are:

1. Records of Pastoral Acts at Trinity Evangelical Lutheran Church, New Holland, Lancaster County, Pennsylvania.
2. George Adam Mann, 1734-1821, A Family on Four Frontiers. By Dorothy Knoff.
3. International Genealogical Society (IGS) Surname Index, 1992. By the Church of Jesus Christ Latter-Day Saints.
4. Pennsylvania Archives, 5th Series, Vol. 7.
5. Official Roster of Soldiers of the American Revolution Buried in Ohio.

Chapter 5

George Carl Mann and his descendants

Descendants of CHARLES (GEORG CARL) MANN

1. CHARLES (GEORG CARL)[3] MANN *(GEORGE BERNARD (JERG BERNHART MOHN)[2], HANS[1])* was born August 06, 1735 in NEW HOLLAND, PENNSYLVANIA. He married ANNA MARIA (MARY).

Sources for chapter 5 are:

1. George Adam Mann, 1734-1821, A Family on Four Frontiers. By Dorothy Knoff.
2. International Genealogical Society (IGS) Surname Index, 1992. By the Church of Jesus Christ Latter-Day Saints.

Chapter 6

<u>George Cunradt Mann and his descendants</u>

Descendants of George Cunradt Mann

1. GEORGE (CUNRADT)[3] MANN   (GEORGE BERNARD (JERG BERNHART MOHN)[2], HANS[1])
   was born April 25, 1737 in NEW HOLLAND, PENNSYLVANIA. He married
   Maria.

   Children of GEORGE MANN and MARIA are:
     i. GEORGE CONRAD[4] MANN, b. March 03, 1763.
        December 25, 1763, Baptized at St. Matthew's Lutheran Church
        in York County, Pennsylvania

     ii. DAVID MANN, b. July 08, 1766.
        August 20, 1766, Baptized at St. Matthew's Lutheran Church in
        York County, Pennsylvania

    iii. JOHN GEORGE MANN, b. August 21, 1768.
     iv. JOHN MANN, b. August 16, 1771.

Sources for chapter 6 are:

1. George Adam Mann, 1734-1821, A Family on Four Frontiers. By Dorothy
   Knoff.
2. International Genealogical Society (IGS) Surname Index, 1992. By
   the Church of Jesus Christ Latter-Day Saints.

Chapter 7

Catrina Mann
and her descendants

The Family of Catrina Mann

1. PETER (HANCE)[2] HERMAN (JACOB[1] HARMON) was born 1733 in GERMANY. He married (1) MARGARET CHOULYN. He married (2) CATARINA MANN May 15, 1764, daughter of GEORGE MANN and MARIA.

   Children of PETER HERMAN and MARGARET CHOULYN are:
   i.   PHILIPPINA[3] HERMAN, b. PEAKED MOUNTAIN, VIRGINIA.
   ii. GEORGE CHARLES HERMAN, b. December 11, 1761, PEAKED MOUNTAIN, VIRGINIA.
   iii. ELIZABETH HERMAN, b. May 06, 1763, PEAKED MOUNTAIN, VIRGINIA.

Sources for chapter 7 are:

1. George Adam Mann, 1734-1821, A Family on Four Frontiers. By Dorothy Knoff.
2. International Genealogical Society (IGS) Surname Index, 1992. By the Church of Jesus Christ Latter-Day Saints.

Chapter 8

John Mann Sr.
and his descendants

Descendants of John Mann Sr.

1.   JOHN SR.[3] MANN   *(GEORGE BERNARD (JERG BERNHART MOHN)*[2]*, HANS*[1]*)* was born 1745 in NEW HOLLAND, LANCASTER COUNTY, PENNSYLVANIA.   He married SUSANNAH PRICE about 1765. Susannah, born May 9, 1750, was the daughter of Augustine Price and Anna Elizabeth Scherp.   She was baptized on August 15, 1753 at Peaked Mountain Church in Virginia. (Augustine, born 1722, was the son of David Preisch and Anna Margareth Preisch, who emigrated from Germany in 1738).

John Mann Sr. owned land on Sinking Creek, and the south side of Johns Creek Mountain and Salt Mountain, at New River, in what is now West Virginia.   On September first, 1801, he appointed his son-in-law Andrew Hatfield as agent to sell land on Sinking Creek, adjacent to Parker Adkins, David Price, and Robert Hunter, in Montgomery County, Virginia.

   Children of JOHN MANN and SUSANNAH PRICE are:
2.   i.   ELIZABETH[4] MANN.
3.   ii.   GEORGE MANN, d. WALKERS CREEK, WEST VIRGINIA.
4.   iii.   COL. JOHN JR. MANN, b. Abt. 1767, VIRGINIA; d. 1833, CYNTHIAN TOWNSHIP, SHELBY COUNTY, OHIO (NEAR NEWPORT).
      iv.   MARY MANN, b. 1769; m. ANDREW HATFIELD JR, March 24, 1798, MONTGOMERY COUNTY, VIRGINIA.   His parents were Andrew Sr, (1737-1813) and Christina Powell (1737-1809).
5.   v.   JACOB MANN, b. September 06, 1788, VIRGINIA; d. March 14, 1857, MIAMI COUNTY, OHIO.

Generation No. 2 of John Mann Sr.

2. ELIZABETH⁴ MANN *(JOHN SR.³, GEORGE BERNARD², HANS¹)*. She married JOHN BATTREL
February 02, 1791 in MONTGOMERY COUNTY, VIRGINIA. In 1803, Elizabeth and John came
to Ohio and lived with her brother Col. John Mann, Jr. In 1808 John Mann and his
brother-in-law John
Battrell were appointed guardians of John and Molly Mann, children
of George, John's deceased brother and Betsy Moyer Mann Harman.
(Probate Court Case #15.) The children stayed originally with the
Battrells, but when they moved west in 1818, stayed with John and
Barbara Mann.

   Children of ELIZABETH MANN and JOHN BATTREL are:
       i.   ELIZABETH⁵ BATTREL, m. DAVID KITE, February 18, 1827, MIAMI COUNTY, OHIO.
6.   ii.   WILLIAM BATTREL, b. 1791, VIRGINIA; d. 1857, DELAWARE COUNTY, INDIANA.
      iii.   JOHN W. BATTREL, b. 1793, VIRGINIA; d. June 27, 1845, DELAWARE COUNTY,
             INDIANA; m. LYDIA WILSON, August 15, 1845, DELAWARE COUNTY, INDIANA.
      iv.   MARY BATTREL, b. 1795, VIRGINIA; m. WILLIAM MERRITT, August 20, 1814, MIAMI
             COUNTY, OHIO.
       v.   ANDREW BATTREL, b. 1799, VIRGINIA; m. DARINDA THOMAS, June 28, 1823, MIAMI
             COUNTY, OHIO.
      vi.   JACOB BATTREL, b. August 23, 1810, OHIO; d. April 03, 1872, DELAWARE
             COUNTY, INDIANA; m. PRISCILLA SIMONTON, August 07, 1831, MIAMI COUNTY,
             OHIO.
      vii.   JOSEPH L. BATTREL, b. 1812; m. MALINDA SWAILS, January 17, 1833, OHIO.
      viii. SUSANNAH BATTREL, b. 1818.

3. GEORGE⁴ MANN *(JOHN SR.³, GEORGE BERNARD², HANS¹)* died in WALKERS CREEK, WEST
VIRGINIA. He married ELIZABETH (BETSY) MOYER August 25, 1790 in MONTGOMERY COUNTY,
VIRGINIA.

   Children of GEORGE MANN and ELIZABETH MOYER are:
       i.   JOHN⁵ MANN. John served as a Private in the War of 1812.
       ii. MOLLY MANN.

Biographical Notes for George Mann.
The Story of George Mann

In the reminisces of Asa Coleman, found in 1834-5 editions of the Troy Times, an early physician of Miami County, Ohio, an interesting story is found concerning George Mann, John and Jacob's brother. The story as it is given:

"John Mann, Jacob Mann, Peter Harman. John Mann was Colonel of the Miami County Militia at the commencement of the War of 1812, Jacob commanded a company of riflemen for some time in the government service on the frontier during the same war.-There was another brother of the Mann's killed by the Indians, and his widow married Peter Harman. The three families came to this county from western Virginia, and settled near each other in Staunton and Elizabeth Townships. The circumstances of George Mann's death, I think worthy of notice. They have been related to me by family members as follows,... The Mann's lived on Walkers Creek, a branch of New River, near Walkers Mountain, West Virginia. George Mann's family consisted of a wife and two children, one infant, the other some three years of age. George, in the spring of 1791 or 2, moved up the creek from the station they had wintered, a mile or two, to a cabin and clearing, to cultivate a crop of corn.-They felt safe as to Indians, as there had been no depredations from them for some time. They had not been there many days when, at night, from the barking of his dogs, he suspected there might be some persons wanting to steal his horses. He stepped outside his cabin, into the dark, towards his stable, and a few rods from the cabin, was set upon by Indians, tomahawked and scalped. He not returning, his wife, suspecting some mischief, barred the door. In a short time the Indians approached the door and demanded admittance.- She, knowing by their voices who were at hand, kept the cabin dark, and the door as secure as her means permitted. They commenced forcing an entrance, and were at the point of succeeding, having the door partly open, when she took a rifle and placing it in the dark, against the breast of the foremost Indian, fired. The Indian fell back and no further attempt was made to enter. After remaining a short time, with one child in her arms, and the other led by the hand, stepped from the door, and escaped to a woody thicket near by, where she remained till daylight, not thinking it safe to attempt an alarm or further escape that night, from the dread scene.   The agony of the brave woman, during the night, can better be imagined than described.   Upon returning to the scene, there was the remains of her dead husband and two dead Indians.   The shot she had fired had killed two savages, who had happened to be standing one directly behind the other while forcing an entrance.   This woman afterwards married Peter Harman, and came to Miami County in 1801 or 2.-   The writer was well acquainted with the family, and the story of her killing the two Indians with one shot, he often heard repeated."

4.   COLONEL JOHN JR.[4] MANN *(JOHN SR.[3], GEORGE BERNARD[2], HANS[1])* was born About. 1767 in VIRGINIA, and died 1833 in CYNTHIAN TOWNSHIP, SHELBY COUNTY, OHIO (NEAR NEWPORT). He married (1) FANNY WILLIAMS April 06, 1791 in MONTGOMERY COUNTY, VIRGINIA, daughter of GEORGE WILLIAMS. He married (2) BARBARA WILLAMS October 23, 1793 in MONTGOMERY COUNTY, VIRGINIA, daughter of MICHAEL WILLIAMS and BARBARA SUMMA. He married (3) RACHAEL BERRY September 23, 1832 in SHELBY COUNTY, OHIO.

Biographical Notes for Colonel John Mann Jr.

The patriarch of the Miami Valley Mann family was Colonel John Mann Jr. He was born about 1767. He and his brother Jacob settled in what became Miami County, Ohio in the late 1790's.

1791, John Mann Sr. gives his consent for John to marry Fanny Williams.

Also in 1791, his son Isaac is born.

1793, John marries Barbara Williams, Fanny's cousin. We assume Fanny died, possibly in childbirth.

1797, John comes with George Williams to locate a claim, and plant corn for John's father-in-law, Michael Williams. They locate a claim on Mad River near Dayton. After this is achieved they return to bring their families back. They return in the fall of 1798. They live near Dayton for a year, then move to Honey Creek, in Elizabeth Township, Miami County, Ohio.

1799, Sergeant John Mann is listed in Virginia Militia records as "having removed to the Miami's." John and Jacob have established themselves as early settlers in Elizabeth Township, in Miami County, Ohio.

1801, Their sister-in-law Betsy Moyer Mann Harman, settles near by in Staunton Township.

1803, By April, their parents, John Sr. and Susannah are living here with them, having sold their 500 acre farm in Virginia. John's sister, Elizabeth Battrell, and her husband John, also come to live with them.

1804, John is serving as a Captain under General Gano, in the Montgomery County Ohio Militia.

1805, In December, John Mann enters land in Cincinnati. The first plot was Range 10, Township 2, Section 25, Part of section 307.20 acres. Residence at time of Entry was Montgomery County, Ohio.(now Miami County, Elizabeth Township The second land entry was Range 9, Township 1. Section 6, Part of section: North ½ and the South ½ fraction 216.16

acres. His residence at time of Entry was Montgomery County, Ohio.(now Miami County, Bethel Township).

1808, John Mann and his brother-in-law John Battrell were appointed guardians of John and Molly Mann, children of George, John's deceased brother and Betsy Moyer Mann Harman. (Probate Court Case #15.) The children stay originally with the Battrells, but when they move west, stay with John and Barbara Mann.

1809, John Mann is serving as a Major in the Montgomery County Ohio Militia.

1812, John Mann is serving of Colonel of the Miami County Militia at the commencement of the War of 1812. (It is likely that he became a Colonel in 1811.) Later during the war, in 1813, when 5000 men are drafted from the state, John becomes Colonel over the 1st Regiment, 2nd Brigade, 5th Division. This 5th division was formed specifically to manage the increase of men on active duty. The counties in this regiment are Montgomery, Preble, Miami, and Darke.

1818, John and Elizabeth Battrell move to Delaware County, Indiana.

1826, George Mann, John and Barbara's son dies, leaving his widow, Margaret Pearson Mann to raise their children Able and Ruth.

1828, John Mann Jr. and Barbara Mann sell their farm in Miami County, Ohio and move to Loramie Township, in Shelby County, Ohio.

1829, John Mann Jr. is listed as Director of School District #2 in Loramie Township.

The 1830 census shows the John Mann household as:

Male	Female
1 10-15 years.	1 50-60 years.
1 10-20 years.	
1 60-70 years.	

1830-1831, Barbara, John's second wife dies.

1832, John Mann Jr. marries Rachael Berry.

1833, John Mann Jr. dies in the latter part of June.

1833, The Executors notice of Col. John Mann's death was placed in the Piqua Gazette, dated 13 July, 1833.

<u>1833</u>, After his death, his youngest daughter, Cynthiana is born to his widow Rachael.

<u>1833</u>, Probate Court, Shelby County, Ohio. Estate package A78 is filed for John Mann. These records show no mention of his deceased son George. All other children are mentioned.

<u>1834</u> The Estate Executor of Col. John Mann's estate files suit against John's widow Rachael Berry Mann seeking land to be sold to satisfy debts.

<u>1835</u>, Ruth and Able Mann file suit against John and Barbara's youngest son, Charles. Charles had been entrusted by John Mann with provision for their father's share of inheritance.

Child of COLONEL JOHN MANN and FANNY WILLIAMS *is:*

7.   i. ISAAC[5] MANN. b. March 24. 1791, VIRGINIA; d. August 28, 1860, ORAN, OHIO.

Children of COLONEL JOHN MANN and BARBARA WILLAMS *are:*

8.   ii. GEORGE[5] MANN, b. VIRGINIA; d. 1826, MIAMI COUNTY, OHIO.
     iii. CHARLES MANN, m. JANE MORRIS, September 13, 1826, MONTGOMERY COUNTY, OHIO.
     iv. FANNY MANN, b. 1797, VIRGINIA; m. (1) MR. CROMER; m. (2) WILLIAM SKILLEN, April 29, 1829, SHELBY COUNTY, OHIO.

Child of COLONEL JOHN MANN and RACHAEL BERRY *is:*

     v. CYNTHIA ANN[5] MANN, b. 1833, SHELBY COUNTY, OHIO.

5. JACOB[4] MANN *(JOHN SR.[3], GEORGE BERNARD[2], HANS[1])* was born September 06, 1788 in VIRGINIA, and died March 14, 1857 in MIAMI COUNTY, OHIO. He married ELIZABETH SHELL December 20, 1814 in MIAMI COUNTY, OHIO. ELIZABETH was born February 21,1796, and died March 15, 1858. They are buried in the Mann Cemetery, located in the northeast ¼ of Section 25, in Elizabeth Township. The cemetery is on the south side of Tipp Elizabeth Road, 1 mile east of State Route 202, on a wooded hill.

Biographical Notes for Major Jacob Mann

An early pioneer in the Miami Valley Mann family was Major Jacob Mann. He and his brother John settled in what became Miami County, Ohio in the late 1790's. Their father owned land where they had resided on Sinking Creek and on the south side of Johns Creek Mountain and Salt Mountain at New River, in what is now West Virginia.

1799, John and Jacob have established themselves as early settlers in Elizabeth Township, in Miami County, Ohio.

1801, His sister-in-law Betsy Moyer Mann Harman, settled near by in Staunton Township.

!801, and for much of his life after, Jacob is noted in Miami county as one of the higher class of hunters. According to Asa Coleman's reminisces, Jacob often made hunting his principal business.

1801-1809, Jacob Mann surveys and lays out early roads in Miami County, Ohio.

1807, Jacob is serving as a Lieutenant in the Ohio Militia. Miami County, Ohio.

1812-13, Several companies of volunteers are organized of which Jacob Mann was a Captain, in the Miami County, Ohio Militia. Later records show him as an Ensign, then a Major, serving under his brother. It is recorded that during the war, he participated in Harrison's campaign to free Fort Wayne. While spying out the land with Captain Logan, another scout, they come upon an ambush planned for Harrison, and when exchanging fire, Jacob shoots the noted Pottawatomie chief, Me-te-a, in the arm, as he was attempting to hide behind a tree, rendering the arm useless for life.

1814, Jacob Mann marries Elizabeth Shell.

Prior to 1830 Jacob Mann erects the first distillery in Miami County of any magnitude.

1857, On March 14, Jacob Mann dies.

1858, On March 15, Elizabeth, Jacob's wife dies.

The Military and Bounty Land Warrant Papers of Major Jacob Mann

State of Ohio

Montgomery County ss On this twenty first day of September One
Thousand Eight Hundred and fifty. Personaly appeared,
before me a Justice of the Peace. for the County and State aforesaid
Jacob Mann, Who being duly sworn according to law on his Oath
Saith. That he is the Identical Jacob Mann, Who was Captain
of a Company Volunteers that was raised in Miami County — And was
ordered on a tour of duty on the frontier with said Company, in the
Early part of said year, by Col. John Mann, who commanded the 1st Reg.
2nd Brigade 8th Division Ohio Militia; That he served out said tour
of Duty — And on his returned That he served as Expressed in
the discharge Annexed. And that he is the Identical Jacob Mann
therein named, and that he served as Ensign to said Company —
And he further saith That Some time in October in the same year
he was drafted from the Reg. Brigade & Division above mentioned
in the Six Months drafted Militia — And that he served the first
part of said term as a Captain, and the latter part as Major
of the Said Reg — and That a short time previous to the Expiration
of his said term he was Ordered home, to assist in making
a New Draft — And that he has served more than Six months
in the War with Great Britian — Exclusive of the time mentioned
in the annexed discharge — That he never received any other
discharge but the one annexed — That he has never received bounty
land for said Service or any other Service, or authorized any person
or persons to do so for him

Sworn & Subscribed to before me   Jacob Mann
This Day & Year above written
John Andrew J.P.

Montgomery County 3s. Before me John Anderson a Justice of the Peace in and for said County personally came Henry Mann and William Geismann, two creditable witness, who being duly sworn according to law deposith and saith they are well acquainted with Jacob Mann and know him to be the identical Jacob Mann who served in the War of Eighteen hundred and twelve of twelve in the Office he states in the foregoing affidavit. And that they are disinterested in his said application, contained in the same for Bounty Land.

Henry Mann
William Geismann

Sworn & subscribed to before me this 21st day of September 1850
John Anderson J.P.

Dayton O. Sepr 21st 1850

Sir

I have the honor of forwarding my Claim for Bounty Land, You will please examine the same and if found entitled you will forward my Certificate to John Anderson J.P. Who is my true and lawful attorney in the premises

Witness
J. T. Kenney
& William Ghertell

Respectfully
your Obt Servt.

Jacob Mann

J. L. Edwards, Esqr
Commissioner of Pensions

Dayton O. Sepr 21st 1850

Sir   I herewith forward you Mr Jacob Mann's application for Bounty Land please Examine the same & forward the result to me at this place

Very Respectfully
your Obt Servt.
John Anderson

To J. L. Edwards Esqr
Commissioner of Pensions
Pension Office
Washington City

TREASURY DEPARTMENT,

THIRD AUDITOR'S OFFICE,

December 24, 1850

It appears from documents on file in this Office, that Jacob Manning a Captain of a Company of Ohio Militia, entered the service on the 14th November, 1812, and served till the 14th March 1813

Jno. S. Gallaher
Auditor

No 95

Treasury Department
3 Auditors Office
May 7 57

The files in this office does not afford
any evidence of the service of Jacob
Mann as Major of Ohio militia

B. F. Gallaher
3d Auditor

Pension Office
Jany. 22d 1851.

Sir—
The papers in the application of Jacob
Mann for bounty land, are respectfully referred to
your office again, to see if said Mann has performed
any other service beside the one mentioned in your certificate— You will perceive that he claims to have performed other tour of duty beside the one mentioned—
Very Respectfully
Yr Obt Sevt.
F. S. Evans
for Commissioner

Jno. S. Gallaher Esq.
3d Auditor
Treas. Dept.

352

Mann, Jacob

Adams' Batt'n (1812-13), Ohio Militia.
(War of 1812.)

Captain *Captain*

CARD NUMBERS.

1	*3779 9619*	22	
2	*9261*	23	
3		24	
4		25	
5		26	
6		27	
7		28	
8		29	
9		30	
10		31	
11		32	
12		33	
13		34	
14		35	
15		36	
16		37	
17		38	
18		39	
19		40	
20		41	
21		42	

Number of personal papers herein 2

Book Mark: _____

See also _____

Subsistence Account of Capt Jacob Mann of

A Detachment of Penna from the Said Company to be

Continued by Edward Mangan — — Second Lieut

entered of Same Commenced the 12th Jany 1813 attached to Major Black's own Batt at Greenville

Commencement	Termination	No. of Days	No. of Rations p day	Rations	System of Acct of Payment		Remarks
					Dolls	Cts	
12th Jany 1813	20 March 1813	68	2	136	20 act	37	20

I certify on honor, that the foregoing accounts is accurate and just, and that I have not drawn the rations in kind from the United States, or received money in lieu thereof, from or owing any part of the time above charged — — — — — —

Received of Lyle Hunt Dep Paymaster Twenty seven dollars and Twenty cents being my Subsistence in full from the 12 day of Jany 1813 to the 20th March 1813 Inclusive having signed Duplicate hereof

Jacob Mann Capt

Jacob Mann Capt

W

Jacob Man

Capt., Capt. Adams Batt'n Co.

Ohio Militia Reg't

___ Inclosures.

(War of 1812.)

Pay accounts	1	Final Statements	
Subsistence accounts	1	Furloughs or L. of A	
Certs. of Dis. for Discharge		Med. Certificates	
C. M. Charges		Med. Des. Lists	
Descriptive Lists		Orders	
Discharge Certificates		Pris. of War Record	
Pension Warrant		Resignations	

Other papers relating to—

Admission to Hosp'l	Furlough or L. of A	
Casualty Sheet	Med. Examination	
Confinement	Misc. Information	
Contracts	Pay or Clothing	
Death or Effects	Personal Reports	
Desertion	Rank	
Discharge from Hosp'l	Transfer to Hosp'l	
Discharge from Service	Transfer to V. R. C.	
Duty	Transportation	

We, the subscribers, do acknowledge to have received of _Lt. Jno. Hawkes(?)_ Pay-master _U. States Army_ the sums annexed to our Names respectively, being in full of our pay for the period herein expressed:

NAMES.	RANK.	Commencement of pay on pay-roll.	Ending of pay.	Time paid for.		Pay per month.	Amount received.		SIGNERS' NAMES.	WITNESSES.	REMARKS.
				months	days	dolls.	dolls.	cts.			
Jacob Mann	_Capt._	_Janu. 1, 187_ _Novr 18, 187_	4	00		40	160	00	_Jacob Mann_	_Fredingborough(?)_	

Jacob Mann

Appears with the rank of Capt. on a

Muster Roll

of a detachment of Drafted Militia commanded by Capt. Jacob Mann, Major G. Adams' Batt'n, Ohio Militia,*

(War of 1812,)

for Mar 14, 1812 to Mrch 14, 1813.

Roll dated ...., 181 .

Commencement of service, Nov 14, 1812.

Expiration of service, Mrch 14, 1813.

Present or absent, Present.

Remarks: Left the Rendezvous that at the Expiration of the term turned Enrolled. was Eligible Major. Gel. was Ordered by Col. Jackson Mann Cand't the 2 Regiment, 2 Brigade, 1 Division of Ohio Militia to the command of the first Battalion of said Regiment and to give up the command of this de-tachment to Ensign John Knight.

Jacob Mann, Capt.

*This company was designated at various times as Captain Jacob Mann's and Ensign John Knight's Company.

Brunham ---------------- Copyist.

(650e)

Jacob Mann

Appears with the rank of Capt. on a

Pay Roll

of a Company of Ohio Militia commanded by Capt. Jacob Mann, and a part of the time by Ensign John Knight, of Major G. Adams Batt'n,*

(War of 1812,)

for Nov 14, 1812 to Mrch 13, 1813.

Roll dated .... Not dated ......, 181 .

Commencement of service or of this settlement, } Nov 14, 1812.

Expiration of service or of this settlement, } Mch 14, 1813.

Term of service charged, ... months, ... days.

Pay per month, ... dollars, ... cents.

Amount of pay, ... dollars, ... cents.

Remarks: ....

*This company was designated at various times as Captain Jacob Mann's and Ensign John Knight's Company.

Brunham ---------------- Copyist.

(572e)

No 95 def 27/50

Jacob Mann Capt & Mg
1st Reg 5 Brigade
5th Division Ohio Militia
War 1812

3d Aud Oct 24/50   Land

Suspended see Let.
to 3. Aud Aug 22/57

Allowed 160 acres

Warrant No 385 issued
and Sent 18th May 1857

John Anderson
Dayton Ohio

Vol 63 Page 55

Children of JACOB MANN and ELIZABETH SHELL are:

    i. JAMES J.[5] MANN, b. June 09, 1815, MIAMI COUNTY, OHIO; d. February 11, 1816, MIAMI COUNTY, OHIO.

9.   ii. PRISCILLA MANN, b. 1817, MIAMI COUNTY, OHIO; d. Aft. 1861.

    iii. MARY MANN, b. 1826, MIAMI COUNTY, OHIO; m. ANDREW SELBY, 1853.

    iv. ISAAC MANN, b. March 28, 1827, MIAMI COUNTY, OHIO; d. January 9, 1927; m. MARY E. GOLDEN, October 12, 1865. ISAAC MANN was buried in MACOUPIN CREEK CEMETERY, MONTGOMERY COUNTY, ILLINOIS. ISAAC served as a 1st Lieutenant in Company C, of the 71st Ohio Infantry during the Civil War.

    v. JACOB MANN, b. November 11, 1828, MIAMI COUNTY, OHIO; d. September 18, 1829, MIAMI COUNTY, OHIO.

10.   vi. JOHN MANN, b. 1830, MIAMI COUNTY, OHIO; d. the Civil War.

    vii. HENRY MANN, b. 1833, MIAMI COUNTY, OHIO.

    viii. CAROLINE MANN, b. 1836, MIAMI COUNTY, OHIO.

Generation No. 3 of John Mann Sr.

6.   WILLIAM⁵ BATTREL *(ELIZABETH⁴ MANN, JOHN SR.³, GEORGE BERNARD², HANS¹)* was born 1791 in VIRGINIA, and died 1857 in DELAWARE COUNTY, INDIANA. He married SUSANNAH CUSTER 1818 in CHAMPAIGN COUNTY, OHIO.

   Children of WILLIAM BATTREL and SUSANNAH CUSTER are:
       i.   ANNA⁶ BATTREL, b. OHIO; m. THOMPSON GIRTON, April 11,
            1839, DELAWARE COUNTY, INDIANA.
      ii.   MARY BATTREL, b. INDIANA; m. DANIEL HAZELBAKER, December
            09, 1852, DELAWARE COUNTY, INDIANA.
     iii.   ELIZABETH BATTREL, b. OHIO; m. ANDREW HAZELBAKER, April
            20, 1848, DELAWARE COUNTY, INDIANA.
11.   iv.   LAURAHOMA BATTREALL, b. about. 1821, OHIO; d. 1860,
            DELAWARE COUNTY, INDIANA.
       v.   CATHERINE BATTREL, b. July 17, 1826, OHIO; m. JOHN
            SELLERS, November 11, 1847.
      vi.   SAMUEL BATTREL, b. 1832; m. MARY ANN HOUSE, April 16,
            1855, DELAWARE COUNTY, INDIANA.

7.   ISAAC⁵ MANN *(COLONEL JOHN JR.⁴, JOHN SR.³, GEORGE BERNARD², HANS¹)* was born March 24, 1791 in VIRGINIA, and died August 28, 1860 in ORAN, OHIO. He married ABIGAIL CATHERINE WILLIAMS 1813 in MIAMI COUNTY, OHIO, daughter of JOHN WILLIAMS and ELIZABETH TAWNEY. CATHERINE died September 9, 1866 in Oran, Ohio. ISAAC and CATHERINE are buried in the Oran Christian Cemetery, Oran, Ohio.

Biographical Sheet for Isaac Mann.

Isaac Mann has been noted in the Sidney Journal as a naturalist. It is family tradition that he was well educated. This may have been so, evidently he was quite successful in his business life.

1812, Isaac Mann serves as a Private in the Miami County, Ohio Militia. He is in a company of riflemen commanded by a Captain John Williams. John Williams later becomes his father-in-law.

1813, Isaac Mann marries Abigail Catherine Williams, daughter of John Williams who is a Captain over riflemen on the frontier during the War of 1812. (Although he died some time later, John Williams death is attributed to wounds he received in the War of 1812.)

In the 1830 census for Cynthian Township, Shelby County Ohio, we find Isaac's family listed as:

	Isaac	30-40 years of age
(2)	M	Under 5 years of age
	M	5-10 years of age
	M	10-15 years of age
	F	30-40 years of age
	F	Under 5 years of age
(2)	F	5 -10 years of age
	F	10-15 years of age

1829, Isaac is sworn in as the Township Overseer of Poor.

1833, The Cynthian Christian Church is organized by the families of Samuel Penrod, the Shorts, the Mann's, the Butts, and others. The meet in a log school house, and later build a church on Panther Run on land donated by Isaac and Catherine Mann. In 1870, the settlement becomes known as Oran. The town receives its name through Orin Mann, son of the postmaster, Charles Mann.

1841, The homes up to this time are made of logs. This year marks the coming of the canal boat, which can transport wood to make frame houses. This was also the year that Isaac Mann starts the first sawmill about, or on the spot where Loramie Banking Company stands. He also builds a large warehouse just north of the Ernst Filling Station along the canal. This frame warehouse is soon purchased by John Willman and Gast.

The Bounty Land
Warrant Papers of
Private Isaac Mann

Piqua Apr 7th 1855

Sir
Enclosed I present to you the Claim of Isaac
Mean for Bounty Land under act of March 3d 1855

I am Sir
Respd, yours
N. F. Wilbur

L. P. Waldo
Court of Pensions

STATE OF OHIO, *Miami* COUNTY. ss.

On this *11th* day of *April* A.D., 185*1*, personally appeared before me *A Notary Public* within and for the County and State aforesaid *Isaac Mann* aged *fifty - nine* years, a resident of the County of *Shelby* in the State of *Ohio* who, being duly sworn according to Law, declares that he is the identical *Isaac Mann* who was a *Private* in the Company commanded by Captain *John Williams* in the Regiment of *Ohio Militia* commanded by *Col. Mann* in the war with great Brittain declared by the United States on the 18th day of June 1812 That he *Volunteered* at *Miami Co. Ohio* on or about the *August* day of A.D. 18*12*, for the term of *Six months* and continued in actual service in said War for the term of *Six Months* and was honorably discharged at *Miami Co Ohio* on or about the *February* day of *March* A.D. 18*13*, as will appear by the muster Rolls of said Company, that he never received a written discharge.

That he makes this declaration for the purpose of obtaining the Bounty land to which he may be entitled under the "Act granting Bounty Lands to certain officers and soldiers, who have been engaged in the military service of the United States," Passed September 28, 1850.

Isaac his *x* mark *Mann*

SWORN TO AND SUBSCRIBED before me the day and year above written. And I hereby certify that I believe the said *Isaac Mann* to be the identical man who performed the military service aforesaid and to be of the age above stated.

N. F. Wilbur
Notary Public.

Piqua, *Ohio April 11th* 185*1*.

Sir :

We herewith present the claim of *Isaac Mann* for Bounty Land under the Act of Congress, passed September 28, 1850, entitled "An Act granting Bounty Land to certain Officers and Soldiers who have been engaged in the military service of the United States." We are Sir, Respectfully yours,

YOUNG & WILBUR.

N. F. Wilbur

To J. L. EDWARDS,
Commissioner of Pensions.

Piqua Feb 26. 1852

Sir
        The Claim of Isaac Mann referred to in the
Circular ~~Amendment report and~~ has been Suspended for proof
of longer Service.
                It will not be possible for Mr Mann
to obtain the proof required So that you may issue
for the Amount that Appears to be due from the Aud
itors reports.
                It is probable that Mr Mann is in an
Error in regard to the time he actually did Serve.
        I am Sir
                Respt Yours
                N. F. Wilber

J. E. Heath
Comr of Pensions

99 025 Sep 17/51

65.937
Isaac Mann

Private & Mus.
Capt Williams
Col. Mann

War 1812   18 act 12
En. Aug 25, 1812
Dis Feb 1813

3 audt office
Jan 28 1852

Isaac Mann served
under Capt Williams
from 23 august to the
26 octr 1812

B A Goodell
J B Saud
At 40 acres march 17/12
W 46.353 - of Ohio.
March 17/12 Ohio.
H F Wilbur
Vol 2 P 174
Piqua
Ohio
2 ō 7 26 Oct 1812

3—347.

No. 65.234
99.628

ACT OF _Mar. 3_, 18_55_

Received _____, 18___

Isaac Mann
Pvt

Capt. John Williams

Maj. Mann

Ohio Mil.

War, 1812

Warrant No. 31.626

For _120_ acres.

In the <u>1850</u> census, Cynthian Township, Shelby County, we find Isaac's family listed as:

Isaac Mann age 58 Farmer, born in Va.
Catherine   age 56   born in Va.
Harrison   age 17   born in Oh.
Lewis   age 20   born in Oh.
Samuel   age 17   born in Oh.
Michael   age 13   born in Oh.
Charles   age 12   born in Oh.
Elizabeth Erwin age 26
Isaac H. Erwin   age 4
Charles Woodard age 6

<u>1855</u>, Isaac Mann receives 120 acres for his service in the War of 1812. The land bounty warrant number is 31626. He gives this land to Lewis Mann.
<u>1860</u>, Isaac Mann dies.

    Children of ISAAC MANN and ABIGAIL WILLIAMS are:

12.   i.   LUCINDA[6] MANN, b. About. 1813; d. February 1872.
13.   ii.   HULDA (HULDY) MANN, b. 1815; d. June 13, 1885, DARKE COUNTY, OHIO.
14.   iii.   SUSANNAH MANN, b. 1817, SHELBY COUNTY, OHIO.
15.   iv.   JOHN F. MANN, b. 1821.
16.   v.   ELIZABETH MANN, b. 1823; d. 1892, SPOKANE, WASHINGTON.
17.   vi.   GEORGE WILLIAM MANN, b. 1827, SHELBY COUNTY, OHIO.
18.   vii.   LEWIS JACKSON MANN, b. November 26, 1829, SHELBY COUNTY, OHIO; d. March 12, 1919, DARKE COUNTY, OHIO.
19.   viii.   ISAAC JR. MANN, b. 1831, SHELBY COUNTY, OHIO; d. September 13, 1876, SHELBY COUNTY, INDIANA.
    ix.   WILLIAM H. HARRISON MANN, b. 1833, SHELBY COUNTY, OHIO; d. July 02, 1882, KANSAS; m. LUCINDA CLAWSON, October 05, 1856, SHELBY COUNTY, OHIO. LUCINDA was the daughter of FRANCES and SARAH CLAWSON.
20.   x.   SAMUEL K. MANN, b. October 09, 1833, SHELBY COUNTY, OHIO; d. May 24, 1880, SHELBY COUNTY, OHIO.
21.   xi.   MICHAEL P. MANN, b. 1837, SHELBY COUNTY, OHIO.
22.   xii.   CHARLES H. MANN, b. 1838, SHELBY COUNTY, OHIO; d. July 18, 1911, PIQUA, OHIO.

8. GEORGE[5] MANN *(COLONEL JOHN JR.[4], JOHN SR.[3], GEORGE BERNARD, HANS[?])* was born in VIRGINIA, and died 1826 in MIAMI COUNTY, OHIO. He married

MARGARET (PEGGY) PEARSON May 23, 1816 *in* MIAMI COUNTY, OHIO, *daughter of* ABLE PEARSON *and* ANN MCCLURE.

   Children of GEORGE MANN *and* MARGARET PEARSON *are:*
23.   i.   RUTH[6] MANN, b. November 09, 1822, MIAMI COUNTY, OHIO; d.
              June 28, 1888, LUDLOW FALLS, OHIO.
24.   ii. ABEL MANN, b. August 19, 1825, MIAMI COUNTY, OHIO; d.
              October 13, 1907, DARKE COUNTY, OHIO.

9. PRISCILLA[5] MANN *(JACOB[4], JOHN SR.[3], GEORGE BERNARD[2], HANS[1])* was born 1817 *in* MIAMI COUNTY, OHIO, *and died Aft.* 1861. *She married* (1) JOSEPH MENDENHALL September 15, 1833 *in* MIAMI COUNTY, OHIO. *She married* (2) JACOB SHROYER January 24, 1861.

   Child of PRISCILLA MANN *and* JOSEPH MENDENHALL *is:*
         i.   ELIZABETH J.[6] MENDENHALL, b. December 30, 1835; d.
              September 28, 1839, SHELBY COUNTY, OHIO.

10. JOHN[5] MANN *(JACOB[4], JOHN SR.[3], GEORGE BERNARD[2], HANS[1])* was born 1830 *in* MIAMI COUNTY, OHIO, *and died in the Civil War.. He married* ANGELINE DENNETT September 11, 1855.

   Child of JOHN MANN *and* ANGELINE DENNETT *is:*
         i.   MARY C.[6] MANN, b. 1856; d. September 05, 1857.

Generation No. 4 of John Mann Sr.

11. LAURAHOMA[6] BATTREALL *(WILLIAM[5] BATTREL, ELIZABETH[4] MANN, JOHN SR.[3], GEORGE BERNARD[2], HANS[1])* was born About. 1821 in OHIO, and died 1860 in DELAWARE COUNTY, INDIANA. She married DAVID SHERRY 1848 in DELAWARE COUNTY, INDIANA.

  Children of LAURAHOMA BATTREALL and DAVID SHERRY are:
      i.   MELISSA[7] SHERRY, b. 1837, INDIANA; d. February 01, 1856, DELAWARE COUNTY, INDIANA; m. ANDREW JACKSON HAZELBAKER, March 01, 1855, DELAWARE COUNTY, INDIANA.
      ii. JOHN W. SHERRY, b. June 17, 1839, DELAWARE COUNTY, INDIANA; d. September 27, 1914, GRANT COUNTY, INDIANA; m. MARY BANNING, 1890.
      iii. WILLIAM PERRY SHERRY, b. January 28, 1841, DELAWARE COUNTY, INDIANA; d. September 18, 1910, DELAWARE COUNTY, INDIANA; m. SUSAN ROSS, December 13, 1867, INDIANA.
25.   iv. SARAH LILLIS SHERRY, b. April 08, 1849, DELAWARE COUNTY, INDIANA; d. January 31, 1919, PORTLAND, OREGON.
      v.   DANIEL BOONE SHERRY, b. October 16, 1853, INDIANA; d. April 13, 1928; m. JOSEPHINE BANNING, June 29, 1887.

12. LUCINDA[6] MANN *(ISAAC[5], COLONEL JOHN JR.[4], JOHN SR.[3], GEORGE BERNARD[2], HANS[1])* was born About. 1813, and died February 1872. She married GEORGE BUTT March 17, 1829 in SHELBY COUNTY, OHIO.

  Children of LUCINDA MANN and GEORGE BUTT are:
      i.   BARBARY ANN[7] BUTT, b. 1830, SHELBY COUNTY, OHIO; m. MATHEW R. RIPPEY, March 17, 1853, SHELBY COUNTY, OHIO.
      ii. MARY JANE BUTT, b. March 15, 1832; d. March 31, 1849.
26.   iii. CATHERINE BUTT, b. 1834, SHELBY COUNTY, OHIO; d. 1904.
27.   iv. JOHN M. BUTT, b. May 03, 1838; d. January 23, 1867.
28.   v.   JACOB J. BUTT, b. August 07, 1841, SHELBY COUNTY, OHIO; d. July 05, 1875.
29.   vi. SARAH BUTT, b. 1842, SHELBY COUNTY, OHIO.
30.   vii. RACHEL A. BUTT, b. 1844, SHELBY COUNTY, OHIO; d. December 04, 1910, SHELBY COUNTY, OHIO.
31.   viii. THOMAS BUTT, b. 1847, SHELBY COUNTY, OHIO.
      ix. ELLEN BUTT, b. 1851.

13.   HULDA (HULDY)[6] MANN (ISAAC[5], COLONEL JOHN JR.[4], JOHN SR.[3], GEORGE BERNARD[2], HANS[1]) was born 1815, and died June 13, 1885 in DARKE COUNTY, OHIO.   She married JOSEPH PLUMMER April 22, 1830 in SHELBY COUNTY, OHIO.   Joseph was born in 1802.

>   Children of HULDA MANN and JOSEPH PLUMMER are:
>   i.   HULDAH[7] PLUMMER, b. 1839.
>   ii.   JOSEPH PLUMMER, b. 1840.
>   iii.   GEORGE PLUMMER, b. 1843.
>   iv.   MARY PLUMMER, b. 1848.

14.   SUSANNAH[6] MANN (ISAAC[5], COLONEL JOHN JR.[4], JOHN SR.[3], GEORGE BERNARD[2], HANS[1]) was born 1817 in SHELBY COUNTY, OHIO.   She married LEWIS S. AUSTIN December 09, 1838 in SHELBY COUNTY, OHIO.   Upon the death of her husband, Lewis, Susannah applied for a Civil War pension based on her son Samuel's death.   Application #314509, Certificate #223056.

>   Children of SUSANNAH MANN and LEWIS AUSTIN are:
>   i.   SAMUEL[7] AUSTIN, b. 1840, SHELBY COUNTY, OHIO.   Samuel
>   served in the 118 Regiment OVI, Company C, during the
>   Civil War.   Samuel died July 30, 1864 in Nashville,
>   Tennessee.   He is buried in the City Cemetery, grave #8901.
>   ii.   MARGARET AUSTIN, b. 1845, SHELBY COUNTY, OHIO; m. LEVI
>   MARTIN.
>   iii.   JOSEPH AUSTIN, b. 1853, SHELBY COUNTY, OHIO.
> 32.   iv.   LUCINDA AUSTIN, b. 1854, SHELBY COUNTY, OHIO.
>   v.   ISAAC AUSTIN, b. February 03, 1855, SHELBY COUNTY, OHIO;
>   d. May 17, 1904; m. MINNIE C. HARSHBARGER, September 22,
>   1890.
>   vi.   CATHERINE AUSTIN, b. 1857.
>   vii.   JESSE AUSTIN, b. December 03, 1861, SHELBY COUNTY, OHIO.

15.   JOHN F.[6] MANN (ISAAC[5], COLONEL JOHN JR.[4], JOHN SR.[3], GEORGE BERNARD[2], HANS[1]) was born 1821.   He married SARAH J. CLAWSON September 30, 1847 in SHELBY COUNTY, OHIO.

Children of JOHN MANN and SARAH CLAWSON are:

33.   *i.*   STEPHEN[7] BLANCHARD MANN, b. January 21, 1852, SHELBY COUNTY, OHIO; d. January 28, 1914, SHELBYVILLE, INDIANA.
34.   *ii.* WILLIAM P. MANN, b. 1852, SHELBY COUNTY, OHIO; d. January 11, 1872, SHELBY COUNTY, INDIANA.
         iii. CHARLES L. MANN, b. February 15, 1857, SHELBY COUNTY, OHIO.
35.   *iv.* ANDREW J. MANN, b. April 28, 1858, SHELBY COUNTY, OHIO; d. October 13, 1929, SHELBYVILLE, INDIANA.
36.   *v.*   MICHAEL MANN, b. April 28, 1858, SHELBY COUNTY, OHIO; d. September 29, 1927, SHELBYVILLE, INDIANA.
         vi. ISAAC ORVIS MANN, b. February 23, 1865, OHIO; d. March 05, 1933, SHELBYVILLE, INDIANA; m. MATTIE PARRISH, May 29, 1887, SHELBY COUNTY, INDIANA.

16. ELIZABETH[6] MANN *(ISAAC[5], COLONEL JOHN JR.[4], JOHN SR.[3], GEORGE BERNARD[2], HANS[1])* was born 1823, and died 1892 in SPOKANE, WASHINGTON. She married JOHN ERWIN December 01, 1844 in SHELBY COUNTY, OHIO.

   Children of ELIZABETH MANN and JOHN ERWIN are:
37.   *i.*   ISAAC HORTON[7] ERWIN, b. September 13, 1847, SHELBY COUNTY, OHIO; d. May 14, 1924, SPOKANE, WASHINGTON.
38.   *ii.* CATHERINE JANE ERWIN, b. 1850.

17. GEORGE WILLIAM[6] MANN *(ISAAC[5], COLONEL JOHN JR.[4], JOHN SR.[3], GEORGE BERNARD[2], HANS[1])* was born 1827 in SHELBY COUNTY, OHIO. He married REBECCA JANE IRWIN (ERWINE) August 01, 1850 in SHELBY COUNTY, OHIO.

   Children of WILLIAM MANN and REBECCA IRWIN (ERWINE) are:
         i.   JOHN[7] MANN, b. October 23, 1850, SHELBY COUNTY, OHIO.
         ii. CHARLES MANN, b. 1860, SHELBY COUNTY, OHIO.
         iii. WILLIAM MANN, b. 1869, SHELBY COUNTY, OHIO.

18.   LEWIS JACKSON[6] MANN (ISAAC[5], COLONEL JOHN JR.[4], JOHN SR.[3], GEORGE BERNARD[2], HANS[1])
was born November 26, 1829 in SHELBY COUNTY, OHIO, and died March 12, 1919 in DARKE
COUNTY, OHIO. He married MARTHA TYLER January 10, 1860 in ORAN OHIO, daughter of
EBENEZER TYLER and MARTHA WINANS CHILDERS.

Biographical Notes for Lewis Jackson Mann

Family tradition states that Lewis had been drafted into the Civil War, but had no desire to go. His brother William lost his arm, and his brother-in-law was killed in Union service. When he received notice of draft, he sent back notice that he was crippled, having a bad back, and was unable to serve. He received notice to appear in Greenville in 6 months to be examined. During the time prior to his examination, he constantly built up callous on his hand with a corn cob. His best friend Samuel Moyer fashioned him a hickory cane. When the day came examined, he picked up his cane and hobbled into town. The physician who examined him asked him how long he had been injured. Lewis told him that he had fallen from a horse several years ago. The doctor then looked at his hand, seeing the build up of callous, and promptly dismissed him. As he walked out of town, bent over and leaning on his cane, he closely observed to make sure of when he was no longer seen. When all was clear, he let out a yell of joy and ran home.

He was known as a superb carpenter. It has been noted that once a visitor from New York purchased a stairway from out of Lewis' house, it being of such high quality.

Lewis bought farms and built houses for all of his children except Dorsey, to whom instead he gave money.

<u>1860</u>, Lewis married Martha Tyler.

<u>1866</u>, Lewis was appointed guardian over Caroline Dunn age 16, Margaret Dunn age 15, and John Dunn age 10, minor heirs of Caldwell Dunn.

<u>1880</u>, Lewis' household is shown in the Bradford, Darke County, Ohio census as follows:

Lewis J.	49	Clement	8
Martha	40	Dorsey	6
John A.	20	Estella	4
Rachel	18	Ortha	2
Lizzie	11		

<u>1900</u>, The children or Rachel Caroline are living with Lewis and Martha.

<u>1919</u>, Lewis died, his wife having preceding him by one year. They are both buried in the Gettysburg Cemetery, Gettysburg, Ohio.

Children of LEWIS MANN and MARTHA TYLER are:

39.   i. JOHN ALLEN[7] MANN, b. April 28, 1860, ORAN, OHIO; d. 1928, GRATIOT COUNTY, MICHIGAN.

40.   ii. RACHAEL CAROLINE MANN, b. March 28, 1862, ORAN, OHIO; d. MICHIGAN.

     iii. LAURA MANN, b. September 17, 1864, ORAN, SHELBY COUNTY, OHIO; d. September 25, 1888, DARKE COUNTY, OHIO.

    iv. ANNA MANN, b. March 19, 1867, ORAN, SHELBY COUNTY, OHIO; d. October 18, 1871, ORAN, SHELBY COUNTY, OHIO.

41.   v. ELIZABETH LOUELLA MANN, b. November 20, 1868, ORAN, OHIO; d. October 23, 1942, BRADFORD, OHIO.

42.   vi. CLEMMENT ELZIE MANN, b. January 06, 1872, DARKE COUNTY, OHIO; d. MUNCIE, INDIANA.

43.   vii. DORSEY VIRGIL MANN, b. May 16, 1874, SHELBY COUNTY, OHIO; d. July 14, 1940, DAYTON, OHIO.

44. viii. ESTELLA MAY MANN, b. August 15, 1875, DARKE COUNTY, OHIO; d. February 17, 1955.

    ix. ORTHA MANN, b. 1878, ADAMS TOWNSHIP, DARKE COUNTY, OHIO.

     x. ISAAC C. MANN, b. February 01, 1882, DARKE COUNTY, OHIO; d. February 03, 1882, DARKE COUNTY, OHIO.

   xi. BERTHA ALVILDA MANN, b. February 14, 1884, DARKE COUNTY, OHIO; d. 1968; m. THEODORE B. HORNER, April 28, 1901.
THEODORE was born Jun 30, 1880 and died in 1942. Both are buried in the Gettysburg Cemetery, Gettysburg, Ohio.

19. ISAAC JR.[6] MANN (ISAAC[5], COLONEL JOHN JR.[4], JOHN SR.[3], GEORGE BERNARD[2], HANS[1]) was born 1831 in SHELBY COUNTY, OHIO, and died September 13, 1876 in SHELBY COUNTY, INDIANA. He married MARY CLAWSON March 10, 1850 in SHELBY CO, OHIO.

Children of ISAAC MANN and MARY CLAWSON are:

45.   i. ELIZA MELISSA[7] MANN, b. November 29, 1852, SHELBY COUNTY, OHIO; d. February 19, 1931, SHELBYVILLE, INDIANA.

    ii. THEODORE MANN, b. About. 1854, OHIO; m. ALAZANNAH STUBBS, March 22, 1876, SHELBY COUNTY, INDIANA.

46.   iii. CHRISTIAN MANN, b. April 12, 1859, SHELBY COUNTY, OHIO; d. February 24, 1928, LIGONIER, INDIANA.

20. SAMUEL K.[6] MANN (ISAAC[5], COLONEL JOHN JR.[4], JOHN SR.[3], GEORGE BERNARD[2], HANS[1]) was born October 09, 1833 in SHELBY COUNTY, OHIO, and died May 24, 1880 in SHELBY COUNTY, OHIO. He married SUSAN COOK October 19, 1854 in SHELBY COUNTY, OHIO.

Child of SAMUEL MANN and SUSAN COOK is:
47.   i.   HENRY ALBERT[7] MANN, b. 1859, SHELBY COUNTY, OHIO.

21.   MICHAEL P.[6] MANN *(ISAAC[6], COLONEL JOHN JR.[4], JOHN SR.[3], GEORGE BERNARD[2], HANS[1])* was born 1837 in SHELBY COUNTY, OHIO. He married ELIZA CLAWSON November 21, 1861 in SHELBY COUNTY, OHIO, daughter of JOSIAH CLAWSON and SARAH.

     Children of MICHAEL MANN and ELIZA CLAWSON are:
          i.   HENDERSON[7] MANN.
          ii. HORACE MANN.

22.   CHARLES H.[6] MANN *(ISAAC[6], COLONEL JOHN JR.[4], JOHN SR.[3], GEORGE BERNARD[2], HANS[1])* was born 1838 in SHELBY COUNTY, OHIO, and died July 18, 1911 in PIQUA, OHIO. He married LUCINDA T. HUGHES May 28, 1866 in SHELBY COUNTY, OHIO.

     Children of CHARLES MANN and LUCINDA HUGHES are:
          i.   MILTON[7] MANN.
          ii.   BABY BOY MANN, b. January 31, 1869, CYNTHIAN TOWNSHIP, SHELBY COUNTY, OHIO.
          iii. ORIN MANN, b. December 31, 1869.
          iv.   LIBBY M. MANN, b. 1871.
          v.   ASA A. MANN, b. February 23, 1875; d. October 11, 1910, PIQUA, OHIO.
          vi.   HERMAN R. MANN, b. May 08, 1884, SHELBY COUNTY, OHIO.

23.   RUTH[6] MANN *(GEORGE[5], COLONEL JOHN JR.[4], JOHN SR.[3], GEORGE BERNARD[2], HANS[1])* was born November 09, 1822 in MIAMI COUNTY, OHIO, and died June 28, 1888 in LUDLOW FALLS, OHIO. She had a daughter with UNKNOWN. She married (1) GEORGE CRESS June 22, 1851 in MONTGOMERY COUNTY, OHIO, son of ABRAM CRESS and MARY PEARSON. Both are buried in the Polk Grove Cemetery, Montgomery, County, Ohio.

     Child of RUTH MANN and UNKNOWN is:
48.   i.   MARY MARGARET A.[7] MANN, b. November 15, 1840.

Children of RUTH MANN and GEORGE CRESS are:

  ii. MARY JANE[7] CRESS, b. April 20, 1853; d. April 16, 1877; m. MICHAEL MADISON KESSLER, October 05, 1872, MIAMI COUNTY, OHIO.

49. iii. ROBERT DAVIS CRESS, b. April 1854, MONTGOMERY COUNTY, OHIO; d. 1948.

50. iv. HENRY CRESS, b. 1856, MONTGOMERY COUNTY, OHIO; d. October 1939, DAYTON, MONTGOMERY COUNTY, OHIO.

51. v. HORATIO GATES CRESS, b. April 1860, MONTGOMERY COUNTY, OHIO; d. March 25, 1943.

24. **ABEL**[6] **MANN** *(GEORGE[5], COLONEL JOHN JR.[4], JOHN SR.[3], GEORGE BERNARD[2], HANS[1])* was born August 19, 1825 in MIAMI COUNTY, OHIO, and died October 13, 1907 in DARKE COUNTY, OHIO. He married (1) ESTHER BURKETT August 17, 1851 in MIAMI COUNTY, OHIO. He married (2) ELIZA DUNCAN October 04, 1892 in MIAMI COUNTY, OHIO. He married (3) CATHERINE HARSHBERGER December 06, 1896 in MIAMI COUNTY, OHIO. He married (4) MARGARET FETTER (PUTERBAUGH) December 13, 1898 in DARKE COUNTY, OHIO, daughter of DANIEL FETTER and PHOEBE POTSENBARGER.

Children of ABEL MANN and ESTHER BURKETT are:

52. i. MARGARET ACHIE[7] MANN, b. January 07, 1853, SHELBY COUNTY, OHIO; d. March 27, 1923, GETTYSBURG, DARKE COUNTY, OHIO.

53. ii. GEORGE SIMEON MANN, b. June 26, 1854; d. May 31, 1945, DARKE COUNTY, OHIO.

54. iii. ELIZABETH E. MANN, b. December 02, 1856, IROQUOIS COUNTY, ILLINOIS; d. April 03, 1925.

55. iv. RACHAEL ANN MANN, b. April 03, 1860, OHIO; d. July 28, 1944, LAURA, OHIO.

56. v. EMMA MANN, b. 1863, INDIANA; d. March 18, 1937, PIQUA, OHIO.

  vi. HULDA JANE MANN, b. 1865; d. November 23, 1881, DARKE COUNTY, OHIO.

57. vii. CHARLES E. MANN, b. 1868, OHIO; d. September 16, 1905, PIQUA, OHIO.

  viii. JOHN W. MANN, b. August 23, 1870, DARKE COUNTY, OHIO; d. June 30, 1871, DARKE COUNTY, OHIO.

Generation No. 5 of John Mann Sr.

25. SARAH LILLIS[7] SHERRY (LAURAHOMA[6] BATTREALL, WILLIAM[5] BATTREL, ELIZABETH[4] MANN, JOHN SR.[3], GEORGE BERNARD[2], HANS[1]) was born April 08, 1849 in DELAWARE COUNTY, INDIANA, and died January 31, 1919 in PORTLAND, OREGON. She married DAVID OWEN SNYDER 1876 in BLACKFORD COUNTY, INDIANA.

    Child of SARAH SHERRY and DAVID SNYDER is:
58.   i.   MARTHA BELL[8] SNYDER, b. 1877, BLACKFORD COUNTY, INDIANA.

26. CATHERINE[7] BUTT (LUCINDA[6] MANN, ISAAC[5], COLONEL JOHN JR.[4], JOHN SR.[3], GEORGE BERNARD[2], HANS[1]) was born 1834 in SHELBY COUNTY, OHIO, and died 1904. She married HENRY MOYER April 16, 1854 in SHELBY COUNTY, OHIO, son of GEORGE MOYER and SARAH ZEMER.

    Children of CATHERINE BUTT and HENRY MOYER are:
        i.   JACOB[8] MOYER, b. 1854, SHELBY COUNTY, OHIO.
        ii. LEVI MOYER, b. 1858, SHELBY COUNTY, OHIO.
59.   iii. WILLIAM H. MOYER, b. 1862, SHELBY COUNTY, OHIO.
        iv. BARBARA MOYER, b. 1865, SHELBY COUNTY, OHIO.
        v.   IDA MOYER, b. 1867, SHELBY COUNTY, OHIO.

27. JOHN M.[7] BUTT (LUCINDA[6] MANN, ISAAC[5], COLONEL JOHN JR.[4], JOHN SR.[3], GEORGE BERNARD[2], HANS[1]) was born May 03, 1838, and died January 23, 1867. He married SARAH MOYER September 02, 1858 in SHELBY COUNTY, OHIO. John is buried in the Oran Christian Cemetery, Oran, Ohio.

    Children of JOHN BUTT and SARAH MOYER are:
        i.   NATHAN[8] BUTT, b. 1858.
        ii. RACHAEL BUTT, b. 1859.

28. JACOB J.[7] BUTT (LUCINDA[6] MANN, ISAAC[5], COLONEL JOHN JR.[4], JOHN SR.[3], GEORGE BERNARD[2], HANS[1]) was born August 07, 1841 in SHELBY COUNTY, OHIO, and died July 05, 1875. He married MELINDA R. PENROD August 22, 1856 in SHELBY COUNTY, OHIO. Jacob is buried in the Oran Christian Cemetery, Oran, Ohio. Upon the death of Jacob, Melinda married Samuel Baker.

Children of JACOB BUTT and MELINDA PENROD are:
    i. WILLIAM[8] BUTT, b. January 03, 1859; d. March 11, 1875.
        William is buried in the Oran Christian Cemetery, Oran,
        Ohio.
    ii. CLEMENT BUTT, b. August 21, 1867, NEWPORT, OHIO.
    iii. FLORA BUTT, b. January 06, 1869, NEWPORT, OHIO; d.
        December 11, 1870, Newport, Ohio. Flora is buried
        in the Oran Christian Cemetery, Oran, Ohio.

29. SARAH[7] BUTT *(LUCINDA[6] MANN, ISAAC[5], COLONEL JOHN JR.[4], JOHN SR.[3], GEORGE BERNARD[2], HANS[1])* was born 1842 in SHELBY COUNTY, OHIO. She married ALSON SHORT May 04, 1860 in SHELBY COUNTY, OHIO, son of ISAAC SHORT and MARY VANDEGRIFT.

Children of SARAH BUTT and ALSON SHORT are:
    i. THOMAS[8] SHORT.
    ii. MARTHA SHORT.
    iii. ALLISON SHORT.
    iv. JASON SHORT.
60.   v. WILLIAM J. SHORT, b. February 12, 1875, SHELBY COUNTY,
        OHIO.

30. RACHEL A.[7] BUTT *(LUCINDA[6] MANN, ISAAC[5], COLONEL JOHN JR.[4], JOHN SR.[3], GEORGE BERNARD[2], HANS[1])* was born 1844 in SHELBY COUNTY, OHIO, and died December 04, 1910 in SHELBY COUNTY, OHIO. She married WILLIAM G. CLAWSON November 07, 1867 in SHELBY COUNTY, OHIO. William died November 4, 1921. Rachel and William are buried in the New Oran Cemetery, Oran, Ohio.

Children of RACHEL BUTT and WILLIAM CLAWSON are:
    i. JAMES ELLIS[8] CLAWSON, b. May 13, 1868, SHELBY COUNTY,
        OHIO; d. December 10, 1887, SHELBY COUNTY, OHIO.
    ii. ELLA (EMMA ELLEN) CLAWSON, b. 1870, SHELBY COUNTY, OHIO;
        m. MR. FISHER.
61.   iii. FREDERICK A. CLAWSON, b. January 1872, SHELBY COUNTY,
        OHIO; d. 1949, SHELBY COUNTY, OHIO.
    iv. NATHAN CLAWSON, b. December 24, 1874, SHELBY COUNTY, OHIO;
        d. March 15, 1876, SHELBY COUNTY, OHIO.

      v. SARAH JANE CLAWSON, b. 1875, SHELBY COUNTY, OHIO; d.
October 11, 1928; m. GEORGE FRANKLIN SWOB, April 09, 1899,
SHELBY COUNTY, OHIO. George served as a Private in
the Spanish American War. Sarah and George are buried
in the Houston Cemetery, Houston, Ohio.

      vi. CORA CLAWSON, b. October 07, 1879, SHELBY COUNTY, OHIO;
d. September 23, 1954 SHELBY COUNTY, OHIO; m. JUSTICE
PENROD, September 26, 1897, SHELBY COUNTY, OHIO. Cora and
Justice are buried in the Houston Cemetery, Houston, Ohio.

62.   vii. FRANK WILLIAM CLAWSON, b. July 18, 1882, SHELBY COUNTY,
OHIO; d. September 02, 1942, SHELBY COUNTY, OHIO.

     viii. GERTRUDE E. CLAWSON, b. November 17, 1884, SHELBY COUNTY,
OHIO; d. 1946; m. JOHN SWOB, October 18, 1905, SHELBY
COUNTY, OHIO.

31. THOMAS[7] BUTT *(LUCINDA[6] MANN, ISAAC[5], COLONEL JOHN JR.[4], JOHN SR.[3], GEORGE BERNARD[2], HANS[1])* was born 1847 in SHELBY COUNTY, OHIO. He married WILIMINA SMEDING July 29, 1868 in SHELBY COUNTY, OHIO.

    Children of THOMAS BUTT and WILIMINA SMEDING are:
      i. EDWARD[8] BUTT, b. February 06, 1868, NEWPORT, OHIO.
      ii. JOHN M. BUTT, b. July 03, 1869, SHELBY COUNTY, OHIO,
SHELBY COUNTY.

32. LUCINDA[7] AUSTIN *(SUSANNAH[6] MANN, ISAAC[5], COLONEL JOHN JR.[4], JOHN SR.[3], GEORGE BERNARD[2], HANS[1])* was born 1854 in SHELBY COUNTY, OHIO. She married WILLIAM SHORT January 12, 1871 in SHELBY COUNTY, OHIO.

    Children of LUCINDA AUSTIN and WILLIAM SHORT are:
      i. VIRGIL[8] SHORT.
      ii. IDA SHORT.
     iii. ABRAHAM SHORT, b. December 17, 1871, SHELBY COUNTY, OHIO.
     iv. CHARLES SHORT, b. January 15, 1873, SHELBY COUNTY, OHIO.
      v. LEONA SHORT, b. January 18, 1875, SHELBY COUNTY, OHIO.
     vi. IVY DELL SHORT, b. January 1877, SHELBY COUNTY, OHIO.
     vii. CORY SHORT, b. July 02, 1877, SHELBY COUNTY, OHIO.

33. STEPHEN[7] BLANCHARD MANN *(JOHN F.[6], ISAAC[5], COLONEL JOHN JR.[4], JOHN SR.[3], GEORGE BERNARD[2], HANS[1])* was born January 21, 1852 in SHELBY COUNTY, OHIO, and died January 28, 1914 in SHELBYVILLE, INDIANA. He married MARTHA JANE PHILLIPS February 15, 1877 in SHELBY COUNTY, INDIANA, daughter of JOHN PHILLIPS and DEBORAH SWINFORD. MARTHA was

born November 8, 1855, and died December 30, 1925. STEVEN and MARTHA are buried in the Snyder Cemetery.

Children of STEPHEN MANN and MARTHA PHILLIPS are:
- i. FRANK[8] R. MANN.
- ii. LAURA ANN MANN, b. About. 1880; m. WILLIAM O. MAHAN, August 30, 1905, SHELBY COUNTY, INDIANA.
- iii. CHARLES MANN, b. 1883, died in infancy.
- iv. BERTHA L. MANN, b. 1883, d. 1913.
- v. William Harvey

34. WILLIAM P.[7] MANN *(JOHN F.[6], ISAAC[5], COLONEL JOHN JR.[4], JOHN SR.[3], GEORGE BERNARD[2], HANS[1])* was born 1852 in SHELBY COUNTY, OHIO, and died January 11, 1872 in SHELBY COUNTY, INDIANA. He married GEORGEANNA PHILLIPS January 11, 1872 in SHELBY COUNTY, INDIANA, daughter of JOHN PHILLIPS and DEBORAH SWINFORD.

Child of WILLIAM MANN and GEORGEANNA PHILLIPS is:
- i. BABY BOY[8] MANN, b. April 12, 1883.

35. ANDREW J.[7] MANN *(JOHN F.[6], ISAAC[5], COLONEL JOHN JR.[4], JOHN SR.[3], GEORGE BERNARD[2], HANS[1])* was born April 28, 1857 in SHELBY COUNTY, OHIO, and died October 13, 1929 in SHELBYVILLE, INDIANA. He married SARAH JANE (JENNIE) HINDS February 22, 1883 in SHELBY COUNTY, INDIANA, daughter of MICHAEL HINDS and SARAH BAILEY. SARAH was born January 17, 1857, and died July 24, 1920. ANDREW and SARAH are buried in Forest Hill Cemetery, SHELBYVILLE, INDIANA.

Children of ANDREW MANN and SARAH HINDS are:
- i. MICHAEL[8] MANN, b. January 14, 1884, SHELBYVILLE, INDIANA.
- ii. BABY BOY MANN, b. July 25, 1885, SHELBYVILLE, INDIANA.
- iii. GLENAMA E. MANN, b. 1887, SHELBY COUNTY, INDIANA; d. July 07, 1888, SHELBYVILLE, INDIANA.
- iv. STANLEY MANN, b. July 04, 1891, SHELBYVILLE, INDIANA; d. January 10, 1965, SHELBYVILLE, INDIANA.
- v. BABY BOY MANN, b. June 01, 1895, SHELBYVILLE, INDIANA.
- vi. BABY GIRL MANN, b. October 23, 1897, SHELBYVILLE, OHIO.

36. MICHAEL[7] MANN *(JOHN F.[6], ISAAC[5], COLONEL JOHN JR.[4], JOHN SR.[3], GEORGE BERNARD[2], HANS[1])* was born April 28, 1858 in SHELBY COUNTY, OHIO, and died September 29, 1927 in SHELBYVILLE, INDIANA. He married

KATHRYN JONES May 18, 1893 *in* SHELBY COUNTY, INDIANA. *Michael and Kate are buried in Forest Hill Cemetery,* SHELBYVILLE, INDIANA.

Children of MICHAEL MANN *and* KATHRYN JONES *are:*

63.   *i.*   ORA LOREN[8] MANN, b. June 15, 1894, SHELBYVILLE, INDIANA; d. April 22, 1966, SHELBYVILLE, INDIANA.
         ii.   BABY BOY MANN, b. August 02, 1896, SHELBYVILLE, INDIANA.

37.   ISAAC HORTON[7] ERWIN *(ELIZABETH[6] MANN, ISAAC[5], COLONEL JOHN JR.[4], JOHN SR.[3], GEORGE BERNARD[2], HANS[1])* was born September 13, 1847 *in* SHELBY COUNTY, OHIO, *and died* May 14, 1924 *in* SPOKANE, WASHINGTON. He married MARY ELLEN WOOTEN July 07, 1869 *in* MOULTRIE, ILLINOIS.

Children of ISAAC ERWIN *and* MARY WOOTEN *are:*

         i.   VIRETTA[8] ERWIN, m. MR. CLAYTON.
        ii.   HECTOR FELIX ERWIN, b. December 25, 1869.
64.   *iii.* THOMAS E. ERWIN, b. December 10, 1871, ILLINOIS; d. June 30, 1950, TONASKET, WASHINGTON.
         iv.   JOSEPHINE ERWIN, b. September 1880, KANSAS; m. THOMAS P. TURNER.
          v.   ISAAC HOMER HORTON, b. November 1885, KANSAS; d. March 21, 1952.
         vi.   PHOEBE ERWIN, b. February 1888, KANSAS; d. SPOKANE, WASHINGTON; m. MR. HANCOCK.

38.   CATHERINE JANE[7] ERWIN *(ELIZABETH[6] MANN, ISAAC[5], COLONEL JOHN JR.[4], JOHN SR.[3], GEORGE BERNARD[2], HANS[1])* was born 1850. She married ABEL FLEMING *in Moultrie County, Illinois.*

Child of CATHERINE ERWIN *and* ABEL FLEMING *is:*
         i.   THEODORE[8] FLEMING.

39.   JOHN ALLEN[7] MANN *(LEWIS JACKSON[6], ISAAC[5], COLONEL JOHN JR.[4], JOHN SR.[3], GEORGE BERNARD[2], HANS[1])* was born April 28, 1860 *in* ORAN, OHIO, *and died* 1928 *in* GRATIOT COUNTY, MICHIGAN. He married MARY WEAVER December 12, 1885 *in* DARKE COUNTY, OHIO.

Children of JOHN MANN and MARY WEAVER are:

  i.   KENNETH[8] MANN.
65. ii. VIRGIL HENRY MANN, b. December 20, 1885, DARKE COUNTY, OHIO.
66. iii. LLOYD B MANN, b. January 1887, DARKE COUNTY, OHIO.
  iv. LEWIS ALFORD MANN, b. May 1888, GRATIOT COUNTY, MICHIGAN; d. 1926, ITHICA, MICHIGAN.
  v.   PEARL ETHEL MANN, b. June 1890, GRATIOT COUNTY, MICHIGAN; m. ROY GRIFFITH.
  vi. HAZEL IRENE MANN, b. September 1896, GRATIOT COUNTY, MICHIGAN; m. EARL BROWN.
  vii. OPHER ALLEN MANN, b. 1899; m. MAY.

40. RACHAEL CAROLINE[7] MANN *(LEWIS JACKSON[6], ISAAC[5], COLONEL JOHN JR.[4], JOHN SR.[3], GEORGE BERNARD[2], HANS[1])* was born March 28, 1862 in ORAN, OHIO, and died in MICHIGAN. She married PERRY A. BLACK January 06, 1888 in DARKE COUNTY, OHIO.

Children of RACHAEL MANN and PERRY BLACK are:

  i. ONDA[8] BLACK, b. 1889; d. 1902.
  ii. BERTHA BLACK, b. March 1892; d. ASHVILLE, NORTH CAROLINA; m. MR. HESTER.

41. ELIZABETH LOUELLA[7] MANN *(LEWIS JACKSON[6], ISAAC[5], COLONEL JOHN JR.[4], JOHN SR.[3], GEORGE BERNARD[2], HANS[1])* was born November 20, 1868 in ORAN, OHIO, and died October 23, 1942 in BRADFORD, OHIO. She married HENRY HALLICK YOUNT December 13, 1885, son of JACK YOUNT and LOUISE FESS.
HENRY was born March 4, 1863 and died August 14, 1929, Darke County, Ohio.

Children of ELIZABETH MANN and HENRY YOUNT are:

  i.   WILBUR METCALF[8] YOUNT, b. June 07, 1886, DARKE COUNTY, OHIO; d. 1978.
  ii. LAURA E. YOUNT, b. 1888; m. (1) SAMUEL E. CAINE;
        m. (2) WILLARD RILEY, December 23, 1905.
  iii. ALMA YOUNT, b. February 1890, DARKE COUNTY, OHIO; m. MR. STOKER.
  iv. DORSEY DOLPHUS YOUNT, b. April 12, 1893; d. December 12, 1901. Buried in the Gettysburg Cemetery, Gettysburg, Ohio.
  v.   FLORIN E. YOUNT, b. February 26, 1896.
67. vi. DEWEY KENNETH YOUNT, b. June 03, 1898, DARKE COUNTY, OHIO; d. September 07, 1940.

42. CLEMMENT ELZIE[7] MANN *(LEWIS JACKSON[6], ISAAC[5], COLONEL JOHN JR.[4], JOHN SR.[3], GEORGE BERNARD[2], HANS[1])* was born January 06, 1872 in DARKE COUNTY, OHIO, and died in MUNCIE, INDIANA. He married (1) DORA MARGARET MARKER, daughter of GEORGE MARKER and LYDIA EBERT. He married (2) LOUETTA ARMSTRONG May 05, 1896.

    Children of CLEMMENT MANN and DORA MARKER are:
68.   i.   RUTH[8] MANN.
       ii.   HELEN MANN, m. SHELDON THORNBURG.
      iii.   LEONARD MANN, m. DOROTHY.
69.   iv.   ELMER MANN.
70.   v.   DAISY MANN.
71.   vi.   ROY WILLIAM MANN, b. February 08, 1900, MUNCIE, INDIANA; d. July 1977.
      vii.   CLARA MANN, b. August 1903; m. TONY BRUNNER.

43. DORSEY VIRGIL[7] MANN *(LEWIS JACKSON[6], ISAAC[5], COLONEL JOHN JR.[4], JOHN SR.[3], GEORGE BERNARD[2], HANS[1])* was born May 16, 1874 in SHELBY COUNTY, OHIO, and died July 14, 1940 in DAYTON, OHIO. He had a daughter with JOSEPHINE THOMPSON, daughter of WILLIAM and MARY THOMPSON. He married MARY JANE (MOLLY) MOYER September 21, 1908 in TROY, OHIO, daughter of SAMUEL MOYER and TERISSA CLAWSON (MCMULLEN).

    Child of DORSEY MANN and JOSEPHINE THOMPSON is:
      i.   EVA[8] THOMPSON, m. WALTER FINE.

    Children of DORSEY MANN and MARY MOYER are:
72.   ii.   JOHN ALLEN SR.[8] MANN, b. June 25, 1909, BRADFORD, OHIO; d. May 07, 1985, PIQUA, OHIO.
73.   iii.   ELLEN VIOLA MANN, b. January 05, 1911, BRADFORD, OHIO; d. December 19, 1992, DAYTON, OHIO.

44. ESTELLA MAY[7] MANN *(LEWIS JACKSON[6], ISAAC[5], COLONEL JOHN JR.[4], JOHN SR.[3], GEORGE BERNARD[2], HANS[1])* was born August 15, 1875 in DARKE COUNTY, OHIO, and died February 17, 1955. She married ELMER HARLACHER January 17, 1895 in DARKE COUNTY, OHIO. Elmer died December 19, 1947. Estella and Elmer are buried in the Greenville Cemetery, Greenville, Ohio.

Child of ESTELLA MANN and ELMER HARLACHER is:
      i.   LETHA[8] HARLACHER, m. WILLIAM COATE.

45. ELIZA MELISSA[7] MANN *(ISAAC JR.[6], ISAAC[5], COLONEL JOHN JR.[4], JOHN SR.[3], GEORGE BERNARD[2], HANS[1])* was born November 29, 1852 in SHELBY COUNTY, OHIO, and died February 19, 1931 in SHELBYVILLE, INDIANA. She married JAMES CHAMBERS DUGAN July 18, 1872 in SHELBY, COUNTY, INDIANA, son of THOMAS DUGAN and REBECCA WALKER.

    Children of ELIZA MANN and JAMES DUGAN are:
74.   *i.*   ALBERT VIRGIL[8] DUGAN, b. June 22, 1872, INDIANA; d. June 14, 1963, SHELBY COUNTY, INDIANA.
75.   *ii.*   CHARLES C. DUGAN, b. April 07, 1877, SHELBY COUNTY, INDIANA; d. January 16, 1951.
76.   *iii.*   DORA B. DUGAN, b. November 1879, INDIANA; d. 1931, SHELBY COUNTY, INDIANA.
      iv.   GILBERT DUGAN, b. May 18, 1882.
       v.   BABY DUGAN, b. May 18, 1885.
      vi.   ROY A. DUGAN, b. February 03, 1888.
     vii.   LILLIAN DUGAN, b. October 09, 1891.
    viii.   GEORGE RUSSELL DUGAN, b. May 12, 1895.

46. CHRISTIAN[7] MANN *(ISAAC JR.[6], ISAAC[5], COLONEL JOHN JR.[4], JOHN SR.[3], GEORGE BERNARD[2], HANS[1])* was born April 12, 1859 in SHELBY COUNTY, OHIO, and died February 24, 1928 in LIGONIER, INDIANA. He married SARAH BLAKE August 29, 1878 in LIGONIER, INDIANA.

    Children of CHRISTIAN MANN and SARAH BLAKE are:
77.   *i.*   ISAAC ORAN[8] MANN, b. About. 1879, NOBLE COUNTY, INDIANA; d. NOBLE COUNTY, INDIANA.
78.   *ii.*   LAURA MAY MANN, b. August 30, 1881, NOBLE COUNTY, INDIANA; d. August 08, 1978.
79.   *iii.*   CORA ETTA MANN, b. June 22, 1887, NOBLE COUNTY, INDIANA; d. September 17, 1946, ELKHART, INDIANA.
80.   *iv.*   EDITH A. MANN, b. December 01, 1889, NOBLE COUNTY, INDIANA; d. May 21, 1979.
81.   *v.*   HARLEY R. MANN, b. February 21, 1892, LIGONIER, NOBLE COUNTY, INDIANA; d. September 29, 1963, SHELBYVILLE, SHELBY COUNTY, INDIANA.

82. vi. ROY RUSSELL MANN, b. March 31, 1895, LIGONIER, INDIANA; d. September 03, 1972, WHITE PIGEON, MICHIGAN.

83. vii. RUTH LAPEARL MANN, b. January 13, 1897, LIGONIER, INDIANA; d. March 08, 1945, CLEARWATER, FLORIDA.

47. HENRY ALBERT⁷ MANN *(SAMUEL K.⁶, ISAAC⁵, COLONEL JOHN JR.⁴, JOHN SR.³, GEORGE BERNARD², HANS¹)* was born 1859 in SHELBY COUNTY, OHIO. He married ELLEN FURMAN April 18, 1877.

Children of HENRY MANN and ELLEN FURMAN are:
    i.   ROY⁸ MANN.
    ii. KILEY MANN, b. May 16, 1878, DAWSON, SHELBY COUNTY, OHIO; d. July 25, 1942.

48. MARY MARGARET A.⁷ MANN *(RUTH⁶, GEORGE⁵, COLONEL JOHN JR.⁴, JOHN SR.³, GEORGE BERNARD², HANS¹)* was born November 15, 1840. She married FRANCIS MARION FOX.

Child of MARY MANN and FRANCIS FOX is:
84.   i.   GRANT⁸ FOX, b. July 28, 1869, MIAMI COUNTY, OHIO; d. 1948.

49. ROBERT DAVIS⁷ CRESS *(RUTH⁶ MANN, GEORGE⁵, COLONEL JOHN JR.⁴, JOHN SR.³, GEORGE BERNARD², HANS¹)* was born April 1854 in MONTGOMERY COUNTY, OHIO, and died 1948. He married HANNAH GOINGS About. 1879.

Children of ROBERT CRESS and HANNAH GOINGS are:
       i.   WALTER E.⁸ CRESS, b. July 1879.
85.   ii. EDNA R. CRESS, b. January 1887; d. May 08, 1985, WEST MILTON, OHIO.
       iii. CHARLES FORREST CRESS, b. February 1892; d. May 26, 1996, WEST MILTON, OHIO; m. BILLIE ROBNETT.

50. HENRY⁷ CRESS *(RUTH⁶ MANN, GEORGE⁵, COLONEL JOHN JR.⁴, JOHN SR.³, GEORGE BERNARD², HANS¹)* was born 1856 in MONTGOMERY COUNTY, OHIO, and died October 1939 in DAYTON, MONTGOMERY COUNTY, OHIO. He married EMMA CURTIS February 01, 1882 in MIAMI COUNTY, OHIO.

Children of HENRY CRESS and EMMA CURTIS are:
86.   i.   CLARENCE C.[8] CRESS, d. 1973.
      ii. BERT SAMUEL CRESS, m. LUCY CLARK.
87.   iii. DESSIE MAE CRESS, d. 1968, WEST MILTON, OHIO.
88.   iv. ERNEST CRESS.
89.   v. DEWEY CRESS.
      vi. EDWIN CRESS.

51.   HORATIO GATES[7] CRESS (RUTH[6] MANN, GEORGE[5], COLONEL JOHN JR.[4], JOHN SR.[3], GEORGE BERNARD[2], HANS[1]) was born April 1860 in MONTGOMERY COUNTY, OHIO, and died March 25, 1943. He married AMANDA SHEARER.

Children of HORATIO CRESS and AMANDA SHEARER are:
      i.   CLARA[8] CRESS.
      ii. ESTELLA B. CRESS, b. October 1884.
    iii. BLANCHE CRESS, b. July 1886.
     iv. MARY E. CRESS, b. June 04, 1893.
      v. HELEN C. CRESS, b. November 1896.

52.   MARGARET ACHIE[7] MANN (ABEL[6], GEORGE[5], COLONEL JOHN JR.[4], JOHN SR.[3], GEORGE BERNARD[2], HANS[1]) was born January 07, 1853 in SHELBY COUNTY, OHIO, and died March 27, 1923 in GETTYSBURG, DARKE COUNTY, OHIO. She married PETER SANGLETON GRISE October 08, 1871 in DARKE COUNTY, OHIO, son of JACOB GRISE and ELIZABETH MYERS.

Children of MARGARET MANN and PETER GRISE are:
90.   i.   SAMANTHA[8] GRISE, b. October 12, 1872, DARKE COUNTY, OHIO; d. April 02, 1902.
      ii. CORA GRISE, b. December 11, 1874, DARKE COUNTY, OHIO; d. August 10, 1875, DARKE COUNTY, OHIO.
91.   iii. CORDA ACHIE GRISE, b. July 30, 1876, DARKE COUNTY, OHIO; d. August 08, 1955, MIAMI COUNTY, OHIO.
92.   iv. ESTHER ANN GRISE, b. June 29, 1878, DARKE COUNTY, OHIO; d. March 22, 1969, MICHIGAN.
93.   v. LOVA CATHERINE GRISE, b. February 09, 1880, DARKE COUNTY, OHIO; d. November 06, 1965, DARKE COUNTY, OHIO.
94.   vi. LAURA JANE GRISE, b. December 13, 1881, DARKE COUNTY, OHIO; d. January 31, 1973, DARKE COUNTY, OHIO.
95.   vii. LILLIE FLORENCE GRISE, b. March 19, 1884, DARKE COUNTY, OHIO; d. January 11, 1980.

96.   *viii.*   RUBEN GRISE, b. July 16, 1886, DARKE COUNTY, OHIO; d. May 18, 1972.
97.   *ix.*   GROVER GRISE, b. September 22, 1888, DARKE COUNTY, OHIO; d. February 22, 1974.
     x.   ALMA GRISE, b. February 26, 1891, DARKE COUNTY, OHIO; d. March 20, 1976, WASHINGTON COURTHOUSE, OHIO.
     xi.   EARL GRISE, b. March 10, 1892, DARKE COUNTY, OHIO; d. March 31, 1892, DARKE COUNTY, OHIO.
98.   *xii.*   ELI C. GRISE, b. December 26, 1895, DARKE COUNTY, OHIO; d. December 08, 1976.

53.   GEORGE SIMEON[7] MANN *(ABEL[6], GEORGE[5], COLONEL JOHN JR.[4], JOHN SR.[3], GEORGE BERNARD[2], HANS[1])* was born June 26, 1854, and died May 31, 1945 in DARKE COUNTY, OHIO. He married MARY CATHERINE SPADE September 01, 1880 in DARKE COUNTY, OHIO. Mary died January 7, 1925. Mary's father
was John G. Spade. George and Mary are buried in the Newcomer Cemetery, Darke County, Ohio.

Children of GEORGE MANN and MARY SPADE are:
     i.   JOHN WALTER[8] MANN, b. July 03, 1881, DARKE COUNTY, OHIO; d. July 09, 1928, DARKE COUNTY, OHIO; m. ADA B. CASHMAN, October 08, 1906, DARKE COUNTY, OHIO.
99.   *ii.*   MARGARET ELSIE MANN, b. January 04, 1886, DARKE COUNTY, OHIO.
     iii.   IRA IRVIN MANN, b. November 20, 1891, DARKE COUNTY, OHIO; d. December 02, 1897, DARKE COUNTY, OHIO. Ira is buried in the Newcomer Cemetery, Darke County, Ohio.

54.   ELIZABETH E.[7] MANN *(ABEL[6], GEORGE[5], COLONEL JOHN JR.[4], JOHN SR.[3], GEORGE BERNARD[2], HANS[1])* was born December 02, 1856 in IROQUOIS COUNTY, ILLINOIS, and died June 25, 1929. She married (1) DAVID MATTHEWS September 03, 1876 in DARKE COUNTY, OHIO, son of CHARLES MATTHEWS and LUCINDA MOTE. She married (2) C.C. TISOR on September 09, 1925.

Children of ELIZABETH MANN and DAVID MATTHEWS are:
100.   *i.*   BERTHA MAE[8] MATTHEWS, b. July 16, 1877, DARKE COUNTY, OHIO; d. August 09, 1947, OHIO.
101.   *ii.*   JOHN H. MATTHEWS, b. 1879; d. 1939.
102.   *iii.*   FORREST MATTHEWS, b. 1889; d. 1967, OHIO.

55. RACHAEL ANN[7] MANN *(ABEL[6], GEORGE[5], COLONEL JOHN JR.[4], JOHN SR.[3], GEORGE BERNARD[2], HANS[1])* was born April 03, 1860 in OHIO, and died July 28, 1944 in LAURA, OHIO. She married ELI NETZLEY December 23, 1890 in DARKE COUNTY, OHIO, son of GEORGE NETZLEY and CATHERINE COFFMAN.

Children of RACHAEL MANN and ELI NETZLEY are:
     i. HARRY[8] NETZLEY, b. May 08, 1891; d. October 22, 1950, MIAMI COUNTY, OHIO; m. ALICE JOSEPHINE WRIGHT on August 11, 1912.
     ii. EVA DOT NETZLEY, b. February 18, 1893; m. ROBERT RAY LESHER, October 21, 1916.
     iii. ALBERT WILLIAM NETZLEY, b. August 12, 1894; m. AUDRA SHUFF, August 14, 1917.
     iv. RAY NETZLEY, b. August 19, 1897; m. ELIZABETH SWINGER, April 08, 1919.
     v. FAY NETZLEY, b. August 19, 1897; d. 1898, OHIO.

56. EMMA[7] MANN *(ABEL[6], GEORGE[5], COLONEL JOHN JR.[4], JOHN SR.[3], GEORGE BERNARD[2], HANS[1])* was born 1863 in INDIANA, and died March 18, 1937 in PIQUA, OHIO. She married (1) JOHN WELBAUM May 06, 1880. She married (2) FRANK COOK about 1900. She married (3) JOHN WICK December 20, 1888 in MIAMI COUNTY, OHIO. She married (4) GEORGE HETZLER April 07, 1927 in COVINGTON, OHIO.

Children of EMMA MANN and JOHN WELBAUM are:
103.   i. WASHINGTON TROY[8] WELBAUM, b. September 21, 1880, DARKE COUNTY, OHIO; d. 1929.
     ii. ORVILLE A. WELBAUM, b. October 29, 1882, DARKE COUNTY, OHIO;   d. June 5, 1909. His son was Jeffery M. WELBAUM.
104.   iii. MARTHA E. WELBAUM, b. March 30, 1884, DARKE COUNTY, OHIO.
     iv. WILLIAM SHERIDAN WELBAUM, b. October 17, 1885, DARKE COUNTY, OHIO.

57. CHARLES E.[7] MANN *(ABEL[6], GEORGE[5], COLONEL JOHN JR.[4], JOHN SR.[3], GEORGE BERNARD[2], HANS[1])* was born 1868 in OHIO, and died September 16, 1905 in PIQUA, OHIO. He married HENRIETTA HELLER September 30, 1893 in DARKE COUNTY, OHIO, daughter of JOHN HELLER and EMMALINE LUKER.

Children of CHARLES MANN and HENRIETTA HELLER are:

105. i. GEORGE IVAN[8] MANN, b. May 29, 1895, DARKE COUNTY, OHIO.
106. ii. JOHN EZRA (JACK) MANN, b. September 10, 1897, MIDLAND COUNTY, MICHIGAN; d. July 22, 1993, CALIFORNIA.
      iii. LESTER LEROY MANN, b. August 11, 1901, MIDLAND COUNTY, MICHIGAN; d. August 05, 1963, GRATIOT COUNTY, MICHIGAN; m. GOLDIE WINN.
      iv. ORA ABEL MANN, b. August 28, 1903, MIDLAND COUNTY, MICHIGAN; d. November 08, 1922, CONNERSVILLE, INDIANA; m. LAURA LOUISE BRATTAIN, July 15, 1922.
107. v. CHARLES FRANK MANN, b. July 18, 1905, MIDLAND COUNTY, MICHIGAN.

Generation No. 6 of John Mann Sr.

58. MARTHA BELL[8] SNYDER (SARAH LILLIS[7] SHERRY, LAURAHOMA[6] BATTREALL, WILLIAM[5] BATTREL, ELIZABETH[4] MANN, JOHN SR.[3], GEORGE BERNARD[2], HANS[1]) was born 1877 in BLACKFORD COUNTY, INDIANA. She married GLEN CLIFTON BOWEN 1896.

Child of MARTHA SNYDER and GLEN BOWEN is:
108.   i.   HERBERT F.[9] BOWEN, b. 1903, MADISON COUNTY, INDIANA.

59. WILLIAM H.[8] MOYER (CATHERINE[7] BUTT, LUCINDA[6] MANN, ISAAC[5], COLONEL JOHN JR.[4], JOHN SR.[3], GEORGE BERNARD[2], HANS[1]) was born 1862 in SHELBY COUNTY, OHIO. He married ANNE C..

Child of WILLIAM MOYER and ANNE is:
     i.   MAUD[9] MOYER, b. August 1891, IDAHO.

60. WILLIAM J.[8] SHORT (SARAH[7] BUTT, LUCINDA[6] MANN, ISAAC[5], COLONEL JOHN JR.[4], JOHN SR.[3], GEORGE BERNARD[2], HANS[1]) was born February 12, 1875 in SHELBY COUNTY, OHIO.

Children of WILLIAM J. SHORT are:
     i.   THOMAS[9] SHORT.
     ii.   MARTHA SHORT.
     iii.   ALLISON SHORT.

61. FREDERICK A.[8] CLAWSON (RACHEL A.[7] BUTT, LUCINDA[6] MANN, ISAAC[5], COLONEL JOHN JR.[4], JOHN SR.[3], GEORGE BERNARD[2], HANS[1]) was born January 19, 1872 in SHELBY COUNTY, OHIO, and died 1949 in SHELBY COUNTY, OHIO. He married CLARA MAY CHARPIAT July 15, 1894 in SHELBY COUNTY, OHIO, daughter of PETER CHARPIAT and EMMA SWEIGART. Clara was born in 1878 and died in 1968. Frederick and Clara are buried in the Houston Cemetery, Houston, Ohio.

Children of FREDERICK CLAWSON and CLARA CHARPIOT are:
     i.   ELFA MARCELLA[9] CLAWSON, b. December 26, 1894, SHELBY COUNTY, OHIO; d. April 07, 1910.
     ii.   PEARL MARIE CLAWSON, b. July 23, 1896, SHELBY COUNTY, OHIO; d. 1977; m. ROBERT CHRISMAN, October 29, 1918.

109.   iii.   CHARLES EDWARD CLAWSON, b. December 27, 1897, SHELBY
                 COUNTY, OHIO; d. 1969.
         iv.   WILLIAM PETER CLAWSON, b. August 30, 1900, SHELBY COUNTY,
                 OHIO.
         v.   WALDO CLAWSON, b. April 16, 1908, SHELBY COUNTY, OHIO.
         vi.   OPAL FRANCES CLAWSON, b. August 03, 1919, SHELBY COUNTY,
                 OHIO; m. PERRY J. BALDWIN.

62.   FRANK WILLIAM[8] CLAWSON (RACHEL A.[7] BUTT, LUCINDA[6] MANN, ISAAC[5],
COLONEL JOHN JR.[4], JOHN SR.[3], GEORGE BERNARD[2], HANS[1]) was born July 18,
1882 in SHELBY COUNTY, OHIO, and died September 02, 1942 in SHELBY
COUNTY, OHIO. He married IONA P. CAIN.

        Children of FRANK CLAWSON and IONA CAIN are:
         i.   VERNISHES EMORY[9] CLAWSON, b. August 23, 1905; d. October
                 05, 1932. Buried in the Houston Cemetery, Houston, Ohio.
         ii.   WILMA IRENE CLAWSON, b. November 01, 1906; d. August 12,
                 1974; m. MR. INDERRIEDEN. Wilma is buried in the Shelby
                 Memory Garden, Shelby County, Ohio.
         iii.   LUCILLE MAE CLAWSON, b. March 13, 1908; d. July 05, 1989;
                 m. OTTO JIM DEETER.
         iv.   RACHEL ANN CLAWSON, b. July 04, 1909; m. MR. ABBOTT.
         v.   CECIL ELSWORTH CLAWSON, b. July 04, 1913; d. July 09,
                 1954. Buried in the Houston Cemetery, Houston, Ohio.
         vi.   FRANK SILVESTER CLAWSON, b. August 23, 1915; d. April 26,
                 1985.
         vii.   RALPH H. CLAWSON, b. July 01, 1917; d. December 31, 1944.
                 Ralph was a PFC in WW2, 9th Division 1st Army.
         viii.   HELEN CLAWSON, b. June 02, 1919; m. HENRY SHAPPIE.

63.   ORA LOREN[8] MANN (MICHAEL[7], JOHN F.[6], ISAAC[5], COLONEL JOHN JR.[4],
JOHN SR.[3], GEORGE BERNARD[2], HANS[1]) was born June 15, 1894 in
SHELBYVILLE, INDIANA, and died April 22, 1966 in SHELBYVILLE, INDIANA.
He married HELEN MCCULLOUGH, daughter of WILLIAM MCCULLOUGH and
FLORENCE MCDONALD.

        Child of ORA MANN and HELEN MCCULLOUGH is:
         i.   BABY BOY[9] MANN, b. November 10, 1920, SHELBYVILLE,
                 INDIANA.

64.   THOMAS E.[8] ERWIN (ISAAC HORTON[7], ELIZABETH[6] MANN, ISAAC[5], COLONEL
JOHN JR.[4], JOHN SR.[3], GEORGE BERNARD[2], HANS[1]) was born December 10, 1871

in ILLINOIS, and died June 30, 1950 in TONASKET, WASHINGTON. He married JESSIE GRACE WRIGHT July 21, 1905 in CHELAN, WASHINGTON, daughter of THOMAS WRIGHT and ELVA ASH.

Children of THOMAS ERWIN and JESSIE WRIGHT are:
- i. WILLIS ISAAC[9] ERWIN, b. July 01, 1906, SPOKANE, WASHINGTON; d. May 10, 1969, TONASKET, WASHINGTON; m. ADELAIDE COLLIER, December 15, 1935, OROVILLE, WASHINGTON.
- ii. GEORGINA ALICE ERWIN, b. March 02, 1908, DEER PARK, WASHINGTON; m. GEORGE T. TINGWALL, December 20, 1929, KELLOGGE, IDAHO.
- iii. JESSIE GRACE ERWIN, b. December 01, 1909, ATTILIA, WASHINGTON; d. December 12, 1988, CHELAN, WASHINGTON; m. OSCAR GRAVES, August 14, 1931, MANSON, WASHINGTON.
- iv. ELSIE ELLEN ERWIN, b. January 30, 1912, CHELAN, WASHINGTON; d. December 28, 1991, SACREMENTO, CALIFORNIA; m. (1) ARTHUR POTVIN; m. (2) ROBERT BIGELOW.
- v. CECIL CHESLEY ERWIN, b. May 17, 1914, CHELAN, WASHINGTON; d. April 16, 1915, CHELAN, WASHINGTON.
- vi. EDNA ADELINE ERWIN, b. July 12, 1916, CHELAN, WASHINGTON; d. October 14, 1985, DEER PARK, WASHINGTON; m. (1) LYMON MORDAN; m. (2) ROBERT KINNY; m. (3) C.F. BRUMFIELD, March 30, 1935.
- vii. EDNA MAY ERWIN, b. July 12, 1916, CHELAN, WASHINGTON; m. CHARLES F. MARTIN.
- viii. HAROLD WRIGHT ERWIN, b. June 11, 1918, CHELAN, WASHINGTON; m. ENID LAREE STOCKER (FACHE), December 04, 1981.
- ix. HAROLD WORTH ERWIN, b. June 11, 1918, CHELAN, WASHINGTON; d. June 27, 1918, CHELAN, WASHINGTON.
- x. BERNICE IRENE ERWIN, b. March 09, 1923, CHELAN, WASHINGTON; m. J.L. RITTER.
- xi. SPENCER GAIL ERWIN, b. January 23, 1926, CHELAN, WASHINGTON; d. May 09, 1963, BREWESTER, WASHINGTON; m. MARY LINDQUIST, November 1944, BREWESTER, WASHINGTON.

65. VIRGIL HENRY[8] MANN (JOHN ALLEN[7], LEWIS JACKSON[6], ISAAC[5], COLONEL JOHN JR.[4], JOHN SR.[3], GEORGE BERNARD[2], HANS[1]) was born December 20, 1885 in DARKE COUNTY, OHIO. He married GLADYS HUNTER in ITHICA, MICHIGAN.

Child of VIRGIL MANN and GLADYS HUNTER is:
- i. HELEN[9] MANN, m. LLOYD FOSTER.

66. LLOYD B[8] MANN (JOHN ALLEN[7], LEWIS JACKSON[6], ISAAC[5], COLONEL JOHN JR.[4], JOHN SR.[3], GEORGE BERNARD[2], HANS[1]) was born January 1887 in DARKE COUNTY, OHIO.

Child of LLOYD B MANN is:
i. CLARK[9] MANN.

67. DEWEY KENNETH[8] YOUNT (ELIZABETH LOUELLA[7] MANN, LEWIS JACKSON[6], ISAAC[5], COLONEL JOHN JR.[4], JOHN SR.[3], GEORGE BERNARD[2], HANS[1]) was born June 03, 1898 in DARKE COUNTY, OHIO, and died September 07, 1940. He married PAULINE G..

Children of DEWEY YOUNT and PAULINE are:
i. KENNETH ELROY[9] YOUNT, b. April 23, 1923; d. November 15, 1941.
ii. KEITH YOUNT, b. 1928.
iii. JOHN YOUNT, b. 1929.
iv. ARLENE YOUNT, b. 1931.
v. JAMES YOUNT, b. 1935.
vi. RUTH ANN YOUNT, b. 1937.
vii. DOROTHY YOUNT, b. 1939.

68. RUTH[8] MANN (CLEMMENT ELZIE[7], LEWIS JACKSON[6], ISAAC[5], COLONEL JOHN JR.[4], JOHN SR.[3], GEORGE BERNARD[2], HANS[1]). She married ELIGE BALDWIN.

Children of RUTH MANN and ELIGE BALDWIN are:
i. MIDGE[9] BALDWIN.
ii. ERNEST BALDWIN.
iii. RICHARD BALDWIN.

69. ELMER[8] MANN (CLEMMENT ELZIE[7], LEWIS JACKSON[6], ISAAC[5], COLONEL JOHN JR.[4], JOHN SR.[3], GEORGE BERNARD[2], HANS[1]). He married GLENNA.

Children of ELMER MANN and GLENNA are:
i. DARLADEEN[9] MANN.
ii. MICKEY MANN.
iii. MARTHA MANN.
iv. TERRY MANN.

70. DAISY[8] MANN (CLEMMENT ELZIE[7], LEWIS JACKSON[6], ISAAC[5], COLONEL JOHN JR.[4], JOHN SR.[3], GEORGE BERNARD[2], HANS[1]). She married CLIFFORD LOUNSBURG.

Children of DAISY MANN and CLIFFORD LOUNSBURG are:
  i.   VERNA[9] LOUNSBURG.
  ii.   GERALD LOUNSBURG.
  iii. ROLAND LOUNSBURG.

71. ROY WILLIAM[8] MANN (CLEMMENT ELZIE[7], LEWIS JACKSON[6], ISAAC[5], COLONEL JOHN JR.[4], JOHN SR.[3], GEORGE BERNARD[2], HANS[1]) was born February 08, 1900 in MUNCIE, INDIANA, and died July 1977. He married DORCAS O. GREEN May 23, daughter of MR. GREEN.

Children of ROY MANN and DORCAS GREEN are:
110.   i.   ROBERT EUGENE[9] MANN, b. MUNCIE, INDIANA.
111.   ii.   BETTY JEANNE MANN, b. January 02, 1924, MUNCIE, Indiana.
112.   iii. ALICE MAE MANN, b. March 16, 1925, MUNCIE, INDIANA.

72. JOHN ALLEN SR.[8] MANN (DORSEY VIRGIL[7], LEWIS JACKSON[6], ISAAC[5], COLONEL JOHN JR.[4], JOHN SR.[3], GEORGE BERNARD[2], HANS[1]) was born June 25, 1909 in BRADFORD, OHIO, and died May 07, 1985 in PIQUA, OHIO. He married NELLIE LOURIE HERRON February 05, 1932 in PIQUA, OHIO, daughter of JOHN HERRON and ZERELDA BLACK.

Children of JOHN MANN and NELLIE HERRON are:
113.   i.   JOHN ALLEN JR.[9] MANN, b. September 26, 1932, PIQUA, OHIO.
114.   ii.   PHYLLIS EILEEN MANN, b. March 02, 1935, CINCINNATI, HAMILTON COUNTY, OHIO.
115.   iii. EDWARD LOUIS SR. MANN, b. January 06, 1937, CINCINNATI, OHIO.
116.   iv.   WILLIAM GEORGE MANN, b. February 04, 1945, PIQUA, OHIO.

73. ELLEN VIOLA[8] MANN (DORSEY VIRGIL[7], LEWIS JACKSON[6], ISAAC[5], COLONEL JOHN JR.[4], JOHN SR.[3], GEORGE BERNARD[2], HANS[1]) was born January 05, 1911 in BRADFORD, OHIO, and died December 19, 1992 in DAYTON, OHIO. She married HARRY BANGS September 17, 1933 in PIQUA, OHIO, son of MR. BANGS.

Child of ELLEN MANN and HARRY BANGS is:
117.   i.   JANE MARIE[9] BANGS, b. October 23, 1936, HAMILTON COUNTY,
             OHIO.

74.   ALBERT VIRGIL[8] DUGAN (ELIZA MELISSA[7] MANN, ISAAC JR.[6], ISAAC[5],
COLONEL JOHN JR.[4], JOHN SR.[3], GEORGE BERNARD[2], HANS[1]) was born June 22,
1872 in INDIANA, and died June 14, 1963 in SHELBY COUNTY, INDIANA. He
married MARY ETTA ANDERSON October 03, 1892 in SHELBY COUNTY, INDIANA.

    Children of ALBERT DUGAN and MARY ANDERSON are:
118.   i.   MYRTLE[9] DUGAN, b. August 30, 1893, SHELBYVILLE, INDIANA;
             d. November 01, 1947, SHELBYVILLE, INDIANA.
119.   ii.   MARQEUERITE DUGAN, b. March 1898, SHELBYVILLE, INDIANA.
120.   iii. MABEL ERNESTINE DUGAN, b. November 1904, SHELBYVILLE,
             INDIANA.
        iv.   ROBERT CORNIELUIS DUGAN, b. June 20, 1907, SHELBYVILLE,
             INDIANA.
121.   v.   EUGENIA MARIE DUGAN, b. May 08, 1915, SHELBYVILLE,
             INDIANA.

75.   CHARLES C.[8] DUGAN (ELIZA MELISSA[7] MANN, ISAAC JR.[6], ISAAC[5], COLONEL
JOHN JR.[4], JOHN SR.[3], GEORGE BERNARD[2], HANS[1]) was born April 07, 1877 in
SHELBY COUNTY, INDIANA, and died January 16, 1951. He married ABBIE M.
SHOULTY November 30, 1898 in SHELBY COUNTY, OHIO.

    Children of CHARLES DUGAN and ABBIE SHOULTY are:
        i.   HERBERT[9] DUGAN, b. About. 1900.
        ii.   IRENE DUGAN, b. July 04, 1903.

76.   DORA B.[8] DUGAN (ELIZA MELISSA[7] MANN, ISAAC JR.[6], ISAAC[5], COLONEL
JOHN JR.[4], JOHN SR.[3], GEORGE BERNARD[2], HANS[1]) was born November 1879 in
INDIANA, and died 1931 in SHELBY COUNTY, INDIANA. She married WALTER
GRIFFEY April 03, 1895 in SHELBY COUNTY, INDIANA, son of LEVI GRIFFEY
and MARY LOGAN.

    Children of DORA DUGAN and WALTER GRIFFEY are:
        i.   IDA MAE[9] GRIFFEY, b. November 02, 1895, INDIANA; m.
             ORVILLE GLENN MYERS, January 07, 1914, SHELBY COUNTY,
             INDIANA.

ii.   EVERETT FRANKLIN GRIFFEY, b. May 1898, INDIANA; d.
      December 27, 1908, SHELBY COUNTY, INDIANA.

122.   iii.   BESSIE CLARINA GRIFFEY, b. October 14, 1900, SHELBYVILLE,
              INDIANA; d. August 24, 1984, RUSH COUNTY, INDIANA.

iv.   JAMES C. GRIFFEY, b. March 11, 1915, SHELBYVILLE, INDIANA;
      d. March 14, 1918, SHELBYVILLE, INDIANA.

77.   ISAAC ORAN[8] MANN (CHRISTIAN[7], ISAAC JR.[6], ISAAC[5], COLONEL JOHN
JR.[4], JOHN SR.[3], GEORGE BERNARD[2], HANS[1]) was born About. 1879 in NOBLE
COUNTY, INDIANA, and died in NOBLE COUNTY, INDIANA. He married MAGGIE
1905 in INDIANA.

      Children of ISAAC MANN and MAGGIE are:
      i.   RAYMOND[9] MANN, m. MILDRED, About. 1936.
      ii.   LUCILLE MANN.
      iii.   RICHARD BUDDY MANN.
      iv.   RALPH MANN.
      v.   HAROLD MANN.
123.   vi.   HARRY CHRIS MANN, b. September 18, 1906, LIGONIER,
              INDIANA; d. April 20, 1971.
      vii.   EDITH MANN, b. About. 1907; m. THOMAS KEAGLE, About. 1928,
              INDIANA.
      viii. MILDRED PEGGY MANN, b. About. 1910; m. RUSSELL DUDLEY,
              About. 1928.
      ix.   ROBERT MANN, b. About. 1912; m. ALMA, About. 1932.
124.   x.   FLORENCE MANN, b. About. 1914.

78.   LAURA MAY[8] MANN (CHRISTIAN[7], ISAAC JR.[6], ISAAC[5], COLONEL JOHN JR.[4],
JOHN SR.[3], GEORGE BERNARD[2], HANS[1]) was born August 30, 1881 in NOBLE
COUNTY, INDIANA, and died August 08, 1978. She married (1) D.S. TROWL
January 10, 1900. She married (2) CARL HITE About. 1918 in INDIANA.

      Children of LAURA MANN and D.S. TROWL are:
      i.   VARON E.[9] TROWL, b. April 1900, NOBLE COUNTY, INDIANA; m.
            HELEN.
125.   ii.   RUTH TROWL, b. April 18, 1904, NOBLE COUNTY, INDIANA.

79.   CORA ETTA[8] MANN (CHRISTIAN[7], ISAAC JR.[6], ISAAC[5], COLONEL JOHN JR.[4],
JOHN SR.[3], GEORGE BERNARD[2], HANS[1]) was born June 22, 1887 in NOBLE
COUNTY, INDIANA, and died September 17, 1946 in ELKHART, INDIANA. She
married CHARLES LONG November 15, 1904 in LIGONIER, INDIANA.

Children of CORA MANN and CHARLES LONG are:
    i.   VIRGIL⁹ LONG, b. About. 1906.
   ii. RICHARD LONG, b. May 31, 1910; d. May 24, 1970, INDIANA.

80. EDITH A.⁸ MANN *(CHRISTIAN⁷, ISAAC JR.⁶, ISAAC⁵, COLONEL JOHN JR.⁴, JOHN SR.³, GEORGE BERNARD², HANS¹)* was born December 01, 1889 in NOBLE COUNTY, INDIANA, and died May 21, 1979. She married WALTER JONES September 27, 1908 in LIGONIER, INDIANA.

   Children of EDITH MANN and WALTER JONES are:
126.   *i.*   LOMA IRENE⁹ JONES, b. July 20, 1909, LIGONIER, INDIANA.
127.   *ii.* DONALD R. JONES, b. March 17, 1911, ELKHART, INDIANA; d. February 23, 1996, ELKHART, INDIANA.
128. *iii.* ERNEST E. JONES, b. July 05, 1917, COATSWORTH, CANADA.
129.   *iv.* DOROTHY GLADYS JONES, b. July 12, 1918, COATSWORTH, CANADA.
130.   *v.* LANCE DARREL JONES, b. 1922, LACOTA, MICHIGAN.
131.   *vi.* PAUL E. JONES, b. March 14, 1929, ELKHART, INDIANA.

81. HARLEY R.⁸ MANN *(CHRISTIAN⁷, ISAAC JR.⁶, ISAAC⁵, COLONEL JOHN JR.⁴, JOHN SR.³, GEORGE BERNARD², HANS¹)* was born February 21, 1892 in LIGONIER, NOBLE COUNTY, INDIANA, and died September 29, 1963 in SHELBYVILLE, SHELBY COUNTY, INDIANA. He married (1) AMY ELOISE WILLS January 13, 1912 in LIGONIER, INDIANA. He married (2) MABEL ERNESTINE DUGAN October 10, 1959 in SHELBYVILLE, INDIANA, daughter of ALBERT DUGAN and MARY ANDERSON.

   Children of HARLEY MANN and AMY WILLS are:
132.   *i.* STEWARD RAYMOND⁹ MANN, b. August 29, 1912, LIGONIER, INDIANA; d. January 18, 1947, ELKHART, INDIANA.
133.   *ii.* KENNETH LEROY MANN, b. December 27, 1914, LIGONIER, INDIANA.

82. ROY RUSSELL⁸ MANN *(CHRISTIAN⁷, ISAAC JR.⁶, ISAAC⁵, COLONEL JOHN JR.⁴, JOHN SR.³, GEORGE BERNARD², HANS¹)* was born March 31, 1895 in

LIGONIER, INDIANA. He died September 03, 1972 in WHITE PIGEON, MICHIGAN. He married NORA MAY CROSS November 23, 1925 in CENTREVILLE, MICHIGAN.

Children of ROY MANN and NORA CROSS are:
134.   i.   HAROLD CHRIS[9] MANN, b. October 15, 1926, ELKHART, INDIANA.
       ii. GERALD BUD MANN, b. About. 1928, ELKHART, INDIANA.
135.   iii. BEVERLY JANE MANN, b. March 10, 1930, ELKHART, INDIANA; d. January 31, 1990.
136.   iv. LEROY RUSSEL MANN, b. November 21, 1931, ELKHART, INDIANA; d. January 31, 1992.

83. RUTH LAPEARL[8] MANN *(CHRISTIAN[7], ISAAC JR.[6], ISAAC[5], COLONEL JOHN JR.[4], JOHN SR.[3], GEORGE BERNARD[2], HANS[1])* was born January 13, 1897 in LIGONIER, INDIANA, and died March 08, 1945 in CLEARWATER, FLORIDA. She married CARL WALTER April 17, 1917 in ELKHART, INDIANA.

Child of RUTH MANN and CARL WALTER is:
137.   i.   LUCILLE BERNICE[9] WALTER, b. April 14, 1918, ELKHART, INDIANA.

84. GRANT[8] FOX *(MARY MARGARET A.[7] MANN, RUTH[6], GEORGE[5], COLONEL JOHN JR.[4], JOHN SR.[3], GEORGE BERNARD[2], HANS[1])* was born July 28, 1869 in MIAMI COUNTY, OHIO, and died 1948. He married FLORETTA PEARSON February 15, 1894 in MIAMI COUNTY, OHIO.

Children of GRANT FOX and FLORETTA PEARSON are:
       i.   RUTH[9] FOX.
       ii. TREVA FOX, b. April 10, 1986, MIAMI COUNTY, OHIO; m. (1) RUSSELL YOUNCE; m. (2) HARRY J. STROHMEYER.

85. EDNA R.[8] CRESS *(ROBERT DAVIS[7], RUTH[6] MANN, GEORGE[5], COLONEL JOHN JR.[4], JOHN SR.[3], GEORGE BERNARD[2], HANS[1])* was born January 1887, and died May 08, 1985 in WEST MILTON, OHIO. She married EARL FALKNOR.

Children of EDNA CRESS and EARL FALKNOR are:
       i.   CATHERINE[9] FALKNOR.
       ii. JEAN FALKNOR.

86.   CLARENCE C.[8] CRESS (HENRY[7], RUTH[6] MANN, GEORGE[5], COLONEL JOHN JR.[4], JOHN SR.[3], GEORGE BERNARD[2], HANS[1]) died 1973. He married DOLLIE KESSLER 1901, daughter of DAVID KESSLER.

Children of CLARENCE CRESS and DOLLIE KESSLER are:
  i. ZELMA[9] CRESS.
  ii. VIRGIL CRESS.
  iii. RUTH CRESS.
  iv. JACK CRESS.
  v. JUNE CRESS.

87.   DESSIE MAE[8] CRESS (HENRY[7], RUTH[6] MANN, GEORGE[5], COLONEL JOHN JR.[4], JOHN SR.[3], GEORGE BERNARD[2], HANS[1]) died 1968 in WEST MILTON, OHIO. She married JOSEPH KELLY.

Children of DESSIE CRESS and JOSEPH KELLY are:
  i. DUANE[9] KELLY.
  ii. DONALD KELLY.
  iii. MAX KELLY.

88.   ERNEST[8] CRESS (HENRY[7], RUTH[6] MANN, GEORGE[5], COLONEL JOHN JR.[4], JOHN SR.[3], GEORGE BERNARD[2], HANS[1]). He married RUTH WERNER.

Children of ERNEST CRESS and RUTH WERNER are:
  i. JANICE[9] CRESS.
  ii. MARVIN CRESS.
  iii. NAOMI CRESS.
  iv. MORRIS CRESS.

89.   DEWEY[8] CRESS (HENRY[7], RUTH[6] MANN, GEORGE[5], COLONEL JOHN JR.[4], JOHN SR.[3], GEORGE BERNARD[2], HANS[1]). He married MARGARET HONEYMAN.

Children of DEWEY CRESS and MARGARET HONEYMAN are:
  i. MARY[9] CRESS.
  ii. MARJORIE JEAN CRESS.
  iii. CAROLYN CRESS.

90.   SAMANTHA[8] GRISE (MARGARET ACHIE[7] MANN, ABEL[6], GEORGE[5], COLONEL JOHN JR.[4], JOHN SR.[3], GEORGE BERNARD[2], HANS[1]) was born October 12, 1872 in

DARKE COUNTY, OHIO, and died April 02, 1902. She married CHARLES EDWARD TRICK September 16, 1888.

Children of SAMANTHA GRISE and CHARLES TRICK are:
        i.   PERRY OTTO⁹ TRICK, b. December 16, 1889; d. May 05, 1918.
138.   ii.   WELMA OPAL TRICK, b. December 13, 1893, DARKE COUNTY, OHIO; d.
              November 17, 1979, BRADFORD, DARKE COUNTY, OHIO.

91. CORDA ACHIE⁸ GRISE (MARGARET ACHIE⁷ MANN, ABEL⁶, GEORGE⁵, COLONEL JOHN JR.⁴, JOHN SR.³, GEORGE BERNARD², HANS¹) was born July 30, 1876 in DARKE COUNTY, OHIO, and died August 08, 1955 in MIAMI COUNTY, OHIO. She married (1) EUGENE JONES May 15, 1892. She married (2) HENRY APPLE February 27, 1899.

Children of CORDA GRISE and EUGENE JONES are:
139.   i.   PERRY⁹ JONES, b. August 13, 1892.
140.   ii.   LAURA JONES, b. July 31, 1895; d. June 10, 1967.

Children of CORDA GRISE and HENRY APPLE are:
        iii. CLARENCE⁹ APPLE. (stepson)
        iv.   RALPH APPLE. (stepson)
        v.   ORVILLE APPLE, b. May 03, 1901; d. 1907.
141.   vi.   MARTHA APPLE, b. October 30, 1904; d. February 26, 1983.

92. ESTHER ANN⁸ GRISE (MARGARET ACHIE⁷ MANN, ABEL⁶, GEORGE⁵, COLONEL JOHN JR.⁴, JOHN SR.³, GEORGE BERNARD², HANS¹) was born June 29, 1878 in DARKE COUNTY, OHIO, and died March 22, 1969 in MICHIGAN. She married JOSEPH BUCHOLZ August 27, 1893 in DARKE COUNTY, OHIO, son of JOHN BUCHOLZ and MARY ODA.

Children of ESTHER GRISE and JOSEPH BUCHOLZ are:
        i.   LOVA⁹ BUCHOLZ, b. September 14, 1895; d. February 23, 1957.
        ii.   HERMAN BUCHOLZ, b. June 28, 1897; d. May 20, 1976; m. BLANCHE
              MERRIETT, December 26, 1917.
142.   iii. GROVER BUCHOLZ, b. December 1903; d. March 04, 1996.
143.   iv.   LORING BUCHOLZ, b. December 14, 1906.
144.   v.   HELEN IRENE BUCHOLZ, b. August 28, 1912.
        vi.   TOILA BUCHOLZ, b. July 10, 1914; d. June 05, 1915.

93. LOVA CATHERINE[8] GRISE *(MARGARET ACHIE[7] MANN, ABEL[6], GEORGE[5], COLONEL JOHN JR.[4], JOHN SR.[3], GEORGE BERNARD[2], HANS[1])* was born February 09, 1880 in DARKE COUNTY, OHIO, and died November 06, 1965 in DARKE COUNTY, OHIO. She married SAMUEL MARTIN BASHORE October 02, 1897 in DARKE COUNTY, OHIO, son of JOHN BASHORE and MARY HITTLE.

Children of LOVA GRISE and SAMUEL BASHORE are:

145. i. MARY BELL[9] BASHORE, b. September 04, 1898, MIAMI COUNTY, OHIO; d. September 27, 1985, OHIO.

146. ii. JESSE E. BASHORE, b. April 17, 1901, MIAMI COUNTY, OHIO; d. April 19, 1974, MIAMI COUNTY, OHIO.

147. iii. EDITH MARGARET BASHORE, b. April 11, 1903, SHELBY COUNTY, OHIO; d. January 21, 1983, GREENVILLE, OHIO.

148. iv. IZORA VIOLA BASHORE, b. July 26, 1905; d. May 22, 1983, GETTYSBURG, OHIO.

v. HARMON WALTER BASHORE, b. May 29, 1908; d. December 10, 1910, in DARKE COUNTY, OHIO.

vi. BERTHA EMMA BASHORE, b. December 28, 1911, DARKE COUNTY, OHIO; m. ARTHUR ROOT, August 29, 1931, DARKE COUNTY, OHIO.

149. vii. VERTIE ALWILDA BASHORE, b. March 02, 1913.

viii. ISAAC C. BASHORE, b. April 18, 1916, DARKE COUNTY, OHIO; d. April 23, 1916, DARKE COUNTY, OHIO.

ix. OLIVE MAY BASHORE, b. March 27, 1917, DARKE COUNTY, OHIO; d. December 04, 1918, OHIO.

150. x. JOHN MARTIN BASHORE, b. February 15, 1920, DARKE COUNTY, OHIO.

151. xi. ORTHA SAMUEL BASHORE, b. March 19, 1923, DARKE COUNTY, OHIO; d. May 12, 1988, PIQUA, OHIO.

152. xii. DOROTHY CATHERINE BASHORE, b. March 19, 1923.

94. LAURA JANE[8] GRISE *(MARGARET ACHIE[7] MANN, ABEL[6], GEORGE[5], COLONEL JOHN JR.[4], JOHN SR.[3], GEORGE BERNARD[2], HANS[1])* was born December 13, 1881 in DARKE COUNTY, OHIO, and died January 31, 1973 in DARKE COUNTY, OHIO. She married OSCAR TROUTWINE October 07, 1899 in DARKE COUNTY, OHIO, son of OSCAR TROUTWINE and LYDIA BESECKER.

Children of LAURA GRISE and OSCAR TROUTWINE are:

153. i. ETHEL LEOTA[9] TROUTWINE, b. September 27, 1899; d. June 01, 1974, MIAMI COUNTY, OHIO.

ii. IRA J. TROUTWINE, b. September 16, 1901; d. January 21, 1986, DARKE COUNTY, OHIO; m. (1) RUBY BROWN, May 25, 1932; m. (2) MABEL WEISEWNBERGER.

95. LILLIE FLORENCE[8] GRISE (MARGARET ACHIE[7] MANN, ABEL[6], GEORGE[5], COLONEL JOHN JR.[4], JOHN SR.[3], GEORGE BERNARD[2], HANS[1]) was born March 19, 1884 in DARKE COUNTY, OHIO, and died January 11, 1980. She married WARREN CLIFFORD WALKER March 28, 1903.

Children of LILLIE GRISE and WARREN WALKER are:
154.   i.   TOILEV[9] WALKER, b. October 16, 1900; d. February 15, 1993.
155.   ii.   RAYMOND WALKER, b. April 03, 1903.
156. iii.   MILLARD WALKER, b. April 05, 1908.
157.   iv.   MARGARET WALKER, b. July 01, 1911.
158.   v.   ELIZABETH MAE WALKER, b. May 24, 1913; d. December 1991.
159.   vi.   EARL WALKER, b. August 10, 1914.
160. vii.   LOUISE WALKER, b. December 28, 1915.
161. viii.   RUTH WALKER, b. May 10, 1917.
162.   ix.   DELORES WALKER, b. July 15, 1922.
163.   x.   HAROLD WALKER, b. July 28, 1923; d. February 07, 1966.

96. RUBEN[8] GRISE (MARGARET ACHIE[7] MANN, ABEL[6], GEORGE[5], COLONEL JOHN JR.[4], JOHN SR.[3], GEORGE BERNARD[2], HANS[1]) was born July 16, 1886 in DARKE COUNTY, OHIO, and died May 18, 1972. He married BERTHA FESSLER January 28, 1905.

Children of RUBEN GRISE and BERTHA FESSLER are:
164.   i.   HELEN IRENE[9] GRISE, b. August 17, 1906; d. September 20, 1945.
165.   ii.   ETOILE GRISE, b. October 20, 1909; d. December 20, 1931.
166. iii.   HARVEY DAVID GRISE, b. April 01, 1916.

97. GROVER[8] GRISE (MARGARET ACHIE[7] MANN, ABEL[6], GEORGE[5], COLONEL JOHN JR.[4], JOHN SR.[3], GEORGE BERNARD[2], HANS[1]) was born September 22, 1888 in DARKE COUNTY, OHIO, and died February 22, 1974. He married LILLIE MAY ARNETTE February 06, 1906.

Children of GROVER GRISE and LILLIE ARNETTE are:
     i.   CARL[9] GRISE, b. November 13, 1906; d. January 22, 1966.
    ii.   MYRON GRISE, b. December 18, 1910; d. 1931.
   iii.   CORDELIA GRISE, b. July 14, 1912; m. DWIGHT KING, April 30, 1951.
    iv.   NORMA GRISE, b. October 14, 1917; d. August 31, 1918.
     v.   MARION GRISE, b. December 23, 1921; d. December 23, 1921.
    vi.   ROBERT GRISE, b. March 10, 1927; d. March 08, 1971.

98.   ELI C.[8] GRISE *(MARGARET ACHIE[7] MANN, ABEL[6], GEORGE[5], COLONEL JOHN JR.[4], JOHN SR.[3], GEORGE BERNARD[2], HANS[1])* was born December 26, 1895 in DARKE COUNTY, OHIO, and died December 08, 1976. He married FERN BOSSERMAN February 22, 1926.

   Child of ELI GRISE and FERN BOSSERMAN is:
167.   *i.*   RICHARD[9] GRISE, b. May 01, 1930.

99.   MARGARET ELSIE[8] MANN *(GEORGE SIMEON[7], ABEL[6], GEORGE[5], COLONEL JOHN JR.[4], JOHN SR.[3], GEORGE BERNARD[2], HANS[1])* was born January 04, 1886 in DARKE COUNTY, OHIO. She married RISLEY O. ULLERY.

   Children of MARGARET MANN and RISLEY ULLERY are:
       i.   KESTON[9] ULLERY, b. January 01, 1906, DARKE COUNTY, OHIO; d. 1908, GREENVILLE, OHIO.
     ii.   MARY ELIZABETH ULLERY, b. July 05, 1908, DARKE COUNTY, OHIO; d. January 24, 1943, WELLBORN, FLORIDA; m. BERNIE R. DENNARD, January 07, 1933.
168. *iii.*   GLADYS GAIL ULLERY, b. August 07, 1910, ANSONIA, OHIO.

100.   BERTHA MAE[8] MATTHEWS *(ELIZABETH E.[7] MANN, ABEL[6], GEORGE[5], COLONEL JOHN JR.[4], JOHN SR.[3], GEORGE BERNARD[2], HANS[1])* was born July 16, 1877 in DARKE COUNTY, OHIO, and died August 09, 1947 in OHIO. She married WILLIAM HENRY SHAFER February 26, 1897.

   Children of BERTHA MATTHEWS and WILLIAM SHAFER are:
169.   *i.*   RUTH[9] SHAFER, b. December 07, 1898, MIAMI COUNTY, OHIO; d. August 18, 1984, MIAMI COUNTY, OHIO.
     ii.   JAMES EDWARD SHAFER, b. December 05, 1909; m. ELIZABETH KISNER, July 16, 1931.
    iii.   HERBERT EUGENE SHAFER, b. April 02, 1913; d. May 23, 1944, EPILALL, FRANCE, DURING WWII.
170.   *iv.*   JOSEPH DAVID SHAFER, b. December 31, 1917, BRADFORD, OHIO; d. July 01, 1989, DAYTON, MONTGOMERY COUNTY, OHIO.

101.   JOHN H.[8] MATTHEWS *(ELIZABETH E.[7] MANN, ABEL[6], GEORGE[5], COLONEL JOHN JR.[4], JOHN SR.[3], GEORGE BERNARD[2], HANS[1])* was born 1879, and died 1939. He married SUSAN NIESLEY October 26, 1906.

Child of JOHN MATTHEWS and SUSAN NIESLEY is:
   i. CLARENCE[9] MATTHEWS.

102. FORREST[8] MATTHEWS *(ELIZABETH E.[7] MANN, ABEL[6], GEORGE[5], COLONEL JOHN JR.[4], JOHN SR.[3], GEORGE BERNARD[2], HANS[1]) was born 1889, and died 1967 in OHIO. He married LEONA MAGGIE FALKNOR.*

   Children of FORREST MATTHEWS and LEONA FALKNOR are:
171.   *i.* RUTH[9] MATTHEWS, b. 1917; d. June 07, 1996.
172.   *ii.* HELEN MATTHEWS, b. 1918.
173.   *iii.* MARIBEL MATTHEWS, b. 1925.

103. WASHINGTON TROY[8] WELBAUM *(EMMA[7] MANN, ABEL[6], GEORGE[5], COLONEL JOHN JR.[4], JOHN SR.[3], GEORGE BERNARD[2], HANS[1]) was born September 21, 1880 in DARKE COUNTY, OHIO, and died 1929. He married LIBBIE WESTFALL December 05, 1901.*

   Children of WASHINGTON WELBAUM and LIBBIE WESTFALL are:
   i. LUCY[9] WELBAUM.
   ii. IDA MAE WELBAUM, b. June 04, 1902, DARKE COUNTY, OHIO.
   iii. INFANT WELBAUM, b. December 1903; d. December 1903.
   iv. CARROL LESTER WELBAUM, b. December 23, 1904, MIAMI COUNTY, OHIO.
   v. BLUEFORD WELBAUM, b. 1906.
174.   *vi.* ORA FRANKLIN WELBAUM, b. March 05, 1908, MIAMI COUNTY, OHIO; d. November 07, 1963, PIQUA, OHIO.
   vii. HAROLD W. WELBAUM, b. 1910.

104. MARTHA E.[8] WELBAUM *(EMMA[7] MANN, ABEL[6], GEORGE[5], COLONEL JOHN JR.[4], JOHN SR.[3], GEORGE BERNARD[2], HANS[1]) was born March 30, 1884 in DARKE COUNTY, OHIO. She married (1) LARKEN HOLE October 24, 1901 in MIAMI COUNTY, OHIO; She married (2) C. LLOYD RASOR about 1907.*

   Children of MARTHA WELBAUM and LARKEN HOLE are:
175.   *i.* HAZEL ESTHER[9] HOLE, b. August 21, 1903, MIAMI COUNTY, OHIO.
   ii. JOHN LEWIS HOLE, b. 1905; d. April 28, 1918.
176.   *iii.* CORDELLA BELLE HOLE, b. April 18, 1906, MIAMI COUNTY, OHIO; d. August 05, 1924, MIAMI COUNTY, OHIO.

105. GEORGE IVAN[8] MANN *(CHARLES E.[7], ABEL[6], GEORGE[5], COLONEL JOHN JR.[4], JOHN SR.[3], GEORGE BERNARD[2], HANS[1])* was born May 29, 1895 in DARKE COUNTY, OHIO. He married PEARL BLANCHE SHONKWILLER August 31, 1915 in ITHICA, MICHIGAN.

Child of GEORGE MANN and PEARL SHONKWILLER is:
   i.   CHARLOTTE[9] MANN, b. May 1918.

106. JOHN EZRA (JACK)[8] MANN *(CHARLES E.[7], ABEL[6], GEORGE[5], COLONEL JOHN JR.[4], JOHN SR.[3], GEORGE BERNARD[2], HANS[1])* was born September 10, 1897 in MIDLAND COUNTY, MICHIGAN, and died July 22, 1993 in CALIFORNIA. He married SOPHIA ADALINE LEIS August 05, 1916 in DARKE COUNTY, OHIO.

Child of JOHN MANN and SOPHIA LEIS is:
   i.   ETHELDA[9] MANN, b. November 1918, CONNORSVILLE, INDIANA; m. EARL BERNARD LINVILLE, January 06, 1942, LAS VEGAS, NEVADA.

107. CHARLES FRANK[8] MANN *(CHARLES E.[7], ABEL[6], GEORGE[5], COLONEL JOHN JR.[4], JOHN SR.[3], GEORGE BERNARD[2], HANS[1])* was born July 18, 1905 in MIDLAND COUNTY, MICHIGAN. He married ELLA LUCILLE MILLER October 30, 1929.

Children of CHARLES MANN and ELLA MILLER are:
   i.   CHARLENE[9] MANN, b. 1931.
   ii.   CHARLES MANN, b. About. 1934.

Generation No. 7 of John Mann Sr.

108. HERBERT F.[9] BOWEN (MARTHA BELL[8] SNYDER, SARAH LILLIS[7] SHERRY, LAURAHOMA[6] BATTREALL, WILLIAM[5] BATTREL, ELIZABETH[4] MANN, JOHN SR.[3], GEORGE BERNARD[2], HANS[1]) was born 1903 in MADISON COUNTY, INDIANA. He married HETTIE BELLE RIDER 1925 in MIDLAND, MICHIGAN.

Child of HERBERT BOWEN and HETTIE RIDER is:
    i.   THOMAS LEE[10] BOWEN, b. 1940, MIDLAND, MICHIGAN.

109. CHARLES EDWARD[9] CLAWSON (FREDERICK A.[8], RACHEL A.[7] BUTT, LUCINDA[6] MANN, ISAAC[5], COLONEL JOHN JR.[4], JOHN SR.[3], GEORGE BERNARD[2], HANS[1]) was born December 27, 1897 in SHELBY COUNTY, OHIO, and died 1969. He married FLORENCE SNOW September 17, 1918. Charles is buried in the Houston Cemetery, Houston, Ohio.

Children of CHARLES CLAWSON and FLORENCE SNOW are:
177.   i.   RICHARD[10] CLAWSON, b. July 11, 1921, SHELBY COUNTY, OHIO.
178.   ii. MAURICE F. CLAWSON, b. August 25, 1923, SHELBY COUNTY,
             OHIO; d. February 26, 1988, PIQUA, OHIO.

110. ROBERT EUGENE[9] MANN (ROY WILLIAM[8], CLEMMENT ELZIE[7], LEWIS JACKSON[6], ISAAC[5], COLONEL JOHN JR.[4], JOHN SR.[3], GEORGE BERNARD[2], HANS[1]) was born in MUNCIE, INDIANA. He married BETTY ARMSTRONG.

Child of ROBERT MANN and BETTY ARMSTRONG is:
    i.   KAREN[10] MANN.

111. BETTY JEANNE[9] MANN (ROY WILLIAM[8], CLEMMENT ELZIE[7], LEWIS JACKSON[6], ISAAC[5], COLONEL JOHN JR.[4], JOHN SR.[3], GEORGE BERNARD[2], HANS[1]) was born January 02, 1924 in MUNCIE, INDIANA. She married LEE JR. QUATE April 12, 1947 in FORT WAYNE, INDIANA, son of LEE QUATE and ELECTRA KING.

Children of BETTY MANN and LEE QUATE are:
179.   i.   RANDALL LEE[10] QUATE, b. November 07, 1947, MUNCIE, INDIANA.
180.   ii.   JEFFERY ALLEN QUATE, b. September 08, 1959, TOLEDO, OHIO.
        iii. VANESSA JEANNE QUATE, b. February 09, 1963, TOLEDO, OHIO.

112. ALICE MAE[9] MANN *(ROY WILLIAM[8], CLEMMENT ELZIE[7], LEWIS JACKSON[6], ISAAC[5], COLONEL JOHN JR.[4], JOHN SR.[3], GEORGE BERNARD[2], HANS[1])* was born March 16, 1925 in MUNCIE, INDIANA. She married EUGENE EARL ROBERTS August 31, 1947, son of EARL ROBERTS and RHODA BIXLER.

Child of ALICE MANN and EUGENE ROBERTS is:
   i.   KELLY[10] ROBERTS.

113. JOHN ALLEN JR.[9] MANN *(JOHN ALLEN SR.[8], DORSEY VIRGIL[7], LEWIS JACKSON[6], ISAAC[5], COLONEL JOHN JR.[4], JOHN SR.[3], GEORGE BERNARD[2], HANS[1])* was born September 26, 1932 in PIQUA, OHIO. He married ROSALYN MARIE JOHNSTON March 15, 1957 in SIDNEY, OHIO, daughter of PARKER LEE JOHNSTON and FLORENCE IRENE GUETH.

Children of JOHN MANN and ROSALYN JOHNSTON are:
   i.   BRENDA LEE[10] MANN, b. August 10, 1958, SIDNEY, OHIO; d. January 14, 1981, GENOA, OHIO; m. WARREN KEITH JR. PALMER, December 16, 1978, SIDNEY, OHIO.
181.   ii.   TIMOTHY ALLEN MANN, b. August 17, 1961, SIDNEY, OHIO.
182.   iii. DEBRA LYNN MANN, b. January 29, 1964, SIDNEY, OHIO.
183.   iv.   SHERRI KAY MANN, b. April 30, 1971, SIDNEY, OHIO.

114. PHYLLIS EILEEN[9] MANN *(JOHN ALLEN SR.[8], DORSEY VIRGIL[7], LEWIS JACKSON[6], ISAAC[5], COLONEL JOHN JR.[4], JOHN SR.[3], GEORGE BERNARD[2], HANS[1])* was born March 02, 1935 in CINCINNATI, HAMILTON COUNTY, OHIO. She married (1) HARRY E. EARLS April 02, 1955 in DAYTON, OHIO, son of RAY EARLS and MARGARET MARY BALDMANN. She married (2) ARTHUR BURDETTE KNOUFF July 08, 1976 in TAZEWELL TENNESSEE, son of LESTER KNOUFF and FLORENCE MILLER.

Children of PHYLLIS MANN and HARRY EARLS are:
184.   i.   JOAN LOURIE[10] EARLS, b. December 17, 1956, PIQUA, OHIO.
185.   ii.   SUSAN ELAINE EARLS, b. April 12, 1958, PIQUA, OHIO.
186.   iii. JOSEPH EDWARD EARLS, b. December 20, 1960, PIQUA, OHIO.

115. EDWARD LOUIS SR.[9] MANN *(JOHN ALLEN SR.[8], DORSEY VIRGIL[7], LEWIS JACKSON[6], ISAAC[5], COLONEL JOHN JR.[4], JOHN SR.[3], GEORGE BERNARD[2], HANS[1])* was born January 06, 1937 in CINCINNATI, OHIO. He married CYNTHIA ANN CLARK May 10, 1958 in COVINGTON, OHIO.

Children of EDWARD MANN and CYNTHIA CLARK are:
  i. EDWARD LOUIS JR.[10] MANN, b. March 24, 1959, PIQUA, OHIO.
187. *ii.* PAMELA ANNETTE MANN, b. February 02, 1962, PIQUA, OHIO.
188. *iii.* CAROLYN DIANE MANN, b. May 30, 1965, PIQUA, OHIO.

116. WILLIAM GEORGE[9] MANN *(JOHN ALLEN SR.[8], DORSEY VIRGIL[7], LEWIS JACKSON[6], ISAAC[6], COLONEL JOHN JR.[4], JOHN SR.[3], GEORGE BERNARD[2], HANS[1])* was born February 04, 1945 in PIQUA, OHIO. He married JULIA ANN DERSHEM August 17, 1968 in COVINGTON, OHIO, daughter of JOSEPH DERSHEM and RUTH SHELLABARGER.

Children of WILLIAM MANN and JULIA DERSHEM are:
  i. WILLIAM GEORGE JR.[10] MANN, b. May 26, 1969, PIQUA, OHIO; d. May 26, 1969, PIQUA, OHIO.
  ii. BABY BOY MANN, b. November 27, 1969, TROY, OHIO; d. November 27, 1969, TROY, OHIO.
  iii. JOSEPH ALLEN MANN, b. April 12, 1972, TROY, OHIO.
  iv. KIMBERLY ANN MANN, b. January 19, 1976, DAYTON, OHIO; d. February 20, 1976, DAYTON, OHIO.

117. JANE MARIE[9] BANGS *(ELLEN VIOLA[8] MANN, DORSEY VIRGIL[7], LEWIS JACKSON[6], ISAAC[6], COLONEL JOHN JR.[4], JOHN SR.[3], GEORGE BERNARD[2], HANS[1])* was born October 23, 1936 in HAMILTON COUNTY, OHIO. She married EUGENE CARL SCHWAIGER July 05, 1958 in MONTGOMERY COUNTY, OHIO.

Children of JANE BANGS and EUGENE SCHWAIGER are:
  i. LINDA[10] SCHWAIGER, b. December 01, 1963, MONTGOMERY COUNTY, OHIO.
189. *ii.* DANIEL SCHWAIGER, b. November 29, 1965, OHIO, MONTGOMERY COUNTY.

118. MYRTLE[9] DUGAN *(ALBERT VIRGIL[8], ELIZA MELISSA[7] MANN, ISAAC JR.[6], ISAAC[5], COLONEL JOHN JR.[4], JOHN SR.[3], GEORGE BERNARD[2], HANS[1])* was born August 30, 1893 in SHELBYVILLE, INDIANA, and died November 01, 1947 in SHELBYVILLE, INDIANA. She married LEONARD FANCHER September 16, 1911.

Children of MYRTLE DUGAN and LEONARD FANCHER are:
  i. ROBERT[10] FANCHER, d. November 18, 1972.
190. *ii.* DONALD FANCHER, b. About. 1913.

119.   MARQEUERITE[9] DUGAN (ALBERT VIRGIL[8], ELIZA MELISSA[7] MANN, ISAAC JR.[6], ISAAC[5], COLONEL JOHN JR.[4], JOHN SR.[3], GEORGE BERNARD[2], HANS[1]) was born March 1898 in SHELBYVILLE, INDIANA.   She married STANLEY BANKER October 04, 1915 in INDIANA.

Children of MARQEUERITE DUGAN and STANLEY BANKER are:
    i.   STANLEY JR.[10] BANKER, b. February 03, 1918, NEW CASTLE, INDIANA.
    ii. MAX BANKER, b. April 10, 1920, KENTUCKY.

120.   MABEL ERNESTINE[9] DUGAN (ALBERT VIRGIL[8], ELIZA MELISSA[7] MANN, ISAAC JR.[6], ISAAC[5], COLONEL JOHN JR.[4], JOHN SR.[3], GEORGE BERNARD[2], HANS[1]) was born November 1904 in SHELBYVILLE, INDIANA.   She married (1) LESTER SMITH About. 1930 in INDIANA.   She married (2) HARLEY R. MANN October 10, 1959 in SHELBYVILLE, INDIANA, son of CHRISTIAN MANN and SARAH BLAKE.

Child of MABEL DUGAN and LESTER SMITH is:
    i.   DONNA JEANNE[10] SMITH, b. May 14, 1931, SHELBYVILLE, INDIANA.

Children of MABEL DUGAN and HARLEY MANN are:
    ii. STEWARD RAYMOND[10] MANN, b. August 29, 1912, LIGONIER, INDIANA; d. January 18, 1947, ELKHART, INDIANA; m. VIRGINIA CRIPE, About. 1935, ELKHART, INDIANA.
    iii. KENNETH LEROY MANN, b. December 27, 1914, LIGONIER, INDIANA; m. FLORENCE M. HEISEL, April 25, 1940, ELKHART, INDIANA.

121.   EUGENIA MARIE[9] DUGAN (ALBERT VIRGIL[8], ELIZA MELISSA[7] MANN, ISAAC JR.[6], ISAAC[5], COLONEL JOHN JR.[4], JOHN SR.[3], GEORGE BERNARD[2], HANS[1]) was born May 08, 1915 in SHELBYVILLE, INDIANA.   She married CLAYTON FROGGE February 17, 1940.

Children of EUGENIA DUGAN and CLAYTON FROGGE are:
191.   i.   SANDRA KAY[10] FROGGE, b. February 22, 1945, SHELBYVILLE, INDIANA.
       ii. SARA ANN FROGGE, b. November 09, 1955, SHELBYVILLE, INDIANA.

122. BESSIE CLARINA⁹ GRIFFEY (DORA B.⁸ DUGAN, ELIZA MELISSA⁷ MANN, ISAAC JR.⁶, ISAAC⁵, COLONEL JOHN JR.⁴, JOHN SR.³, GEORGE BERNARD², HANS¹) was born October 14, 1900 in SHELBYVILLE, INDIANA, and died August 24, 1984 in RUSH COUNTY, INDIANA. She married WILLIAM T. ROSS 1924 in URBANA, CHAMPAIGN COUNTY, ILLINOIS, son of MARION ROSS and FLORENTINE COWEN.

Children of BESSIE GRIFFEY and WILLIAM ROSS are:
- i. WILLIAM ARTHUR¹⁰ ROSS, b. November 01, 1925, MONTICELLO, PIATT COUNTY, ILLINOIS; d. September 23, 1995, GREENFIELD, HANCOCK COUNTY, INDIANA; m. (1) MAVERNE MARIE MARKS; m. (2) SARAH JANE BOGUE, April 28, 1946, RUSHVILLE, RUSH COUNTY, INDIANA.
- ii. KATHERINE CLARINA ROSS, b. August 07, 1928, SHELBYVILLE, INDIANA; m. WILLIAM JR. ELLISON, June 10, 1951, RUSHVILLE, RUSH COUNTY, INDIANA.
- 192. iii. LARRY THOMAS ROSS, b. February 22, 1942, ARLINGTON, RUSH COUNTY, INDIANA.

123. HARRY CHRIS⁹ MANN (ISAAC ORAN⁸, CHRISTIAN⁷, ISAAC JR.⁶, ISAAC⁵, COLONEL JOHN JR.⁴, JOHN SR.³, GEORGE BERNARD², HANS¹) was born September 18, 1906 in LIGONIER, INDIANA, and died April 20, 1971. He married KATHERINE BASTELA About. 1928 in ILLINOIS.

Children of HARRY MANN and KATHERINE BASTELA are:
- i. HARRY CHRIS JR.¹⁰ MANN, b. January 07, 1930; d. 1965.
- 193. ii. LUCILLE KATHERINE MANN, b. September 24, 1931, CHICAGO, ILLINOIS.

124. FLORENCE⁹ MANN (ISAAC ORAN⁸, CHRISTIAN⁷, ISAAC JR.⁶, ISAAC⁵, COLONEL JOHN JR.⁴, JOHN SR.³, GEORGE BERNARD², HANS¹) was born About. 1914. She married RACK RASK About. 1930 in MICHIGAN.

Children of FLORENCE MANN and RACK RASK are:
- i. LARRY RACK¹⁰ RASK, b. June 07, 1951.
- ii. LINDA RACK RASK, b. About. 1953.

125. RUTH⁹ TROWL (LAURA MAY⁸ MANN, CHRISTIAN⁷, ISAAC JR.⁶, ISAAC⁵, COLONEL JOHN JR.⁴, JOHN SR.³, GEORGE BERNARD², HANS¹) was born April 18, 1904 in NOBLE COUNTY, INDIANA. She married R. SHELBY BOWLES About. 1924 in INDIANA.

Children of RUTH TROWL and R. BOWLES are:
    i.   ROBERT[10] BOWLES, b. About. 1925.
    ii. BILLIE BOWLES, b. About. 1927.

126. LOMA IRENE[9] JONES (EDITH A.[8] MANN, CHRISTIAN, ISAAC JR.[6], ISAAC[5], COLONEL JOHN JR.[4], JOHN SR.[3], GEORGE BERNARD[2], HANS[1]) was born July 20, 1909 in LIGONIER, INDIANA. She married IRVING REINGHARD CARLBERG November 20, 1926 in GOSHEN, INDIANA.

  Children of LOMA JONES and IRVING CARLBERG are:
194.   *i.*   LEONARD R.[10] CARLBERG, b. May 08. 1928, SOUTH HAVEN, MICHIGAN.
195.   *ii.* NANCY CARLBERG, b. August 07, 1937, SOUTH HAVEN, MICHIGAN.
      iii. NORMAN CARLBERG, b. August 07, 1937, SOUTH HAVEN, MICHIGAN.

127. DONALD R.[9] JONES (EDITH A.[8] MANN, CHRISTIAN, ISAAC JR.[6], ISAAC[5], COLONEL JOHN JR.[4], JOHN SR.[3], GEORGE BERNARD[2], HANS[1]) was born March 17, 1911 in ELKHART, INDIANA, and died February 23, 1996 in ELKHART, INDIANA. He married MARY STURM March 17, 1935 in ELKHART, INDIANA.

  Children of DONALD JONES and MARY STURM are:
196.   *i.*   SALLY ANN[10] JONES, b. October 14, 1936, ELKHART, INDIANA.
197.   *ii.* CAROL JONES, b. April 01, 1945, ELKHART, INDIANA.
198.   *iii.* LINDA KATHLEEN JONES, b. December 02, 1952, ELKHART, INDIANA.

128. ERNEST E.[9] JONES (EDITH A.[8] MANN, CHRISTIAN, ISAAC JR.[6], ISAAC[5], COLONEL JOHN JR.[4], JOHN SR.[3], GEORGE BERNARD[2], HANS[1]) was born July 05, 1917 in COATSWORTH, CANADA. He married JEANETTE ALBERT About. 1937 in INDIANA.

  Children of ERNEST JONES and JEANETTE ALBERT are:
    i.   RONALD[10] JONES.
    ii. KATHIE JONES.
   iii. EDWARD JONES.
   iv. MARGORIE JONES.
    v. JACK JONES, b. About. 1938, ELKHART, INDIANA.

129. DOROTHY GLADYS[9] JONES (EDITH A.[8] MANN, CHRISTIAN[7], ISAAC JR.[6], ISAAC[6], COLONEL JOHN JR.[4], JOHN SR.[3], GEORGE BERNARD[2], HANS[1]) was born July 12, 1918 in COATSWORTH, CANADA. She married ALBERT STRUKEL June 30, 1948 in ELKHART, INDIANA.

Children of DOROTHY JONES and ALBERT STRUKEL are:
199.   i.   SANDRA[10] STRUKEL, b. About. 1950, ELKHART, INDIANA.
      ii.   MICHAEL STRUKEL, b. About. 1952, ELKHART, INDIANA.

130. LANCE DARREL[9] JONES (EDITH A.[8] MANN, CHRISTIAN[7], ISAAC JR.[6], ISAAC[6], COLONEL JOHN JR.[4], JOHN SR.[3], GEORGE BERNARD[2], HANS[1]) was born 1922 in LACOTA, MICHIGAN. He married RUTH GORDON August 29, 1941 in GOSHEN, INDIANA.

Children of LANCE JONES and RUTH GORDON are:
      i.   DIANA SUE[10] JONES, b. March 09, 1944, ELKHART, INDIANA.
200.   ii.   STEPHEN D. JONES, b. August 19, 1946, ELKHART, INDIANA.
201.   iii.   RUTH ANN JONES, b. August 30, 1950, ELKHART, INDIANA.
202.   iv.   SARA JANE JONES, b. September 16, 1954, ELKHART, INDIANA.

131. PAUL E.[9] JONES (EDITH A.[8] MANN, CHRISTIAN[7], ISAAC JR.[6], ISAAC[6], COLONEL JOHN JR.[4], JOHN SR.[3], GEORGE BERNARD[2], HANS[1]) was born March 14, 1929 in ELKHART, INDIANA. He married MARGARET WATKINS 1941 in INDIANA.

Child of PAUL JONES and MARGARET WATKINS is:
203.   i.   JOHN E.[10] JONES, b. About. April 1953, ELKHART, INDIANA; d. 1989, ELKHART, INDIANA.

132. STEWARD RAYMOND[9] MANN (HARLEY R.[8], CHRISTIAN[7], ISAAC JR.[6], ISAAC[6], COLONEL JOHN JR.[4], JOHN SR.[3], GEORGE BERNARD[2], HANS[1]) was born August 29, 1912 in LIGONIER, INDIANA, and died January 18, 1947 in ELKHART, INDIANA. He married VIRGINIA CRIPE About. 1935 in ELKHART, INDIANA.

Child of STEWARD MANN and VIRGINIA CRIPE is:
204.   i.   CHERRIE LOU[10] MANN, b. 1937, ELKHART, INDIANA.

133. KENNETH LEROY[9] MANN (HARLEY R.[8], CHRISTIAN[7], ISAAC JR.[6], ISAAC[6], COLONEL JOHN JR.[4], JOHN SR.[3], GEORGE BERNARD[2], HANS[1]) was born December 27, 1914 in LIGONIER, INDIANA. He married FLORENCE M. HEISEL April 25, 1940 in ELKHART, INDIANA.

Children of KENNETH MANN and FLORENCE HEISEL are:
205.   i.   SUSAN LEE[10] MANN, b. October 08, 1948, ELKHART, INDIANA.
206.   ii.   KATHY JEAN MANN, b. September 15, 1950, ELKHART, INDIANA.

134.   HAROLD CHRIS[9] MANN (ROY RUSSELL[8], CHRISTIAN[7], ISAAC JR.[6], ISAAC[5], COLONEL JOHN JR.[4], JOHN SR.[3], GEORGE BERNARD[2], HANS[1]) was born October 15, 1926 in ELKHART, INDIANA. He married MARTHA KUSSMAN About. 1955.

Children of HAROLD MANN and MARTHA KUSSMAN are:
207.   i.   MARY MARIE[10] MANN, b. July 08, 1956.
208.   ii.   MARSHA MARIE MANN, b. September 13, 1957.
209.   iii.   HAROLD CHRIS JR. MANN, b. November 03, 1959.
        iv.   MARJORIE MARIE MANN, b. June 1969.

135.   BEVERLY JANE[9] MANN (ROY RUSSELL[8], CHRISTIAN[7], ISAAC JR.[6], ISAAC[5], COLONEL JOHN JR.[4], JOHN SR.[3], GEORGE BERNARD[2], HANS[1]) was born March 10, 1930 in ELKHART, INDIANA, and died January 31, 1990. She married (1) MR. ROGERS About. 1950 in INDIANA. She married (2) HAROLD WHISLER About. 1970 in MICHIGAN.

Children of BEVERLY MANN and MR. ROGERS are:
210.   i.   GENE[10] ROGERS, b. About. 1952.
        ii.   MONTE ROGERS, b. About. 1953.

Child of BEVERLY MANN and HAROLD WHISLER is:
        iii.   DAVID[10] WHISLER, b. About. 1972.

136.   LEROY RUSSEL[9] MANN (ROY RUSSELL[8], CHRISTIAN[7], ISAAC JR.[6], ISAAC[5], COLONEL JOHN JR.[4], JOHN SR.[3], GEORGE BERNARD[2], HANS[1]) was born November 21, 1931 in ELKHART, INDIANA, and died January 31, 1992. He married SHIRLEY HINGE About. 1950 in INDIANA.

Children of LEROY MANN and SHIRLEY HINGE are:
        i.   SARA[10] MANN, b. About. 1951.
        ii.   KATHLEEN MANN, b. About. 1953.
        iii.   MICHAEL MANN, b. About. 1955.

137.   LUCILLE BERNICE[9] WALTER (RUTH LAPEARL[8] MANN, CHRISTIAN[7], ISAAC JR.[6], ISAAC[5], COLONEL JOHN JR.[4], JOHN SR.[3], GEORGE BERNARD[2], HANS[1]) was

born April 14, 1918 in ELKHART, INDIANA. She married LOWELL SHAUM
August 08, 1935 in ELKHART, INDIANA.

Children of LUCILLE WALTER and LOWELL SHAUM are:
211.   i.   GARY LOWELL[10] SHAUM, b. May 03, 1942, ELKHART, INDIANA.
212.   ii.   LEWIS DEAN SHAUM, b. May 13, 1945.

138. WELMA OPAL[9] TRICK (SAMANTHA[8] GRISE, MARGARET ACHIE[7] MANN, ABEL[6],
GEORGE[5], COLONEL JOHN JR.[4], JOHN SR.[3], GEORGE BERNARD[2], HANS[1]) was born
December 13, 1893 in DARKE COUNTY, OHIO, and died November 17, 1979 in
BRADFORD, DARKE COUNTY, OHIO. She married JAMES L. JOHNSON February
24, 1909 in DARKE COUNTY, OHIO.

Children of WELMA TRICK and JAMES JOHNSON are:
        i.   RUBY[10] JOHNSON, b. 1911; m. ROBERT ROGERS.
213.   ii.   CHARLES DALE JOHNSON, b. April 03, 1914; d. October 20,
              1972.
214.   iii. CHALMER EDWARD JOHNSON, b. December 31, 1915; d. June 02,
              1985, PIQUA, MIAMI COUNTY, OHIO.
215.   iv.   JAY JOHNSON, b. July 03, 1918.
216.   v.   MAC JOHNSON, b. October 05, 1924.
217.   vi.   JACK JOHNSON, b. October 15, 1928, GETTYSBURG, DARKE
              COUNTY, OHIO; d. August 01, 1993, SAN ANTONIO, TEXAS.
218.   vii. PHYLLIS JOHNSON, b. September 11, 1938.

139. PERRY[9] JONES (CORDA ACHIE[8] GRISE, MARGARET ACHIE[7] MANN, ABEL[6],
GEORGE[5], COLONEL JOHN JR.[4], JOHN SR.[3], GEORGE BERNARD[2], HANS[1]) was born
August 13, 1892. He married ANNA HEISEY 1915.

Children of PERRY JONES and ANNA HEISEY are:
219.   i.   RACHEL[10] JONES, b. January 30, 1916.
220.   ii.   ELSIE CORDA JONES, b. April 15, 1920; d. November 23,
              1987.

140. LAURA[9] JONES (CORDA ACHIE[8] GRISE, MARGARET ACHIE[7] MANN, ABEL[6],
GEORGE[5], COLONEL JOHN JR.[4], JOHN SR.[3], GEORGE BERNARD[2], HANS[1]) was born
July 31, 1895, and died June 10, 1967. She married RUSSELL FURNAS May
14, 1918.

Children of LAURA JONES and RUSSELL FURNAS are:

136

221.   *i.*   THERM RODNEY[10] FURNAS, b. April 09, 1919.
222.   *ii.* HELEN MAE FURNAS, b. May 18, 1920.

141. MARTHA[9] APPLE (CORDA ACHIE[8] GRISE, MARGARET ACHIE[7] MANN, ABEL[6], GEORGE[5], COLONEL JOHN JR.[4], JOHN SR.[3], GEORGE BERNARD[2], HANS[1]) was born October 30, 1904, and died February 26, 1983. She married (1) MR. HOUSER. She married (2) CHARLES WARNER November 22, 1922.

   Children of MARTHA APPLE and CHARLES WARNER are:
          i.   ELSIE[10] WARNER, b. September 24, 1923; d. September 24, 1923.
223.   *ii.* GLENNA WARNER, b. December 13, 1925.
224.   *iii.* ROBERT WARNER, b. April 02, 1928.
225.   *iv.* RICHARD WARNER, b. September 27, 1931.

142. GROVER[9] BUCHOLZ (ESTHER ANN[8] GRISE, MARGARET ACHIE[7] MANN, ABEL[6], GEORGE[5], COLONEL JOHN JR.[4], JOHN SR.[3], GEORGE BERNARD[2], HANS[1]) was born December 1903, and died March 04, 1996. He married CLARA MCKAY January 05, 1932.

   Child of GROVER BUCHOLZ and CLARA MCKAY is:
226.   *i.*   GROVER JR.[10] BUCHOLZ, b. December 03, 1932.

143. LORING[9] BUCHOLZ (ESTHER ANN[8] GRISE, MARGARET ACHIE[7] MANN, ABEL[6], GEORGE[5], COLONEL JOHN JR.[4], JOHN SR.[3], GEORGE BERNARD[2], HANS[1]) was born December 14, 1906. He married MARGORIE FLEGAL May 31, 1930.

   Children of LORING BUCHOLZ and MARGORIE FLEGAL are:
227.   *i.*   JAMES ROGER[10] BUCHOLZ, b. March 30, 1933.
228.   *ii.* JOYCE IRENE BUCHOLZ, b. March 30, 1933.
229.   *iii.* BARBARA BUCHOLZ, b. February 27, 1941.

144. HELEN IRENE[9] BUCHOLZ (ESTHER ANN[8] GRISE, MARGARET ACHIE[7] MANN, ABEL[6], GEORGE[5], COLONEL JOHN JR.[4], JOHN SR.[3], GEORGE BERNARD[2], HANS[1]) was born August 28, 1912. She married GEORGE JACOB SMITH October 06, 1934.

   Children of HELEN BUCHOLZ and GEORGE SMITH are:
230.   *i.*   GARY LYNN[10] SMITH, b. December 13, 1936.
231.   *ii.* RUBY ELLEN SMITH, b. September 07, 1940.
232.   *iii.* KENNETH WARD SMITH, b. October 09, 1947.

145. MARY BELL[9] BASHORE *(LOVA CATHERINE[8] GRISE, MARGARET ACHIE[7] MANN, ABEL[6], GEORGE[5], COLONEL JOHN JR.[4], JOHN SR.[3], GEORGE BERNARD[2], HANS[1])* was born September 04, 1898 in MIAMI COUNTY, OHIO, and died September 27, 1985 in OHIO.   She married THOMAS HILL January 22, 1918 in DARKE COUNTY, OHIO, son of JAMES HILL and NELLIE THOMPSON.

   Children of MARY BASHORE and THOMAS HILL are:
233.   i.   GLENNA MAE[10] HILL, b. September 28, 1918.
234.   ii.   KENNETH HILL, b. January 09, 1922; d. June 26, 1961.

146. JESSE E.[9] BASHORE *(LOVA CATHERINE[8] GRISE, MARGARET ACHIE[7] MANN, ABEL[6], GEORGE[5], COLONEL JOHN JR.[4], JOHN SR.[3], GEORGE BERNARD[2], HANS[1])* was born April 17, 1901 in MIAMI COUNTY, OHIO, and died April 19, 1974 in MIAMI COUNTY, OHIO.   He married (1) OPAL HECATHORN January 10, 1923 in DARKE COUNTY, OHIO.   He married (2) AOUDA F. RIFFELL on March 5, 1936.   He married (3) LOVA GORMAN on January 22, 1940.

   Child of JESSE BASHORE and AOUDA RIFFELL is:
235.   i.   ALICE FAYE[10] RIFFELL, b. December 11, 1939.

   Child of JESSE BASHORE and OPAL HECATHORN is:
        ii.   KATHERINE[10] BASHORE, b. March 24, 1924; d. March 24, 1924.

   Child of JESSE BASHORE and LOVA GORMAN is:
236.   iii.   WAYNE[10] BASHORE, b. April 15, 1942.

147. EDITH MARGARET[9] BASHORE *(LOVA CATHERINE[8] GRISE, MARGARET ACHIE[7] MANN, ABEL[6], GEORGE[5], COLONEL JOHN JR.[4], JOHN SR.[3], GEORGE BERNARD[2], HANS[1])* was born April 11, 1903 in SHELBY COUNTY, OHIO, and died January 21, 1983 in GREENVILLE, OHIO.   She married WILLIE E. REDMAN December 18, 1920 in DARKE COUNTY, OHIO, son of CHARLES REDMAN and ALMA HARRIS.

   Children of EDITH BASHORE and WILLIE REDMAN are:
237.   i.   DALE E.[10] REDMAN, b. February 15, 1922, DARKE COUNTY, OHIO.
238.   ii.   NORMAN REDMAN, b. January 13, 1927, DARKE COUNTY, OHIO.
239.   iii.   NANCY JANE REDMAN, b. November 22, 1937, DARKE COUNTY, OHIO.

148. IZORA VIOLA[9] BASHORE *(LOVA CATHERINE[8] GRISE, MARGARET ACHIE[7] MANN, ABEL[6], GEORGE[5], COLONEL JOHN JR.[4], JOHN SR.[3], GEORGE BERNARD[2], HANS[1])* was born July 26, 1905, and died May 22, 1983 in GREENVILLE, OHIO. She married LOUIS HERMAN STROBEL October 30, 1924 in DARKE COUNTY, OHIO.

    Children of IZORA BASHORE and LOUIS STROBEL are:
240.   i.   LEWIS[10] STROBEL, b. April 02, 1926; d. February 22, 1995.
241.   ii.   FLORENCE STROBEL, b. February 07, 1928.
242.   iii. MARY LOUISE STROBEL, b. March 03, 1929.
243.   iv.   CARL RICHARD STROBEL, b. July 14, 1938.
244.   v.   LUTHER STROBEL, b. September 07, 1940.

149. VERTIE ALWILDA[9] BASHORE *(LOVA CATHERINE[8] GRISE, MARGARET ACHIE[7] MANN, ABEL[6], GEORGE[5], COLONEL JOHN JR.[4], JOHN SR.[3], GEORGE BERNARD[2], HANS[1])* was born March 02, 1913. She married HARRY HORNER February 28, 1934 in DARKE COUNTY, OHIO.

    Children of VERTIE BASHORE and HARRY HORNER are:
245.   i.   H. DEAN[10] HORNER, b. August 15, 1935.
246.   ii.   DONNA HORNER, b. April 16, 1938.
247.   iii. HERMAN HORNER, b. November 19, 1939.

150. JOHN MARTIN[9] BASHORE *(LOVA CATHERINE[8] GRISE, MARGARET ACHIE[7] MANN, ABEL[6], GEORGE[5], COLONEL JOHN JR.[4], JOHN SR.[3], GEORGE BERNARD[2], HANS[1])* was born February 15, 1920 in DARKE COUNTY, OHIO. He died August 26, 1992, in PIQUA, OH. He married DOROTHY WION February 25, 1939 in WINCHESTER, INDIANA, daughter of JOHN WION and DORA VANATTA.

    Children of JOHN BASHORE and DOROTHY WION are:
248.   i.   PHYLLIS JOAN[10] BASHORE, b. June 15, 1940, MIAMI COUNTY, OHIO.
249.   ii.   SAMUEL WILLIAM BASHORE, b. January 07, 1942, MIAMI COUNTY, OHIO.
250.   iii. DONALD JAMES BASHORE, b. October 11, 1946, MIAMI COUNTY, OHIO.
        iv.   LARRY JOE BASHORE, b. April 12, 1951, MIAMI COUNTY, OHIO.
251.   v.   DEBORAH ARLENE BASHORE, b. May 14, 1953, MIAMI COUNTY, OHIO.
252.   vi.   RICHARD LEE BASHORE, b. December 25, 1959, MIAMI COUNTY, OHIO.

151. ORTHA SAMUEL[9] BASHORE *(LOVA CATHERINE[8] GRISE, MARGARET ACHIE[7] MANN, ABEL[6], GEORGE[5], COLONEL JOHN JR.[4], JOHN SR.[3], GEORGE BERNARD[2],*

HANS⁷) was born March 19, 1923 in DARKE COUNTY, OHIO, and died May 12, 1988 in PIQUA, OHIO. He married GOLDIE MENDENHALL February 07, 1942.

Children of ORTHA BASHORE and GOLDIE MENDENHALL are:
253.   i.   KENNETH¹⁰ BASHORE, b. December 31, 1942.
254.   ii.   HARRY BASHORE, b. March 21, 1947.

152.   DOROTHY CATHERINE⁹ BASHORE *(LOVA CATHERINE⁸ GRISE, MARGARET ACHIE⁷ MANN, ABEL⁶, GEORGE⁵, COLONEL JOHN JR.⁴, JOHN SR.³, GEORGE BERNARD², HANS⁷)* was born March 19, 1923. She married IVAN RHOADES December 14, 1940.

Children of DOROTHY BASHORE and IVAN RHOADES are:
255.   i.   NOVA¹⁰ RHOADES, b. March 16, 1942.
        ii.   DUANE RHOADES, b. January 21, 1945; d. June 1950.
256.   iii. NINA RHOADES, b. April 11, 1946.

153.   ETHEL LEOTA⁹ TROUTWINE *(LAURA JANE⁸ GRISE, MARGARET ACHIE⁷ MANN, ABEL⁶, GEORGE⁵, COLONEL JOHN JR.⁴, JOHN SR.³, GEORGE BERNARD², HANS⁷)* was born September 27, 1899, and died June 01, 1974 in MIAMI COUNTY, OHIO. She married (1) HOMER SMITH September 10, 1919. She married (2) LANDON ODA 1971.

Child of ETHEL TROUTWINE and HOMER SMITH is:
257.   i.   KENNETH LEO¹⁰ SMITH, b. February 13, 1920; d. February 05, 1945,
              ENGLAND DURING WW II.

154.   TOILEY⁹ WALKER *(LILLIE FLORENCE⁸ GRISE, MARGARET ACHIE⁷ MANN, ABEL⁶, GEORGE⁵, COLONEL JOHN JR.⁴, JOHN SR.³, GEORGE BERNARD², HANS⁷)* was born October 16, 1900, and died February 15, 1993. She married EARL MILLER.

Children of TOILEY WALKER and EARL MILLER are:
258.   i.   LOWELL¹⁰ MILLER, b. December 14, 1919, BRADFORD, OHIO; d. April 11,
              1993, INDIANA.
259.   ii.   DOROTHY MILLER, b. September 05, 1921.
260.   iii. JUANITA MILLER, b. September 25, 1923.
261.   iv.   ALICE MILLER, b. January 31, 1926.
262.   v.   RUBY MILLER, b. January 19, 1929.

155. RAYMOND[9] WALKER *(LILLIE FLORENCE[8] GRISE, MARGARET ACHIE[7] MANN, ABEL[6], GEORGE[5], COLONEL JOHN JR.[4], JOHN SR.[3], GEORGE BERNARD[2], HANS[1])* was born April 03, 1903. He married NINA WORTHINGTON March 01, 1929.

Children of RAYMOND WALKER and NINA WORTHINGTON are:
263.   i. BETTY[10] WALKER, b. July 25, 1930.
264.   ii. NORMA WALKER, b. March 19, 1933.
265. iii. ROBERT WALKER, b. September 22, 1934.
266.   iv. EVELYN WALKER, b. December 24, 1935.
        v. PHYLISS WALKER, b. January 15, 1939.

156. MILLARD[9] WALKER *(LILLIE FLORENCE[8] GRISE, MARGARET ACHIE[7] MANN, ABEL[6], GEORGE[5], COLONEL JOHN JR.[4], JOHN SR.[3], GEORGE BERNARD[2], HANS[1])* was born April 05, 1908. He married VIRGIE CLARK January 1927.

Children of MILLARD WALKER and VIRGIE CLARK are:
        i. JUNE[10] WALKER, b. March 05, 1929.
       ii. JAMES WALKER, b. June 21, 1931.
      iii. LARRY WALKER, b. April 01, 1947.

157. MARGARET[9] WALKER *(LILLIE FLORENCE[8] GRISE, MARGARET ACHIE[7] MANN, ABEL[6], GEORGE[5], COLONEL JOHN JR.[4], JOHN SR.[3], GEORGE BERNARD[2], HANS[1])* was born July 01, 1911. She married (1) ROBERT BAKER. She married (2) WILLARD SWERKING.

Child of MARGARET WALKER and ROBERT BAKER is:
        i. VIRGINIA[10] BAKER, m. MARTIN WALDREN.

158. ELIZABETH MAE[9] WALKER *(LILLIE FLORENCE[8] GRISE, MARGARET ACHIE[7] MANN, ABEL[6], GEORGE[5], COLONEL JOHN JR.[4], JOHN SR.[3], GEORGE BERNARD[2], HANS[1])* was born May 24, 1913, and died December 1991. She married RICHARD KONZ April 19, 1934.

Children of ELIZABETH WALKER and RICHARD KONZ are:
267.   i. CHARLES[10] KONZ, b. July 29, 1934.
       ii. MARVIN KONZ, b. November 24, 1935; m. DARLENE MUNS, December 23, 1954.
268. iii. RITA KONZ, b. April 08, 1937.
       iv. DONALD KONZ, b. February 03, 1939.

159. EARL[9] WALKER *(LILLIE FLORENCE[8] GRISE, MARGARET ACHIE[7] MANN, ABEL[6], GEORGE[5], COLONEL JOHN JR.[4], JOHN SR.[3], GEORGE BERNARD[2], HANS[1])* was born August 10, 1914. He married RUTH VALENTINE September 01, 1934.

   Children of EARL WALKER and RUTH VALENTINE are:
269.   i.   MARGARET[10] WALKER, b. January 04, 1935.
        ii.   HOWARD WALKER, b. December 23, 1938; d. February 07, 1985.
       iii.   LARRY WALKER, b. August 10, 1945.
        iv.   THOMAS WALKER, b. September 15, 1952.

160. LOUISE[9] WALKER *(LILLIE FLORENCE[8] GRISE, MARGARET ACHIE[7] MANN, ABEL[6], GEORGE[5], COLONEL JOHN JR.[4], JOHN SR.[3], GEORGE BERNARD[2], HANS[1])* was born December 28, 1915. She married MARTIN CROMES July 03, 1933.

   Children of LOUISE WALKER and MARTIN CROMES are:
270.   i.   PAUL[10] CROMES, b. December 27, 1933.
271.   ii.   MARION CROMES, b. September 28, 1935.
272.   iii.   DELBERT CROMES, b. August 23, 1937.
273.   iv.   WANDA CROMES, b. May 13, 1939.
274.   v.   BENNY CROMES, b. April 27, 1944.
275.   vi.   DANNY CROMES, b. December 19, 1945.

161. RUTH[9] WALKER *(LILLIE FLORENCE[8] GRISE, MARGARET ACHIE[7] MANN, ABEL[6], GEORGE[5], COLONEL JOHN JR.[4], JOHN SR.[3], GEORGE BERNARD[2], HANS[1])* was born May 10, 1917. She married MICHAEL KULP November 20, 1940.

   Children of RUTH WALKER and MICHAEL KULP are:
         i.   PATRICK[10] KULP, b. August 11, 1943.
        ii.   DIANE KULP, b. June 30, 1946; m. THOMAS GRIFFIN.
       iii.   DEBORAH KULP, b. December 04, 1952.

162. DELORES[9] WALKER *(LILLIE FLORENCE[8] GRISE, MARGARET ACHIE[7] MANN, ABEL[6], GEORGE[5], COLONEL JOHN JR.[4], JOHN SR.[3], GEORGE BERNARD[2], HANS[1])* was born July 15, 1922. She married JAMES COVAULT August 31, 1940.

   Child of DELORES WALKER and JAMES COVAULT is:
         i.   SANDRA[10] COVAULT, b. February 19, 1942; m. DOUG CHRISTIAN.

163. HAROLD[9] WALKER *(LILLIE FLORENCE[8] GRISE, MARGARET ACHIE[7] MANN, ABEL[6], GEORGE[5], COLONEL JOHN JR.[4], JOHN SR.[3], GEORGE BERNARD[2], HANS[1])* was

born July 28, 1923, and died February 07, 1966. He married HELEN HISSONG September 13, 1941.

Children of HAROLD WALKER and HELEN HISSONG are:
     i.   LINDA[10] WALKER, b. February 07, 1943; m. BRUCE WEATHERHEAD.
276. ii. HAROLD GENE WALKER, b. January 11, 1945.
     iii. SHIRLEY WALKER, b. August 08, 1949; m. MR. THORPE.
     iv. JACK WALKER, b. March 31, 1954.

164. HELEN IRENE[9] GRISE *(RUBEN[8], MARGARET ACHIE[7] MANN, ABEL[6], GEORGE[5], COLONEL JOHN JR.[4], JOHN SR.[3], GEORGE BERNARD[2], HANS[1])* was born August 17, 1906, and died September 20, 1945. She married CARL COOK April 1930.

Child of HELEN GRISE and CARL COOK is:
277.   i. PHYLISS[10] COOK, b. October 03, 1931.

165. ETOILE[9] GRISE *(RUBEN[8], MARGARET ACHIE[7] MANN, ABEL[6], GEORGE[5], COLONEL JOHN JR.[4], JOHN SR.[3], GEORGE BERNARD[2], HANS[1])* was born October 20, 1909, and died December 20, 1931. She married HAROLD FOLKERTH February 18, 1931.

Child of ETOILE GRISE and HAROLD FOLKERTH is:
278.   i. HAROLD[10] FOLKERTH, b. December 06, 1931.

166. HARVEY DAVID[9] GRISE *(RUBEN[8], MARGARET ACHIE[7] MANN, ABEL[6], GEORGE[5], COLONEL JOHN JR.[4], JOHN SR.[3], GEORGE BERNARD[2], HANS[1])* was born April 01, 1916. He married HILDA BRANDT September 05, 1938.

Child of HARVEY GRISE and HILDA BRANDT is:
279.   i. PATRICK[10] GRISE, b. November 30, 1951.

167. RICHARD[9] GRISE *(ELI C.[8], MARGARET ACHIE[7] MANN, ABEL[6], GEORGE[5], COLONEL JOHN JR.[4], JOHN SR.[3], GEORGE BERNARD[2], HANS[1])* was born May 01, 1930. He married SUSAN HOWELL August 26, 1950.

Children of RICHARD GRISE and SUSAN HOWELL are:
280.   i. SHERYL[10] GRISE, b. January 13, 1952.
281. ii. GAIL GRISE, b. June 23, 1953.

282.   iii.   SANDRA GRISE, b. January 18, 1958.

168.   GLADYS GAIL[9] ULLERY (MARGARET ELSIE[8] MANN, GEORGE SIMEON[7], ABEL[6], GEORGE[5], COLONEL JOHN JR.[4], JOHN SR.[3], GEORGE BERNARD[2], HANS[1]) was born August 07, 1910 in ANSONIA, OHIO. She married PAUL LINK MILLER July 27, 1940.

   Children of GLADYS ULLERY and PAUL MILLER are:
       i.   JUDITH LYNN[10] MILLER, b. July 08, 1941, DAYTON, OHIO.
      ii.   MARY DEE MILLER, b. January 21, 1943, DAYTON, OHIO; m.
            JOHN FARLEY, May 21, 1978.
     iii.   PETER LINK MILLER, b. January 25, 1947.
      iv.   PAUL LINK MILLER, b. January 25, 1947; m. DOROTHY CRIDEL,
            June 1982.

169.   RUTH[9] SHAFER (BERTHA MAE[8] MATTHEWS, ELIZABETH E.[7] MANN, ABEL[6], GEORGE[5], COLONEL JOHN JR.[4], JOHN SR.[3], GEORGE BERNARD[2], HANS[1]) was born December 07, 1898 in MIAMI COUNTY, OHIO, and died August 18, 1984 in MIAMI COUNTY, OHIO. She married ALBERT THOMPSON January 25, 1919 in MIAMI COUNTY, OHIO.

   Children of RUTH SHAFER and ALBERT THOMPSON are:
283.   i.   DALE EVERETT[10] THOMPSON, b. December 03, 1920, MIAMI
              COUNTY, OHIO.
284.   ii.   DELMAR LEROY THOMPSON, b. March 28, 1922, MIAMI COUNTY,
              OHIO.
285.   iii.   ROBERT LEE THOMPSON, b. January 28, 1924, MIAMI COUNTY,
              OHIO.
286.   iv.   BETTY LOU THOMPSON, b. January 28, 1924.
         v.   ESTHER ARLENE THOMPSON, b. December 16, 1926, MIAMI
              COUNTY, OHIO; m. RUSSELL SMITH, June 22, 1943, MIAMI
              COUNTY, OHIO.

170.   JOSEPH DAVID[9] SHAFER (BERTHA MAE[8] MATTHEWS, ELIZABETH E.[7] MANN, ABEL[6], GEORGE[5], COLONEL JOHN JR.[4], JOHN SR.[3], GEORGE BERNARD[2], HANS[1]) was born December 31, 1917 in BRADFORD, OHIO, and died July 01, 1989 in DAYTON, MONTGOMERY COUNTY, OHIO. He married MARLENE BRUMBAUGH.

   Children of JOSEPH SHAFER and MARLENE BRUMBAUGH are:
287.   i.   JOSEPH DAVID[10] SHAFER, b. February 01, 1956.
        ii.   RICHARD E. SHAFER, b. August 06, 1958.

171. RUTH[9] MATTHEWS (FORREST[8], ELIZABETH E.[7] MANN, ABEL[6], GEORGE[5], COLONEL JOHN JR.[4], JOHN SR.[3], GEORGE BERNARD[2], HANS[1]) was born 1917, and died June 07, 1996. She married HAROLD PEARSON June 17, 1936.

   Child of RUTH MATTHEWS and HAROLD PEARSON is:
288.   i.   MARILYN SUE[10] PEARSON, b. 1946.

172. HELEN[9] MATTHEWS (FORREST[8], ELIZABETH E.[7] MANN, ABEL[6], GEORGE[5], COLONEL JOHN JR.[4], JOHN SR.[3], GEORGE BERNARD[2], HANS[1]) was born 1918. She married MELVIN KELLER September 09, 1939.

   Child of HELEN MATTHEWS and MELVIN KELLER is:
289.   i.   LYNN[10] KELLER, b. 1941.

173. MARIBEL[9] MATTHEWS (FORREST[8], ELIZABETH E.[7] MANN, ABEL[6], GEORGE[5], COLONEL JOHN JR.[4], JOHN SR.[3], GEORGE BERNARD[2], HANS[1]) was born 1925. She married ROBERT MCGARRY 1950.

   Children of MARIBEL MATTHEWS and ROBERT MCGARRY are:
         i.   DANIEL[10] MCGARRY.
        ii.   ROGER MCGARRY.
       iii.   JULIE MCGARRY.
        iv.   ROBERT MCGARRY.

174. ORA FRANKLIN[9] WELBAUM (WASHINGTON TROY[8], EMMA[7] MANN, ABEL[6], GEORGE[5], COLONEL JOHN JR.[4], JOHN SR.[3], GEORGE BERNARD[2], HANS[1]) was born March 05, 1908 in MIAMI COUNTY, OHIO, and died November 07, 1963 in PIQUA, OHIO. He married ANNA.

   Child of ORA WELBAUM and ANNA is:
         i.   ORA HAROLD[10] WELBAUM.

175. HAZEL ESTHER[9] HOLE (MARTHA E.[8] WELBAUM, EMMA[7] MANN, ABEL[6], GEORGE[5], COLONEL JOHN JR.[4], JOHN SR.[3], GEORGE BERNARD[2], HANS[1]) was born August 21, 1903 in MIAMI COUNTY, OHIO. She married CLARENCE CLYDE COVULT October 09, 1922 in MIAMI COUNTY, OHIO.

   Child of HAZEL HOLE and CLARENCE COVULT is:

    i.   LOIS V.[10] COVULT, b. February 29, 1924, PIQUA, OHIO; d. 1967; m. RALPH DEETER, August 23, 1945, MIAMI COUNTY, OHIO.

176.   CORDELLA BELLE[9] HOLE *(MARTHA E.[8] WELBAUM, EMMA[7] MANN, ABEL[6], GEORGE[5], COLONEL JOHN JR.[4], JOHN SR.[3], GEORGE BERNARD[2], HANS[1])* was born April 18, 1906 in MIAMI COUNTY, OHIO, and died August 05, 1924 in MIAMI COUNTY, OHIO.   She married CARL WILLIAM KESSLER August 05, 1924 in MIAMI COUNTY, OHIO.

    Child of CORDELLA HOLE and CARL KESSLER is:
    i.   THOMAS[10] KESSLER.

Generation No. 8 of John Mann Sr.

177. RICHARD[10] CLAWSON *(CHARLES EDWARD[9], FREDERICK A.[8], RACHEL A.[7] BUTT, LUCINDA[6] MANN, ISAAC[5], COLONEL JOHN JR.[4], JOHN SR.[3], GEORGE BERNARD[2], HANS[1])* was born July 11, 1921 in SHELBY COUNTY, OHIO. He married RUTH MIDDY June 26, 1945.

Children of RICHARD CLAWSON and RUTH MIDDY are:
    i.   GARY[11] CLAWSON, m. DONNA.
    ii.   RICHARD CLAWSON.
    iii. BEVERLY CLAWSON.

178. MAURICE F.[10] CLAWSON *(CHARLES EDWARD[9], FREDERICK A.[8], RACHEL A.[7] BUTT, LUCINDA[6] MANN, ISAAC[5], COLONEL JOHN JR.[4], JOHN SR.[3], GEORGE BERNARD[2], HANS[1])* was born August 25, 1923 in SHELBY COUNTY, OHIO, and died February 26, 1988 in PIQUA, OHIO. He married CATHERINE MEEKER.

Child of MAURICE CLAWSON and CATHERINE MEEKER is:
    i.   FREDERICK[11] CLAWSON.

179. RANDALL LEE[10] QUATE *(BETTY JEANNE[9] MANN, ROY WILLIAM[8], CLEMMENT ELZIE[7], LEWIS JACKSON[6], ISAAC[5], COLONEL JOHN JR.[4], JOHN SR.[3], GEORGE BERNARD[2], HANS[1])* was born November 07, 1947 in MUNCIE, INDIANA. He married PATRICIA ANN OSBORNE September 30, 1967 in TOLEDO, OHIO.

Children of RANDALL QUATE and PATRICIA OSBORNE are:
    i.   MARGARET ANN (PEGGY)[11] QUATE, b. September 25, 1975, TOLEDO, OHIO.
    ii.   SARA ANN QUATE, b. November 17, 1978, TOLEDO, OHIO.

180. JEFFERY ALLEN[10] QUATE *(BETTY JEANNE[9] MANN, ROY WILLIAM[8], CLEMMENT ELZIE[7], LEWIS JACKSON[6], ISAAC[5], COLONEL JOHN JR.[4], JOHN SR.[3], GEORGE BERNARD[2], HANS[1])* was born September 08, 1959 in TOLEDO, OHIO. He married LOUNIE SUE JEFFERS May 05, 1979 in WHITEHOUSE, OHIO.

Children of JEFFERY QUATE and LOUNIE JEFFERS are:
    i.   NICOLE MARIE[11] QUATE, b. December 11, 1979, TOLEDO, OHIO.
    ii.   JESSICA LEE QUATE, b. March 06, 1982, TOLEDO, OHIO.

181. TIMOTHY ALLEN[10] MANN *(JOHN ALLEN JR.[9], JOHN ALLEN SR.[8], DORSEY VIRGIL[7], LEWIS JACKSON[6], ISAAC[5], COLONEL JOHN JR.[4], JOHN SR.[3], GEORGE BERNARD[2], HANS[1])* was born August 17, 1961 in SIDNEY, OHIO.

   Children of TIMOTHY ALLEN MANN are:
    i. ELIZABETH MARIE (BETSY)[11] MANN, b. March 16, 1986, SIDNEY, OHIO. Her son MAVEN LEE BRADLEY was born JULY 20, 2009.
    ii. SHAYNA RACHELLE MANN, b. June 26, 1994, SIDNEY, OHIO.

182. DEBRA LYNN[10] MANN *(JOHN ALLEN JR.[9], JOHN ALLEN SR.[8], DORSEY VIRGIL[7], LEWIS JACKSON[6], ISAAC[5], COLONEL JOHN JR.[4], JOHN SR.[3], GEORGE BERNARD[2], HANS[1])* was born January 29, 1964 in SIDNEY, OHIO. She married JEFFERY MICHAEL DONALD WAGNER September 05, 1981 in McCARTYVILLE, OHIO.

   Children of DEBRA MANN and JEFFERY WAGNER are:
    i. MICHAEL LEE[11] WAGNER, b. February 06, 1982, LIMA, OHIO. He married ANGELA CHENOWETH on April 24, 2004.   Their son LUKE MICHAEL was born on December 17, 2008.
    ii. JUSTIN HENRY WAGNER, b. November 17, 1986, PIQUA, OHIO. He married MEGAN ANNE MORELOCK on October 2, 2010.
    iii. MEGAN LYNN WAGNER, b. August 09, 1988, PIQUA, OHIO.

183. SHERRI KAY[10] MANN *(JOHN ALLEN JR.[9], JOHN ALLEN SR.[8], DORSEY VIRGIL[7], LEWIS JACKSON[6], ISAAC[5], COLONEL JOHN JR.[4], JOHN SR.[3], GEORGE BERNARD[2], HANS[1])* was born April 30, 1971 in SIDNEY, OHIO. She married KENNETH ANDREW JENSEN March 20, 1992 in ANNA, OHIO.

   Children of SHERRI MANN and KENNETH JENSEN is:
    i. ANDREW LOUIS[11] JENSEN, b. June 24, 1996, LIMA, ALLEN COUNTY, OHIO.
    ii. AARON PARKER JENSEN, b. January 9, 1999.

184. JOAN LOURIE[10] EARLS *(PHYLLIS EILEEN[9] MANN, JOHN ALLEN SR.[8], DORSEY VIRGIL[7], LEWIS JACKSON[6], ISAAC[5], COLONEL JOHN JR.[4], JOHN SR.[3], GEORGE BERNARD[2], HANS[1])* was born December 17, 1956 in PIQUA, OHIO. She married (1) JAY ALLEN MOON March 21, 1975 in PIQUA, OHIO. She married (2) CARL STEPHEN CRAWFORD April 04, 1987, son of CARL CRAWFORD and ALBERTA FOURMAN.

   Child of JOAN EARLS and JAY MOON is:
   290.   i. ANGEL RENEE[11] MOON, b. July 08, 1977, PIQUA, OHIO.

185. SUSAN ELAINE[10] EARLS *(PHYLLIS EILEEN[9] MANN, JOHN ALLEN SR.[8], DORSEY VIRGIL[7], LEWIS JACKSON[6], ISAAC[5], COLONEL JOHN JR.[4], JOHN SR.[3], GEORGE BERNARD[2], HANS[1])* was born April 12, 1958 in PIQUA, OHIO. She married DAVID SCHNEIDER September 24, 1977 in SIDNEY, OHIO, son of CHESTER SCHNEIDER and EILEEN BUENTE.

   Children of SUSAN EARLS and DAVID SCHNEIDER are:
      i.   JOHN ALLEN[11] SCHNEIDER, b. November 12, 1981, PIQUA, OHIO.
      ii. STACY LYNN SCHNEIDER, b. October 15, 1986, PIQUA, OHIO.

186. JOSEPH EDWARD[10] EARLS *(PHYLLIS EILEEN[9] MANN, JOHN ALLEN SR.[8], DORSEY VIRGIL[7], LEWIS JACKSON[6], ISAAC[5], COLONEL JOHN JR.[4], JOHN SR.[3], GEORGE BERNARD[2], HANS[1])* was born December 20, 1960 in PIQUA, OHIO. He married (1) PEGGY SUE COMPTON March 10, 1979 in COVINGTON, OHIO, daughter of ELMER COMPTON and CHRISTINE WILSON. He married (2) CANDRA M. MOWERY December 1991.

   Child of JOSEPH EARLS and PEGGY COMPTON is:
      i.   JASON WAYNE[11] EARLS, b. September 07, 1979, SIDNEY, OHIO. His children are AUTUMN EARLS, b. 2001, and AUSTIN EARLS, b. 2003

   Child of JOSEPH EARLS and CANDRA MOWERY is:
      ii. RYAN JOSEPH[11] EARLS, b. December 30, 1986. His son is STEVEN EARLS, b.2007.

187. PAMELA ANNETTE[10] MANN *(EDWARD LOUIS SR.[9], JOHN ALLEN SR.[8], DORSEY VIRGIL[7], LEWIS JACKSON[6], ISAAC[5], COLONEL JOHN JR.[4], JOHN SR.[3], GEORGE BERNARD[2], HANS[1])* was born February 02, 1962 in PIQUA, OHIO. She married (1) RICKEY SCOTT SHANNON June 19, 1981 in PIQUA, OHIO, son of HAROLD SHANNON and JUDY FLOSS. She married (2) Donald Palmer.

   Children of PAMELA MANN and RICKEY SHANNON are:
      i.   RICHARD SCOTT[11] SHANNON, b. April 08, 1982, PIQUA, OHIO.
           Richard died August 11, 1997
      ii. NICHOLAS EDWARD SHANNON, b. February 23, 1984, PIQUA, OHIO.
      iii. CHRISTOPHER ADAM SHANNON, b. February 23, 1984, PIQUA, OHIO.

188. CAROLYN DIANE[10] MANN *(EDWARD LOUIS SR.[9], JOHN ALLEN SR.[8], DORSEY VIRGIL[7], LEWIS JACKSON[6], ISAAC[5], COLONEL JOHN JR.[4], JOHN SR.[3], GEORGE BERNARD[2], HANS[1])* was born May 30, 1965 in PIQUA, OHIO. She married GARY MILLER July 14, 1984 in PIQUA, OHIO, son of GARY MILLER and ELOISE HARMON.

   Children of CAROLYN MANN and GARY MILLER are:
        i.   GARY ALLEN JR.[11] MILLER, b. December 04, 1984, DAYTON, OHIO.
       ii.   ANDREW MICHAEL BRIAN MILLER, b. September 21, 1986. ANDREW'S children
              are CHEYENNE, b. 2006 and McKenzie, born 2008.

189. DANIEL[10] SCHWAIGER *(JANE MARIE[9] BANGS, ELLEN VIOLA[8] MANN, DORSEY VIRGIL[7], LEWIS JACKSON[6], ISAAC[5], COLONEL JOHN JR.[4], JOHN SR.[3], GEORGE BERNARD[2], HANS[1])* was born November 29, 1965 in OHIO, MONTGOMERY COUNTY. He married CHRISTINA.

   Children of DANIEL SCHWAIGER and CHRISTINA are:
        i.   JACOB DANIEL[11] SCHWAIGER, b. December 14, 1990.
       ii.   KATILYN SCHWAIGER, b. June 22, 1995.

190. DONALD[10] FANCHER *(MYRTLE[9] DUGAN, ALBERT VIRGIL[8], ELIZA MELISSA[7] MANN, ISAAC JR.[6], ISAAC[5], COLONEL JOHN JR.[4], JOHN SR.[3], GEORGE BERNARD[2], HANS[1])* was born About. 1913.

   Children of DONALD FANCHER are:
        i.   RALPH[11] FANCHER, b. About. 1927.
       ii.   PATTY FANCHER, b. About. 1929.

191. SANDRA KAY[10] FROGGE *(EUGENIA MARIE[9] DUGAN, ALBERT VIRGIL[8], ELIZA MELISSA[7] MANN, ISAAC JR.[6], ISAAC[5], COLONEL JOHN JR.[4], JOHN SR.[3], GEORGE BERNARD[2], HANS[1])* was born February 22, 1945 in SHELBYVILLE, INDIANA. He married MR. ROWE March 28, 1962 in INDIANA.

   Children of SANDRA FROGGE and MR. ROWE are:
        i.   JEFFERY S.[11] ROWE, b. February 14, 1963.
       ii.   DOUGLAS ROWE, b. About. 1965.

192.   LARRY THOMAS[10] ROSS *(BESSIE CLARINA[9] GRIFFEY, DORA B.[8] DUGAN, ELIZA MELISSA[7] MANN, ISAAC JR.[6], ISAAC[5], COLONEL JOHN JR.[4], JOHN SR.[3], GEORGE BERNARD[2], HANS[1])* was born February 22, 1942 in ARLINGTON, RUSH COUNTY, INDIANA. He married ROBERTA DIANE CHAPMAN August 05, 1967 in HYDE PARK, LAMOILLE COUNTY, VERMONT, daughter of ROBERT CHAPMAN and MILDRED NETZBAND.

   Children of LARRY ROSS and ROBERTA CHAPMAN are:
        i.   KIMBERLY ELLEN[11] ROSS, b. January 13, 1973, SEOUL, SOUTH
              KOREA.
        ii. LAURA ANN ROSS, b. April 17, 1976, SAN ANGELO, TOM GREEN
              COUNTY, TEXAS.

193.   LUCILLE KATHERINE[10] MANN *(HARRY CHRIS[9], ISAAC ORAN[8], CHRISTIAN[7], ISAAC JR.[6], ISAAC[5], COLONEL JOHN JR.[4], JOHN SR.[3], GEORGE BERNARD[2], HANS[1])* was born September 24, 1931 in CHICAGO, ILLINOIS. She married HILTON A. TONEY June 06, 1951.

   Children of LUCILLE MANN and HILTON TONEY are:
291.   i.   RONALD HILTON[11] TONEY, b. May 08, 1952.
292.   ii. CYNTHIA MARIE TONEY, b. March 29, 1955.
293.   iii. SUSANNE CHRISTINE TONEY, b. January 01, 1958.

194.   LEONARD R.[10] CARLBERG *(LOMA IRENE[9] JONES, EDITH A.[8] MANN, CHRISTIAN[7], ISAAC JR.[6], ISAAC[5], COLONEL JOHN JR.[4], JOHN SR.[3], GEORGE BERNARD[2], HANS[1])* was born May 08, 1928 in SOUTH HAVEN, MICHIGAN. He married ALICE STANTZ 1957 in ELKHART, INDIANA.

   Children of LEONARD CARLBERG and ALICE STANTZ are:
        i.   SCOTT[11] CARLBERG, b. About. 1958, ELKHART, INDIANA.
        ii. WILLIAM CARLBERG, b. About. 1961, ELKHART, INDIANA.
        iii. HELSHMAN CARLBERG, b. About. 1963, ELKHART, INDIANA.

195.   NANCY[10] CARLBERG *(LOMA IRENE[9] JONES, EDITH A.[8] MANN, CHRISTIAN[7], ISAAC JR.[6], ISAAC[5], COLONEL JOHN JR.[4], JOHN SR.[3], GEORGE BERNARD[2], HANS[1])* was born August 07, 1937 in SOUTH HAVEN, MICHIGAN. She married DON KORRECKI 1957.

Children of NANCY CARLBERG and DON KORRECKI are:
  i.   AMY[11] KORRECKI, b. About. 1960.
  ii.   CINDY KORRECKI, b. About. 1962.
  iii. BONNIE KORRECKI, b. About. 1965.
  iv.   DIANE KORRECKI, b. About. 1967.

196.   SALLY ANN[10] JONES (DONALD R.[9], EDITH A.[8] MANN, CHRISTIAN[7], ISAAC JR.[6], ISAAC[5], COLONEL JOHN JR.[4], JOHN SR.[3], GEORGE BERNARD[2], HANS[1]) was born October 14, 1936 in ELKHART, INDIANA.   She married MIKE PIERPORT About. 1960 in ELKHART, INDIANA.

  Children of SALLY JONES and MIKE PIERPORT are:
    i.   DENISE[11] PIERPORT, b. About. 1962, ELKHART, INDIANA.
    ii.   PAMELA PIERPORT, b. About. 1965, ELKHART, INDIANA.
    iii. MARY PIERPORT, b. About. 1966, ELKHART, INDIANA.
    iv.   CAROLE PIERPORT, b. About. 1967, ELKHART, INDIANA.
    v.   GEORGE PIERPORT, b. About. 1968, ELKHART, INDIANA.

197.   CAROL[10] JONES (DONALD R.[9], EDITH A.[8] MANN, CHRISTIAN[7], ISAAC JR.[6], ISAAC[5], COLONEL JOHN JR.[4], JOHN SR.[3], GEORGE BERNARD[2], HANS[1]) was born April 01, 1945 in ELKHART, INDIANA.   She married (1) MR. DIETZ About. 1960 in ELKHART, INDIANA.   She married (2) PHILLIP SMITH September 29, 1962 in ELKHART, INDIANA.

  Child of CAROL JONES and MR. DIETZ is:
    i.   LORI ANN[11] DIETZ, b. March 22, 1962.

  Children of CAROL JONES and PHILLIP SMITH are:
    ii.   MICHAEL RAY[11] SMITH, b. May 22, 1963, ELKHART, INDIANA.
    iii. CHRISTINE MARIE SMITH, b. May 07, 1965, ELKHART, INDIANA.
    iv.   TRACY RENEE SMITH, b. October 04, 1968, ELKHART, INDIANA.

198.   LINDA KATHLEEN[10] JONES (DONALD R.[9], EDITH A.[8] MANN, CHRISTIAN[7], ISAAC JR.[6], ISAAC[5], COLONEL JOHN JR.[4], JOHN SR.[3], GEORGE BERNARD[2], HANS[1]) was born December 02, 1952 in ELKHART, INDIANA.   She married ROGER HOLDREN January 18, 1967 in SOUTH BEND INDIANA.

  Children of LINDA JONES and ROGER HOLDREN are:
    i.   TOMMIE RAY[11] HOLDREN, b. March 17, 1969, ELKHART, INDIANA.
    ii.   ROGER HOLDREN, b. October 18, 1970, ELKHART, INDIANA.

199.   SANDRA[10] STRUKEL (DOROTHY GLADYS[9] JONES, EDITH A.[8] MANN, CHRISTIAN[7], ISAAC JR.[6], ISAAC[5], COLONEL JOHN JR.[4], JOHN SR.[3], GEORGE BERNARD[2], HANS[1]) was born About. 1950 in ELKHART, INDIANA. She married MR. FREES About. 1970 in INDIANA.

    Children of SANDRA STRUKEL and MR. FREES are:
        i.   SANDRA[11] FREES, b. About. 1966, ELKHART, INDIANA.
        ii. MELISSA FREES, b. About. 1975, ELKHART, INDIANA.

200.   STEPHEN D.[10] JONES (LANCE DARREL[9], EDITH A.[8] MANN, CHRISTIAN[7], ISAAC JR.[6], ISAAC[5], COLONEL JOHN JR.[4], JOHN SR.[3], GEORGE BERNARD[2], HANS[1]) was born August 19, 1946 in ELKHART, INDIANA. He married ELIZABETH KIDDER August 29, 1965 in ELKHART, INDIANA.

    Children of STEPHEN JONES and ELIZABETH KIDDER are:
        i.   ROBERT LANCE[11] JONES, b. January 02, 1965.
294.   ii. MARK RICHARD JONES, b. February 09, 1967, ELKHART, INDIANA.

201.   RUTH ANN[10] JONES (LANCE DARREL[9], EDITH A.[8] MANN, CHRISTIAN[7], ISAAC JR.[6], ISAAC[5], COLONEL JOHN JR.[4], JOHN SR.[3], GEORGE BERNARD[2], HANS[1]) was born August 30, 1950 in ELKHART, INDIANA. She married DENNIS FLICKENGER June 13, 1968 in ELKHART, INDIANA.

    Children of RUTH JONES and DENNIS FLICKENGER are:
        i.   MICHAEL ALLEN[11] FLICKENGER, b. April 24, 1968, ELKHART, INDIANA.
        ii. TRAY ANDREW FLICKENGER, b. August 17, 1971, ELKHART, INDIANA.

202.   SARA JANE[10] JONES (LANCE DARREL[9], EDITH A.[8] MANN, CHRISTIAN[7], ISAAC JR.[6], ISAAC[5], COLONEL JOHN JR.[4], JOHN SR.[3], GEORGE BERNARD[2], HANS[1]) was born September 16, 1954 in ELKHART, INDIANA. She married HARRY K. KASPRAZAK About. 1974 in INDIANA.

Children of SARA JONES and HARRY KASPRAZAK are:
- i.   JASON TODD[11] KASPRAZAK, b. August 20, 1976, ELKHART, INDIANA.
- ii. HEATHER RENEE KASPRAZAK, b. February 16, 1981, ELKHART, INDIANA.

203.   JOHN E.[10] JONES *(PAUL E.[9], EDITH A.[8] MANN, CHRISTIAN[7], ISAAC JR.[6], ISAAC[5], COLONEL JOHN JR.[4], JOHN SR.[3], GEORGE BERNARD[2], HANS[1])* was born About. April 1953 in ELKHART, INDIANA, and died 1989 in ELKHART, INDIANA. He married SHARON HAFER 1973 in INDIANA.

Children of JOHN JONES and SHARON HAFER are:
- i.   CHERRIE J.[11] JONES, b. 1974, ELKHART, INDIANA.
- ii. TOMMIE J. JONES, b. About. 1975, ELKHART, INDIANA.
- iii. ICENA J. JONES, b. About. 1977, ELKHART, INDIANA.
- iv. ROBIN JONES, b. About. 1979, ELKHART, INDIANA.

204.   CHERRIE LOU[10] MANN *(STEWARD RAYMOND[9], HARLEY R.[8], CHRISTIAN[7], ISAAC JR.[6], ISAAC[5], COLONEL JOHN JR.[4], JOHN SR.[3], GEORGE BERNARD[2], HANS[1])* was born 1937 in ELKHART, INDIANA. She married JOHN R. SCHEETS September 25, 1955 in ELKHART, INDIANA.

Children of CHERRIE MANN and JOHN SCHEETS are:
- i.   LORI[11] SCHEETS, b. February 21, 1958.
- 295. ii. PATRICK SCHEETS, b. July 13, 1959, ELKHART, INDIANA.
- iii. JON SCHEETS, b. January 02, 1964, ELKHART, INDIANA.

205.   SUSAN LEE[10] MANN *(KENNETH LEROY[9], HARLEY R.[8], CHRISTIAN[7], ISAAC JR.[6], ISAAC[5], COLONEL JOHN JR.[4], JOHN SR.[3], GEORGE BERNARD[2], HANS[1])* was born October 08, 1948 in ELKHART, INDIANA. She married FLOYD GREEN March 13, 1969 in ELKHART, INDIANA.

Children of SUSAN MANN and FLOYD GREEN are:
- i.   ANDREW PAUL[11] GREEN, b. October 04, 1970, ELKHART, INDIANA.
- ii. JENNIFER RENEE GREEN, b. June 26, 1973, ELKHART, INDIANA.

206.   KATHY JEAN[10] MANN *(KENNETH LEROY[9], HARLEY R.[8], CHRISTIAN[7], ISAAC JR.[6], ISAAC[5], COLONEL JOHN JR.[4], JOHN SR.[3], GEORGE BERNARD[2], HANS[1])* was

born September 15, 1950 in ELKHART, INDIANA. She married D.J. RIENDEAU About. 1969 in ELKHART, INDIANA.

Children of KATHY MANN and D.J. RIENDEAU are:
    i.   CHRISTA[11] RIENDEAU, b. January 05, 1970, ELKHART, INDIANA.
    ii. BRIAN RIENDEAU, b. July 16, 1977, ELKHART, INDIANA.

207. MARY MARIE[10] MANN (HAROLD CHRIS[9], ROY RUSSELL[8], CHRISTIAN[7], ISAAC JR.[6], ISAAC[5], COLONEL JOHN JR.[4], JOHN SR.[3], GEORGE BERNARD[2], HANS[1]) was born July 08, 1956. She married JEFFREY HAGAN About. 1976 in MICHIGAN.

Children of MARY MANN and JEFFREY HAGAN are:
    i.   MELODY LYNN[11] HAGAN, b. August 30, 1978.
    ii. GREGORY ALAN HAGAN, b. June 29, 1980.
    iii. KASEY HAGAN, b. December 13, 1981.

208. MARSHA MARIE[10] MANN (HAROLD CHRIS[9], ROY RUSSELL[8], CHRISTIAN[7], ISAAC JR.[6], ISAAC[5], COLONEL JOHN JR.[4], JOHN SR.[3], GEORGE BERNARD[2], HANS[1]) was born September 13, 1957. She married JOHN ALEXANDER SWEINHAGAN About. 1977 in MICHIGAN.

Children of MARSHA MANN and JOHN SWEINHAGAN are:
    i.   THOMAS ALEXANDER[11] SWEINHAGAN, b. About. 1978.
    ii. AMBER NICOLE SWEINHAGAN, b. About. 1980.

209. HAROLD CHRIS JR.[10] MANN (HAROLD CHRIS[9], ROY RUSSELL[8], CHRISTIAN[7], ISAAC JR.[6], ISAAC[5], COLONEL JOHN JR.[4], JOHN SR.[3], GEORGE BERNARD[2], HANS[1]) was born November 03, 1959. He married DEBORAH A. OLDENBERG July 07, 1983 in MICHIGAN.

Children of HAROLD MANN and DEBORAH OLDENBERG are:
    i.   KIMBERLY ANN[11] MANN, b. July 14, 1978.
    ii. KARLIEN RAE MANN, b. January 10, 1981.
    iii. HAROLD CHRIS III MANN, b. January 13, 1987.

210. GENE[10] ROGERS (BEVERLY JANE[9] MANN, ROY RUSSELL[8], CHRISTIAN[7], ISAAC JR.[6], ISAAC[5], COLONEL JOHN JR.[4], JOHN SR.[3], GEORGE BERNARD[2], HANS[1]) was born about 1952. He married DEBBIE about 1972 in MICHIGAN.

Children of GENE ROGERS and DEBBIE are:
    i. CHAD[11] ROGERS, b. about 1972.
  ii. JAIME ROGERS, b. about 1975.

211. GARY LOWELL[10] SHAUM (LUCILLE BERNICE[9] WALTER, RUTH LAPEARL[8] MANN, CHRISTIAN[7], ISAAC JR.[6], ISAAC[5], COLONEL JOHN JR.[4], JOHN SR.[3], GEORGE BERNARD[2], HANS[1]) was born May 03, 1942 in ELKHART, INDIANA. He married SHEILA KAY LOVEJOY May 03, 1942 in ELKHART, INDIANA.

Children of GARY SHAUM and SHEILA LOVEJOY are:
      i. SHELLY DENISE[11] SHAUM, b. January 14, 1967, ELKHART, INDIANA.
296. ii. MICHAEL GARY SHAUM, b. November 23, 1970, ELKHART, INDIANA.

212. LEWIS DEAN[10] SHAUM (LUCILLE BERNICE[9] WALTER, RUTH LAPEARL[8] MANN, CHRISTIAN[7], ISAAC JR.[6], ISAAC[5], COLONEL JOHN JR.[4], JOHN SR.[3], GEORGE BERNARD[2], HANS[1]) was born May 13, 1945. He married (1) TANIA JANE FRANCESE June 1965 in PITTSVILLE, MISSISSIPPI. He married (2) KAREN PEARL BRILL August 09, 1975 in ELKHART, INDIANA.

Child of LEWIS SHAUM and TANIA FRANCESE is:
      i. CYNTHIA JANE[11] SHAUM, b. January 21, 1966.

Children of LEWIS SHAUM and KAREN BRILL are:
    ii. ERNEST DUANE[11] SHAUM, b. September 17, 1976, ELKHART, INDIANA.
  iii. SARAH JANE SHAUM, b. August 04, 1979, ELKHART, INDIANA.

213. CHARLES DALE[10] JOHNSON (WELMA OPAL[9] TRICK, SAMANTHA[8] GRISE, MARGARET ACHIE[7] MANN, ABEL[6], GEORGE[5], COLONEL JOHN JR.[4], JOHN SR.[3], GEORGE BERNARD[2], HANS[1]) was born April 03, 1914, and died October 20, 1972. He married DOROTHY THOMPSON.

Children of CHARLES JOHNSON and DOROTHY THOMPSON are:
     i. RONNIE[11] JOHNSON.
    ii. JOANN JOHNSON.
  iii. PENNY JOHNSON.
  iv. JENA JOHNSON.

214. CHALMER EDWARD[10] JOHNSON (WELMA OPAL[9] TRICK, SAMANTHA[8] GRISE, MARGARET ACHIE[7] MANN, ABEL[6], GEORGE[5], COLONEL JOHN JR.[4], JOHN SR.[3], GEORGE BERNARD[2], HANS[1]) was born December 31, 1915, and died June 02, 1985 in PIQUA, MIAMI COUNTY, OHIO. He married EVELYN WARREN.

Child of CHALMER JOHNSON and EVELYN WARREN is:
297.   i.   ROBERT[11] JOHNSON, b. January 30, 1943.

215. JAY[10] JOHNSON (WELMA OPAL[9] TRICK, SAMANTHA[8] GRISE, MARGARET ACHIE[7] MANN, ABEL[6], GEORGE[5], COLONEL JOHN JR.[4], JOHN SR.[3], GEORGE BERNARD[2], HANS[1]) was born July 03, 1918. He married BETTE TRYDLE.

Children of JAY JOHNSON and BETTE TRYDLE are:
        i.   GARY[11] JOHNSON.
        ii.   CAROLL JOHNSON, m. JAN MOTTINGER.
        iii. JAYNIE JOHNSON.

216. MAC[10] JOHNSON (WELMA OPAL[9] TRICK, SAMANTHA[8] GRISE, MARGARET ACHIE[7] MANN, ABEL[6], GEORGE[5], COLONEL JOHN JR.[4], JOHN SR.[3], GEORGE BERNARD[2], HANS[1]) was born October 05, 1924. He married THEDA HILE.

Child of MAC JOHNSON and THEDA HILE is:
        i.   STEVE[11] JOHNSON.

217. JACK[10] JOHNSON (WELMA OPAL[9] TRICK, SAMANTHA[8] GRISE, MARGARET ACHIE[7] MANN, ABEL[6], GEORGE[5], COLONEL JOHN JR.[4], JOHN SR.[3], GEORGE BERNARD[2], HANS[1]) was born October 15, 1928 in GETTYSBURG, DARKE COUNTY, OHIO, and died August 01, 1993 in SAN ANTONIO, TEXAS. He married VALERIE.

Children of JACK JOHNSON and VALERIE are:
        i.   KELLIE H.[11] JOHNSON, m. MR. GOMBERT.
        ii.   ANDREA S. JOHNSON, m. MR. ROSZEL.
        iii. STEPHANIE JOHNSON, m. MR. HUMPHREYS.
        iv.   VALERIE D. JOHNSON.

218. PHYLLIS[10] JOHNSON (WELMA OPAL[9] TRICK, SAMANTHA[8] GRISE, MARGARET ACHIE[7] MANN, ABEL[6], GEORGE[5], COLONEL JOHN JR.[4], JOHN SR.[3], GEORGE BERNARD[2], HANS[1]) was born September 11, 1938. She married HARRY STUBBLES.

Child of PHYLLIS JOHNSON and HARRY STUBBLES is:
    i.   SHARREN[11] STUBBLES.

219. RACHEL[10] JONES *(PERRY[9], CORDA ACHIE[8] GRISE, MARGARET ACHIE[7] MANN, ABEL[6], GEORGE[5], COLONEL JOHN JR.[4], JOHN SR.[3], GEORGE BERNARD[2], HANS[1])* was born January 30, 1916. She married MAX WOLF January 30, 1941.

    Child of RACHEL JONES and MAX WOLF is:
        i.   PHILLIP MAX[11] WOLF, b. February 08, 1941.

220. ELSIE CORDA[10] JONES *(PERRY[9], CORDA ACHIE[8] GRISE, MARGARET ACHIE[7] MANN, ABEL[6], GEORGE[5], COLONEL JOHN JR.[4], JOHN SR.[3], GEORGE BERNARD[2], HANS[1])* was born April 15, 1920, and died November 23, 1987. She married CLARENCE FESSLER 1915.

    Children of ELSIE JONES and CLARENCE FESSLER are:
        i.   WILLIAM JOE[11] FESSLER, b. August 13, 1944; d. December 24, 1965.
298.   ii. TIMOTHY RALPH FESSLER, b. December 23, 1955.
299. iii. GREGORY ALAN FESSLER, b. April 17, 1957.

221. THERM RODNEY[10] FURNAS *(LAURA[9] JONES, CORDA ACHIE[8] GRISE, MARGARET ACHIE[7] MANN, ABEL[6], GEORGE[5], COLONEL JOHN JR.[4], JOHN SR.[3], GEORGE BERNARD[2], HANS[1])* was born April 09, 1919. He married ANTONINETTE (ANN) BAJOK December 24, 1941.

    Children of THERM FURNAS and ANTONINETTE BAJOK are:
        i.   RUSSELL EDWARD[11] FURNAS, b. January 16, 1947.
300.   ii. CAROL LOUISE FURNAS, b. April 04, 1949.

222. HELEN MAE[10] FURNAS *(LAURA[9] JONES, CORDA ACHIE[8] GRISE, MARGARET ACHIE[7] MANN, ABEL[6], GEORGE[5], COLONEL JOHN JR.[4], JOHN SR.[3], GEORGE BERNARD[2], HANS[1])* was born May 18, 1920. She married LEO SAMPSON March 17, 1939.

    Children of HELEN FURNAS and LEO SAMPSON are:
301.   i.   RODNEY LEE[11] SAMPSON, b. November 02, 1939.
302.   ii. JAMES ALLEN SAMPSON, b. June 23, 1941.

303.   iii.   JEANETTE MARIE SAMPSON, b. March 25, 1947.
304.   iv.   STEVEN LEE SAMPSON, b. November 15, 1952.

223.   GLENNA[10] WARNER *(MARTHA[9] APPLE, CORDA ACHIE[8] GRISE, MARGARET ACHIE[7] MANN, ABEL[6], GEORGE[5], COLONEL JOHN JR.[4], JOHN SR.[3], GEORGE BERNARD[2], HANS[1])* was born December 13, 1925.   She married KENNETH SHELLHAUS January 05, 1944.

   Children of GLENNA WARNER and KENNETH SHELLHAUS are:
        i.   LEE ALAN[11] SHELLHAUS, m. BETTY SUE BRAMLETTE, March 28, 1973.
        ii.   DEBBIE SHELLHAUS.
        iii.   CONNIE KAY SHELLHAUS, b. January 1949; m. MARK W. GOLDNER, June 08, 1974.

224.   ROBERT[10] WARNER *(MARTHA[9] APPLE, CORDA ACHIE[8] GRISE, MARGARET ACHIE[7] MANN, ABEL[6], GEORGE[5], COLONEL JOHN JR.[4], JOHN SR.[3], GEORGE BERNARD[2], HANS[1])* was born April 02, 1928.   He married ANN KIRBY November 13, 1947.

   Children of ROBERT WARNER and ANN KIRBY are:
        i.   BARBARA[11] WARNER, b. 1947; d. April 1948.
        ii.   RICHARD WARNER, b. February 17, 1948.
        iii.   MARY WARNER, b. May 10, 1949.
        iv.   BRUCE WARNER, b. May 24, 1952.
        v.   RANDY WARNER, b. March 26, 1956.
        vi.   KAREN SUE WARNER, b. April 04, 1961.

225.   RICHARD[10] WARNER *(MARTHA[9] APPLE, CORDA ACHIE[8] GRISE, MARGARET ACHIE[7] MANN, ABEL[6], GEORGE[5], COLONEL JOHN JR.[4], JOHN SR.[3], GEORGE BERNARD[2], HANS[1])* was born September 27, 1931.   He married DOROTHY MINGER April 02, 1956.

   Children of RICHARD WARNER and DOROTHY MINGER are:
        i.   RANDY[11] WARNER, b. March 26, 1956.
        ii.   MARK WARNER, b. April 1958.

226.   GROVER JR.[10] BUCHOLZ *(GROVER[9], ESTHER ANN[8] GRISE, MARGARET ACHIE[7] MANN, ABEL[6], GEORGE[5], COLONEL JOHN JR.[4], JOHN SR.[3], GEORGE BERNARD[2], HANS[1])* was born December 03, 1932.   He married VIRGINIA WHITMARE February 03, 1951.

Children of GROVER BUCHOLZ and VIRGINIA WHITMARE are:
- i. JULIE[11] BUCHOLZ, b. August 01, 1951.
- ii. JAMES BUCHOLZ, b. June 17, 1953.
- iii. JANICE BUCHOLZ, b. May 18, 1954.
- iv. JOSEPH BUCHOLZ, b. June 23, 1955.
- v. JEANETTE BUCHOLZ, b. February 14, 1957.
- vi. JOHN BUCHOLZ, b. September 25, 1958.
- vii. JEFFERY BUCHOLZ, b. January 27, 1960.

227. JAMES ROGER[10] BUCHOLZ (LORING[9], ESTHER ANN[8] GRISE, MARGARET ACHIE[7] MANN, ABEL[6], GEORGE[5], COLONEL JOHN JR.[4], JOHN SR.[3], GEORGE BERNARD[2], HANS[1]) was born March 30, 1933. He married GEORGEANNA HOLEBEK October 31, 1953.

Children of JAMES BUCHOLZ and GEORGEANNA HOLEBEK are:
- 305. i. JAMES[11] BUCHOLZ, b. September 23, 1954.
- 306. ii. KIM·JOSEPH BUCHOLZ, b. March 13, 1957.
- 307. iii. ELDON BUCHOLZ, b. May 02, 1960.
- iv. KELLY BUCHOLZ, b. January 03, 1962; m. MARV BLIGHT, May 03, 1986.
- v. LEON GERALD BUCHOLZ, b. July 05, 1966; m. JANICE TOOMEV, February 04, 1989.

228. JOYCE IRENE[10] BUCHOLZ (LORING[9], ESTHER ANN[8] GRISE, MARGARET ACHIE[7] MANN, ABEL[6], GEORGE[5], COLONEL JOHN JR.[4], JOHN SR.[3], GEORGE BERNARD[2], HANS[1]) was born March 30, 1933. She married ANDREW BARANCIK November 05, 1952.

Children of JOYCE BUCHOLZ and ANDREW BARANCIK are:
- 308. i. ELLEN ANN[11] BARANCIK, b. May 22, 1955.
- 309. ii. JEFFERY BARANCIK, b. July 14, 1956.
- 310. iii. CURTIS ANDREW BARANCIK, b. January 15, 1958.
- iv. DAVID MARK BARANCIK, b. March 09, 1959; d. March 09, 1959.
- 311. v. JILL BARANCIK, b. October 04, 1961.
- vi. SHEILA MARIE BARANCIK, b. March 03, 1963; m. KEVIN BATES, June 03, 1989.

229. BARBARA[10] BUCHOLZ (LORING[9], ESTHER ANN[8] GRISE, MARGARET ACHIE[7] MANN, ABEL[6], GEORGE[5], COLONEL JOHN JR.[4], JOHN SR.[3], GEORGE BERNARD[2],

HANS¹) was born February 27, 1941. She married FREDERICK LEE TUPICA June 13, 1963.

    Children of BARBARA BUCHOLZ and FREDERICK TUPICA are:
312.   i. TONY LEE¹¹ TUPICA, b. November 16, 1963.
        ii. JOLE SUE TUPICA, b. May 26, 1968.
        iii. LYNN ANN TUPICA, b. May 14, 1971.

230. GARY LYNN¹⁰ SMITH (HELEN IRENE⁹ BUCHOLZ, ESTHER ANN⁸ GRISE, MARGARET ACHIE⁷ MANN, ABEL⁶, GEORGE⁵, COLONEL JOHN JR.⁴, JOHN SR.³, GEORGE BERNARD², HANS¹) was born December 13, 1936. He married GRETCHEN MARIE HUGHES April 27, 1957.

    Children of GARY SMITH and GRETCHEN HUGHES are:
313.   i. JODY LYNN¹¹ SMITH, b. February 26, 1958.
314.   ii. AUDREY SMITH, b. October 04, 1963.

231. RUBY ELLEN¹⁰ SMITH (HELEN IRENE⁹ BUCHOLZ, ESTHER ANN⁸ GRISE, MARGARET ACHIE⁷ MANN, ABEL⁶, GEORGE⁵, COLONEL JOHN JR.⁴, JOHN SR.³, GEORGE BERNARD², HANS¹) was born September 07, 1940. She married GERALD KIENITZ April 25, 1959.

    Children of RUBY SMITH and GERALD KIENITZ are:
315.   i.   STEVEN KENT¹¹ KIENITZ, b. April 20, 1960.
        ii. ALAN JAY KIENITZ, b. September 19, 1961; d. December 31, 1961.
316.   iii. SALLY JO KIENITZ, b. July 25, 1963.
317.   iv. ADAM TROY KIENITZ, b. November 29, 1964.
        v.   PATRICK GERALD KIENITZ, b. May 10, 1967; m. DEBRA NORTHRUP, July 27, 1990.
318.   vi. JERRY TODD KIENITZ, b. August 02, 1968.

232. KENNETH WARD¹⁰ SMITH (HELEN IRENE⁹ BUCHOLZ, ESTHER ANN⁸ GRISE, MARGARET ACHIE⁷ MANN, ABEL⁶, GEORGE⁵, COLONEL JOHN JR.⁴, JOHN SR.³, GEORGE BERNARD², HANS¹) was born October 09, 1947. He married LORETTA ANN PALASZEKI November 16, 1973.

Children of KENNETH SMITH and LORETTA PALASZEKI are:
       i.   JAMES BRADLY[11] SMITH, b. June 24, 1971.
319.   ii. NICHOLAS JACOB SMITH, b. March 19, 1975.
      iii. STEPHANIE LEIGH SMITH, b. May 20, 1978.

233.   GLENNA MAE[10] HILL *(MARY BELL[9] BASHORE, LOVA CATHERINE[8] GRISE, MARGARET ACHIE[7] MANN, ABEL[6], GEORGE[5], COLONEL JOHN JR.[4], JOHN SR.[3], GEORGE BERNARD[2], HANS[1])* was born September 28, 1918. She married ROBERT BRANDT February 09, 1941.

Children of GLENNA HILL and ROBERT BRANDT are:
320.   i.   ROBERT[11] BRANDT, b. October 03, 1942.
321.   ii. MARY ANN BRANDT, b. July 28, 1944.
322.   iii. DONALD BRANDT, b. March 06, 1948.

234.   KENNETH[10] HILL *(MARY BELL[9] BASHORE, LOVA CATHERINE[8] GRISE, MARGARET ACHIE[7] MANN, ABEL[6], GEORGE[5], COLONEL JOHN JR.[4], JOHN SR.[3], GEORGE BERNARD[2], HANS[1])* was born January 09, 1922, and died June 26, 1961. He married EDNA BARNETT December 17, 1945.

Children of KENNETH HILL and EDNA BARNETT are:
323.   i.   THOMAS JAMES[11] HILL, b. April 30, 1947.
324.   ii. CONNIE EILEEN HILL, b. October 15, 1948.
      iii. GARY EUGENE HILL, b. October 15, 1948; m. SHIRLEY CULLERS, April 12, 1969.

235.   ALICE FAYE[10] RIFFELL *(JESSE E.[9] BASHORE, LOVA CATHERINE[8] GRISE, MARGARET ACHIE[7] MANN, ABEL[6], GEORGE[5], COLONEL JOHN JR.[4], JOHN SR.[3], GEORGE BERNARD[2], HANS[1])* was born December 11, 1939. She married RONALD STEPHENS July 27, 1957.

Child of ALICE RIFFELL and RONALD STEPHENS is:
      i.   RICHARD JAY[11] STEPHENS, b. September 25, 1962; d. 1977.

236.   WAYNE[10] BASHORE *(JESSE E.[9], LOVA CATHERINE[8] GRISE, MARGARET ACHIE[7] MANN, ABEL[6], GEORGE[5], COLONEL JOHN JR.[4], JOHN SR.[3], GEORGE BERNARD[2], HANS[1])* was born April 15, 1942. He married (1) JUDITH ANN REED February 12, 1961. He married (2) ALICE KALASHIAN August 29, 1970. He married (3) EMMA L. BERNHART February 08, 1973.

Children of WAYNE BASHORE and JUDITH REED are:
325.   i.   PHILLIP KIRK[11] BASHORE, b. May 20, 1961.
         ii.   ANTHONY WAYNE BASHORE, b. 1964.
         iii. SHAWN FREDRIC BASHORE, b. March 04, 1966.

237.   DALE E.[10] REDMAN *(EDITH MARGARET[9] BASHORE, LOVA CATHERINE[8] GRISE, MARGARET ACHIE[7] MANN, ABEL[6], GEORGE[5], COLONEL JOHN JR.[4], JOHN SR.[3], GEORGE BERNARD[2], HANS[1])* was born February 15, 1922 in DARKE COUNTY, OHIO. He married (1) MYRTLE P. KUHLMAN April 24, 1943 in GREENVILLE, OHIO. He married (2) VIOLET FAEHR June 12, 1970. He married (3) HELEN CRAWFORD February 19, 1971.

Children of DALE REDMAN and MYRTLE KUHLMAN are:
326.   i.   JUDITH ANN[11] REDMAN, b. August 13, 1944, DARKE COUNTY, OHIO.
327.   ii.   ONDA LEE REDMAN, b. December 30, 1946, DARKE COUNTY, OHIO.
328.   iii. BETTY LOU REDMAN, b. December 09, 1948, DARKE COUNTY, OHIO.
329.   iv.   ANITA KAY REDMAN, b. June 19, 1951, DARKE COUNTY, OHIO.
330.   v.   RITA MAY REDMAN, b. June 19, 1951, DARKE COUNTY, OHIO.

238.   NORMAN[10] REDMAN *(EDITH MARGARET[9] BASHORE, LOVA CATHERINE[8] GRISE, MARGARET ACHIE[7] MANN, ABEL[6], GEORGE[5], COLONEL JOHN JR.[4], JOHN SR.[3], GEORGE BERNARD[2], HANS[1])* was born January 13, 1927 in DARKE COUNTY, OHIO. He married MARY ALICE SHARP December 29, 1945 in GREENVILLE, OHIO.

Children of NORMAN REDMAN and MARY SHARP are:
331.   i.   STEPHEN RAY[11] REDMAN, b. November 04, 1948, GREENVILLE, OHIO.
332.   ii.   ALICE REGINA REDMAN, b. October 21, 1953, DARKE COUNTY, OHIO.

239.   NANCY JANE[10] REDMAN *(EDITH MARGARET[9] BASHORE, LOVA CATHERINE[8] GRISE, MARGARET ACHIE[7] MANN, ABEL[6], GEORGE[5], COLONEL JOHN JR.[4], JOHN SR.[3], GEORGE BERNARD[2], HANS[1])* was born November 22, 1937 in DARKE COUNTY, OHIO. She married (1) JOHN PAUL THIEBEAU June 09, 1956 in VERSAILLES, OHIO, son of CHALMER THIEBEAU and GEORGIANNA BATTY. She married (2) DELBERT STUMP.

Children of NANCY REDMAN and JOHN THIEBEAU are:

333. *i.* JANE ANN[11] THIEBEAU, b. January 30, 1959, GREENVILLE, OHIO.

     ii. JERRY NICHOLAS THIEBEAU, b. October 25, 1961, GREENVILLE, OHIO.

334. *iii.* JOHN PAUL WILLIAM THIEBEAU, b. August 27, 1963, GREENVILLE, OHIO.

335. *iv.* CHRISTINA MARIE THIEBEAU, b. July 24, 1964, GREENVILLE, OHIO.

336. *v.* KATHERINE LOUISE THIEBEAU, b. September 26, 1965, DARKE COUNTY, OHIO.

240. LEWIS[10] STROBEL *(IZORA VIOLA[9] BASHORE, LOVA CATHERINE[8] GRISE, MARGARET ACHIE[7] MANN, ABEL[6], GEORGE[5], COLONEL JOHN JR.[4], JOHN SR.[3], GEORGE BERNARD[2], HANS[1])* was born April 02, 1926, and died February 22, 1995. He married MARGARET BAIL June 12, 1948.

Children of LEWIS STROBEL and MARGARET BAIL are:

337. *i.* STEVEN[11] STROBEL, b. May 07, 1957.

     ii. MICHAEL STROBEL, b. July 29, 1959; m. TINA WATNE, October 23, 1990.

241. FLORENCE[10] STROBEL *(IZORA VIOLA[9] BASHORE, LOVA CATHERINE[8] GRISE, MARGARET ACHIE[7] MANN, ABEL[6], GEORGE[5], COLONEL JOHN JR.[4], JOHN SR.[3], GEORGE BERNARD[2], HANS[1])* was born February 07, 1928. She married PAUL BEAVER March 07, 1946.

Children of FLORENCE STROBEL and PAUL BEAVER are:

338. *i.* JOYCE[11] BEAVER, b. December 13, 1948.

339. *ii.* CHERYL BEAVER, b. December 13, 1949.

242. MARY LOUISE[10] STROBEL *(IZORA VIOLA[9] BASHORE, LOVA CATHERINE[8] GRISE, MARGARET ACHIE[7] MANN, ABEL[6], GEORGE[5], COLONEL JOHN JR.[4], JOHN SR.[3], GEORGE BERNARD[2], HANS[1])* was born March 03, 1929. She married ELDEAN HAMILTON January 01, 1949.

Children of MARY STROBEL and ELDEAN HAMILTON are:

340. *i.* ANNA LOUISE[11] HAMILTON, b. March 15, 1952.

341. *ii.* DUANE HAMILTON, b. December 22, 1954.

243. CARL RICHARD[10] STROBEL *(IZORA VIOLA[9] BASHORE, LOVA CATHERINE[8] GRISE, MARGARET ACHIE[7] MANN, ABEL[6], GEORGE[5], COLONEL JOHN JR.[4], JOHN SR.[3], GEORGE BERNARD[2], HANS[1])* was born July 14, 1938. He married BETTY BEISNER November 25, 1960.

    Children of CARL STROBEL and BETTY BEISNER are:
        i.   BRIAN RICHARD[11] STROBEL, b. December 16, 1968.
        ii. BRENT ALAN STROBEL, b. December 12, 1970.
342. *iii.* BRUCE CHARLES STROBEL, b. March 10, 1973.
343. *iv.* CARLA ANN STROBEL, b. March 15, 1974.

244. LUTHER[10] STROBEL *(IZORA VIOLA[9] BASHORE, LOVA CATHERINE[8] GRISE, MARGARET ACHIE[7] MANN, ABEL[6], GEORGE[5], COLONEL JOHN JR.[4], JOHN SR.[3], GEORGE BERNARD[2], HANS[1])* was born September 07, 1940. He married JUDY GROFF June 27, 1964.

    Children of LUTHER STROBEL and JUDY GROFF are:
344.   *i.* LEE ANN MARIE[11] STROBEL, b. March 19, 1967.
        ii. AMY ELIZABETH STROBEL, b. August 18, 1974.

245. H. DEAN[10] HORNER *(VERTIE ALWILDA[9] BASHORE, LOVA CATHERINE[8] GRISE, MARGARET ACHIE[7] MANN, ABEL[6], GEORGE[5], COLONEL JOHN JR.[4], JOHN SR.[3], GEORGE BERNARD[2], HANS[1])* was born August 15, 1935. He married EDITH KELLY.

    Children of H. HORNER and EDITH KELLY are:
345.   *i.* SHERRY[11] HORNER, b. March 11, 1961.
346. *ii.* SCOTT HORNER, b. March 11, 1961.

246. DONNA[10] HORNER *(VERTIE ALWILDA[9] BASHORE, LOVA CATHERINE[8] GRISE, MARGARET ACHIE[7] MANN, ABEL[6], GEORGE[5], COLONEL JOHN JR.[4], JOHN SR.[3], GEORGE BERNARD[2], HANS[1])* was born April 16, 1938. She married (1) LAVON WRIGHT. She married (2) ROBERT REED January 01, 1963.

    Children of DONNA HORNER and ROBERT REED are:
347.   *i.* LAVON[11] WRIGHT REED, b. August 31, 1959.
348. *ii.* REX WRIGHT REED, b. March 14, 1961.
349. *iii.* DEBORAH REED, b. February 22, 1965.

247. HERMAN[10] HORNER *(VERTIE ALWILDA[9] BASHORE, LOVA CATHERINE[8] GRISE, MARGARET ACHIE[7] MANN, ABEL[6], GEORGE[5], COLONEL JOHN JR.[4], JOHN SR.[3], GEORGE BERNARD[2], HANS[1])* was born November 19, 1939. He married (1) JOYCE NOLLEY October 25, 1969. He married (2) CORA ADAMS CREMEANS November 1983.

Child of HERMAN HORNER and JOYCE NOLLEY *is:*
   i. DAVID[11] HORNER, b. December 08, 1970.

248. PHYLLIS JOAN[10] BASHORE *(JOHN MARTIN[9], LOVA CATHERINE[8] GRISE, MARGARET ACHIE[7] MANN, ABEL[6], GEORGE[5], COLONEL JOHN JR.[4], JOHN SR.[3], GEORGE BERNARD[2], HANS[1])* was born June 15, 1940 *in* MIAMI COUNTY, OHIO. She married HARVEY JR. CRICK July 13, 1959 *in* RICHMOND, INDIANA.

Children of PHYLLIS BASHORE and HARVEY CRICK *are:*
   i. NANCY[11] CRICK, b. June 08, 1963, LOGAN COUNTY, OHIO.
   ii. JOANNE CRICK, b. October 23, 1965, LOGAN COUNTY, OHIO.
   iii. SUSAN CRICK, b. February 19, 1971, DARKE COUNTY, OHIO; m. MARK SMITH, April 19, 1997.

249. SAMUEL WILLIAM[10] BASHORE *(JOHN MARTIN[9], LOVA CATHERINE[8] GRISE, MARGARET ACHIE[7] MANN, ABEL[6], GEORGE[5], COLONEL JOHN JR.[4], JOHN SR.[3], GEORGE BERNARD[2], HANS[1])* was born January 07, 1942 *in* MIAMI COUNTY, OHIO. He married ZONA LOUISE PETERS October 12, 1963 *in* DARKE COUNTY, OHIO.

Children of SAMUEL BASHORE and ZONA PETERS *are:*
   i. DALE ALLEN[11] BASHORE, b. June 14, 1965, GREENVILLE, OHIO; m. LYNN ADELE HELMKE, March 07, 1986.
350.   *ii.* CYNTHIA LYNN BASHORE, b. October 20, 1967, GREENVILLE, OHIO.
351.   *iii.* TERRY LEE BASHORE, b. July 25, 1969.

250. DONALD JAMES[10] BASHORE *(JOHN MARTIN[9], LOVA CATHERINE[8] GRISE, MARGARET ACHIE[7] MANN, ABEL[6], GEORGE[5], COLONEL JOHN JR.[4], JOHN SR.[3], GEORGE BERNARD[2], HANS[1])* was born October 11, 1946 *in* MIAMI COUNTY, OHIO. He married (1) LINDA SWANK December 16, 1967 *in* RICHMOND, INDIANA. He married (2) JANE STEPHENS. He married (3) TISH MANIX October 11, 1990.

Child of DONALD BASHORE and LINDA SWANK is:
    i. BONNIE JEAN[11] BASHORE, b. July 01, 1968.

251. DEBORAH ARLENE[10] BASHORE (JOHN MARTIN[9], LOVA CATHERINE[8] GRISE, MARGARET ACHIE[7] MANN, ABEL[6], GEORGE[5], COLONEL JOHN JR.[4], JOHN SR.[3], GEORGE BERNARD[2], HANS[1]) was born May 14, 1953 in MIAMI COUNTY, OHIO. She married BARRY M. BROWN April 25, 1972 in BRADFORD, OHIO.

    Children of DEBORAH BASHORE and BARRY BROWN are:
      i. BRADY ARTHUR[11] BROWN, b. December 14, 1972, PIQUA, OHIO.
     ii. CASEY ANN BROWN, b. April 25, 1974; d. April 26, 1974.

252. RICHARD LEE[10] BASHORE (JOHN MARTIN[9], LOVA CATHERINE[8] GRISE, MARGARET ACHIE[7] MANN, ABEL[6], GEORGE[5], COLONEL JOHN JR.[4], JOHN SR.[3], GEORGE BERNARD[2], HANS[1]) was born December 25, 1959 in MIAMI COUNTY, OHIO. He married KARLA KAY STUMP October 16, 1990 in GREENVILLE, OHIO.

    Children of RICHARD BASHORE and KARLA STUMP are:
      i. ANISSA JANE[11] BASHORE, b. October 14, 1991, DARKE COUNTY, OHIO.
     ii. RICHARD ADDISON BASHORE, b. December 03, 1994, GREENVILLE, OHIO.

253. KENNETH[10] BASHORE (ORTHA SAMUEL[9], LOVA CATHERINE[8] GRISE, MARGARET ACHIE[7] MANN, ABEL[6], GEORGE[5], COLONEL JOHN JR.[4], JOHN SR.[3], GEORGE BERNARD[2], HANS[1]) was born December 31, 1942. He married JANET RIFFELL August 04, 1963.

    Children of KENNETH BASHORE and JANET RIFFELL are:
352.   i. MELISSA[11] BASHORE, b. October 08, 1966.
     ii. SHARRON MARIE BASHORE, b. July 26, 1969.
    iii. SANDRA K. BASHORE, b. July 26, 1969.

254. HARRY[10] BASHORE (ORTHA SAMUEL[9], LOVA CATHERINE[8] GRISE, MARGARET ACHIE[7] MANN, ABEL[6], GEORGE[5], COLONEL JOHN JR.[4], JOHN SR.[3], GEORGE BERNARD[2], HANS[1]) was born March 21, 1947. He married DIANA ROBBINS December 18, 1966.

Children of HARRY BASHORE and DIANA ROBBINS are:
353.   i.   ANITA DARLENE[11] BASHORE, b. December 27, 1969.
      ii. BRIAN SCOTT BASHORE, b. April 14, 1971; m. ANGELA KAY
              LEMASTER, May 18, 1996.
     iii. AMBER RENEE BASHORE, b. June 20, 1977.
     iv. ALYSSIA ANN BASHORE, b. November 01, 1979.

255. NOVA[10] RHOADES (DOROTHY CATHERINE[9] BASHORE, LOVA CATHERINE[8] GRISE, MARGARET ACHIE[7] MANN, ABEL[6], GEORGE[5], COLONEL JOHN JR.[4], JOHN SR.[3], GEORGE BERNARD[2], HANS[1]) was born March 16, 1942. She married ALLEN ROGERS June 12, 1960.

Children of NOVA RHOADES and ALLEN ROGERS are:
354.   i.   DURINDA[11] ROGERS, b. March 20, 1961.
      ii. SHELLY KAY ROGERS, b. September 13, 1964; m. WILLIAM CLYDE
              LANE, October 13, 1984.

256. NINA[10] RHOADES (DOROTHY CATHERINE[9] BASHORE, LOVA CATHERINE[8] GRISE, MARGARET ACHIE[7] MANN, ABEL[6], GEORGE[5], COLONEL JOHN JR.[4], JOHN SR.[3], GEORGE BERNARD[2], HANS[1]) was born April 11, 1946. She married LOWELL D. UNGER January 30, 1965.

Children of NINA RHOADES and LOWELL UNGER are:
355.   i.   KIMBERLY ANN[11] UNGER, b. March 31, 1967.
356.   ii. CRAIG DUANE UNGER, b. January 16, 1969.
     iii. KATHERINE JANELL UNGER, b. September 07, 1971.

257. KENNETH LEO[10] SMITH (ETHEL LEOTA[9] TROUTWINE, LAURA JANE[8] GRISE, MARGARET ACHIE[7] MANN, ABEL[6], GEORGE[5], COLONEL JOHN JR.[4], JOHN SR.[3], GEORGE BERNARD[2], HANS[1]) was born February 13, 1920, and died February 05, 1945 in ENGLAND DURING WW II. He married MONA WIFORD August 11, 1940.

Children of KENNETH SMITH and MONA WIFORD are:
357.   i.   KENNETH LEE[11] SMITH, b. April 24, 1942.
358.   ii. JAMES ALLAN SMITH, b. July 05, 1944, PIQUA, OHIO.

258. LOWELL[10] MILLER (TOILEY[9] WALKER, LILLIE FLORENCE[8] GRISE, MARGARET ACHIE[7] MANN, ABEL[6], GEORGE[5], COLONEL JOHN JR.[4], JOHN SR.[3], GEORGE

BERNARD[9], HANS[1] / was born December 14, 1919 in BRADFORD, OHIO, and died April 11, 1993 in INDIANA. He married LEDA CHANEY December 10, 1941.

Children of LOWELL MILLER and LEDA CHANEY are:
359.   i.   ANNE M.[11] MILLER, b. December 10, 1943.
360.   ii.   DENNIS WAYNE MILLER, b. February 05, 1945.
361.   iii. BETH J. MILLER, b. March 19, 1951.

259. DOROTHY[10] MILLER (TOILEY[9] WALKER, LILLIE FLORENCE[8] GRISE, MARGARET ACHIE[7] MANN, ABEL[6], GEORGE[5], COLONEL JOHN JR.[4], JOHN SR.[3], GEORGE BERNARD[2], HANS[1] / was born September 05, 1921. She married MAX SHARP April 29, 1944.

Children of DOROTHY MILLER and MAX SHARP are:
     i.   SUSAN DEE[11] SHARP.
     ii.   CYNTHIS SHARP, b. January 06, 1948.
     iii. RICKLIN SHARP, b. August 31, 1950.

260. JUANITA[10] MILLER (TOILEY[9] WALKER, LILLIE FLORENCE[8] GRISE, MARGARET ACHIE[7] MANN, ABEL[6], GEORGE[5], COLONEL JOHN JR.[4], JOHN SR.[3], GEORGE BERNARD[2], HANS[1] / was born September 25, 1923. She married LOUIS SHELLABARGER August 25, 1950.

Children of JUANITA MILLER and LOUIS SHELLABARGER are:
     i.   RANDALL[11] SHELLABARGER, b. June 21, 1952.
     ii.   ROGER SHELLABARGER, b. September 25, 1954; m. KATHY DECKER, December 11, 1976.
     iii. BONNIE SHELLABARGER, b. February 23, 1957.

261. ALICE[10] MILLER (TOILEY[9] WALKER, LILLIE FLORENCE[8] GRISE, MARGARET ACHIE[7] MANN, ABEL[6], GEORGE[5], COLONEL JOHN JR.[4], JOHN SR.[3], GEORGE BERNARD[2], HANS[1] / was born January 31, 1926. She married WILLIAM SAMS October 18, 1947.

Children of ALICE MILLER and WILLIAM SAMS are:
     i.   BECKY[11] SAMS, b. September 21, 1951.
     ii.   KATHY SAMS, b. August 27, 1955.
     iii. VICKY SAMS, b. February 07, 1957.

262. RUBY[10] MILLER (TOILEY[9] WALKER, LILLIE FLORENCE[8] GRISE, MARGARET ACHIE[7] MANN, ABEL[6], GEORGE[5], COLONEL JOHN JR.[4], JOHN SR.[3], GEORGE BERNARD[2], HANS[1]) was born January 19, 1929. She married RICHARD WEAVER July 30, 1949.

        Children of RUBY MILLER and RICHARD WEAVER are:
            i.   JAMES[11] WEAVER, b. March 30, 1953.
            ii. JULIA WEAVER, b. June 03, 1955.
            iii. DAVID WEAVER, b. March 28, 1957.

263. BETTY[10] WALKER (RAYMOND[9], LILLIE FLORENCE[8] GRISE, MARGARET ACHIE[7] MANN, ABEL[6], GEORGE[5], COLONEL JOHN JR.[4], JOHN SR.[3], GEORGE BERNARD[2], HANS[1]) was born July 25, 1930. She married ROGER FRIEND November 06, 1948.

        Children of BETTY WALKER and ROGER FRIEND are:
            i.   RITA[11] FRIEND, b. July 13, 1950.
            ii. DAVID FRIEND, b. May 07, 1952.
            iii. DEBBIE FRIEND, b. March 21, 1957.
            iv. MARK FRIEND, b. May 18, 1958.

264. NORMA[10] WALKER (RAYMOND[9], LILLIE FLORENCE[8] GRISE, MARGARET ACHIE[7] MANN, ABEL[6], GEORGE[5], COLONEL JOHN JR.[4], JOHN SR.[3], GEORGE BERNARD[2], HANS[1]) was born March 19, 1933. She married ROBERT MOTHMILLER June 08, 1957.

        Child of NORMA WALKER and ROBERT MOTHMILLER is:
            i.   CHRISTINE[11] MOTHMILLER, b. March 06, 1959.

265. ROBERT[10] WALKER (RAYMOND[9], LILLIE FLORENCE[8] GRISE, MARGARET ACHIE[7] MANN, ABEL[6], GEORGE[5], COLONEL JOHN JR.[4], JOHN SR.[3], GEORGE BERNARD[2], HANS[1]) was born September 22, 1934. He married BETTY BOGGS July 10, 1953.

        Child of ROBERT WALKER and BETTY BOGGS is:
            i.   TERRY[11] WALKER, b. January 20, 1955.

266. EVELYN[10] WALKER (RAYMOND[9], LILLIE FLORENCE[8] GRISE, MARGARET ACHIE[7] MANN, ABEL[6], GEORGE[5], COLONEL JOHN JR.[4], JOHN SR.[3], GEORGE BERNARD[2],

HANS¹) was born December 24, 1935. She married CHARLES PASTORI November 27, 1954.

Children of EVELYN WALKER and CHARLES PASTORI are:
    i. LINDA¹¹ PASTORI, b. January 16, 1956.
    ii. ANNETTE PASTORI, b. January 16, 1959.

267. CHARLES¹⁰ KONZ *(ELIZABETH MAE⁹ WALKER, LILLIE FLORENCE⁸ GRISE, MARGARET ACHIE⁷ MANN, ABEL⁶, GEORGE⁵, COLONEL JOHN JR.⁴, JOHN SR.³, GEORGE BERNARD², HANS¹)* was born July 29, 1934. He married SHIRLEY WHITEHEAD March 12, 1954.

Children of CHARLES KONZ and SHIRLEY WHITEHEAD are:
    i. DEBRA¹¹ KONZ, b. September 02, 1955.
    ii. TAMMIE KONZ, b. November 04, 1958.
    iii. MICHAEL KONZ, b. July 10, 1960.

268. RITA¹⁰ KONZ *(ELIZABETH MAE⁹ WALKER, LILLIE FLORENCE⁸ GRISE, MARGARET ACHIE⁷ MANN, ABEL⁶, GEORGE⁵, COLONEL JOHN JR.⁴, JOHN SR.³, GEORGE BERNARD², HANS¹)* was born April 08, 1937. She married CLAYTON LEON WHITEAKER February 05, 1955.

Children of RITA KONZ and CLAYTON WHITEAKER are:
    i. KATHY¹¹ WHITEAKER, b. October 19, 1955.
    ii. RICK WHITEAKER, b. March 12, 1959.

269. MARGARET¹⁰ WALKER *(EARL⁹, LILLIE FLORENCE⁸ GRISE, MARGARET ACHIE⁷ MANN, ABEL⁶, GEORGE⁵, COLONEL JOHN JR.⁴, JOHN SR.³, GEORGE BERNARD², HANS¹)* was born January 04, 1935. She married DALE FORREST January 16, 1954.

Children of MARGARET WALKER and DALE FORREST are:
    i. NICHOLAS¹¹ FORREST.
    ii. JOHN FORREST.

270. PAUL¹⁰ CROMES *(LOUISE⁹ WALKER, LILLIE FLORENCE⁸ GRISE, MARGARET ACHIE⁷ MANN, ABEL⁶, GEORGE⁵, COLONEL JOHN JR.⁴, JOHN SR.³, GEORGE BERNARD², HANS¹)* was born December 27, 1933. He married BETTY SCHIMMEL January 25, 1953.

Children of PAUL CROMES and BETTY SCHIMMEL are:
    i. KENDRA[11] CROMES, b. May 30, 1953.
    ii. JANE ANNA CROMES, b. April 20, 1954.
    iii. LYNETTE CROMES, b. April 16, 1956; m. ANDY WRIGHT.
362.   *iv.* MARTIN CROMES, b. September 24, 1960.

271. MARION[10] CROMES *(LOUISE[9] WALKER, LILLIE FLORENCE[8] GRISE, MARGARET ACHIE[7] MANN, ABEL[6], GEORGE[5], COLONEL JOHN JR.[4], JOHN SR.[3], GEORGE BERNARD[2], HANS[1])* was born September 28, 1935. He married NANCY TROST May 19, 1956.

Children of MARION CROMES and NANCY TROST are:
    i. CHARLES[11] CROMES, b. January 16, 1957; d. January 16, 1957.
    ii. DOUGLAS CROMES, b. January 15, 1958; m. ROBIN.
363.   *iii.* MICHAEL CROMES, b. February 12, 1959.
    iv. KAREN LYNN CROMES, b. October 03, 1964.

272. DELBERT[10] CROMES *(LOUISE[9] WALKER, LILLIE FLORENCE[8] GRISE, MARGARET ACHIE[7] MANN, ABEL[6], GEORGE[5], COLONEL JOHN JR.[4], JOHN SR.[3], GEORGE BERNARD[2], HANS[1])* was born August 23, 1937. He married LOUISE ENSMINGER June 26, 1958.

Children of DELBERT CROMES and LOUISE ENSMINGER are:
    i. DEBRA[11] CROMES, b. July 24, 1958.
    ii. JEFFERY CROMES, b. September 28, 1959.
    iii. CHRISTOPHER STEVEN CROMES, b. November 16, 1960.
    iv. TAWANA ELAINE CROMES, b. April 18, 1963; m. RALPH PIKE.

273. WANDA[10] CROMES *(LOUISE[9] WALKER, LILLIE FLORENCE[8] GRISE, MARGARET ACHIE[7] MANN, ABEL[6], GEORGE[5], COLONEL JOHN JR.[4], JOHN SR.[3], GEORGE BERNARD[2], HANS[1])* was born May 13, 1939. She married JAMES FAVORITE September 08, 1956.

Children of WANDA CROMES and JAMES FAVORITE are:
    i. RANDY[11] FAVORITE, b. February 11, 1957; m. BECKY.
    ii. JAMES FAVORITE, b. May 17, 1958; m. JENNIFER.
    iii. JULIA FAVORITE, b. August 07, 1960; m. ROBERT POUGE.

274. BENNY[10] CROMES *(LOUISE[9] WALKER, LILLIE FLORENCE[8] GRISE, MARGARET ACHIE[7] MANN, ABEL[6], GEORGE[5], COLONEL JOHN JR.[4], JOHN SR.[3], GEORGE*

BERNARD², HANS¹) was born April 27, 1944. He married GAYLE FREEMAN September 27, 1967.

Children of BENNY CROMES and GAYLE FREEMAN are:
i. DAVID¹¹ CROMES, b. July 30, 1968.
ii. MATTHEW L. CROMES, b. December 01, 1970.

275. DANNY¹⁰ CROMES (LOUISE⁹ WALKER, LILLIE FLORENCE⁸ GRISE, MARGARET ACHIE⁷ MANN, ABEL⁶, GEORGE⁵, COLONEL JOHN JR.⁴, JOHN SR.³, GEORGE BERNARD², HANS¹) was born December 19, 1945. He married JOANNE EURY September 19, 1964.

Children of DANNY CROMES and JOANNE EURY are:
i. DANIEL KEVIN¹¹ CROMES, b. July 22, 1967.
ii. DENISE NICOLE CROMES, b. October 20, 1970.
iii. MELISSA CROMES, b. September 02, 1972.

276. HAROLD GENE¹⁰ WALKER (HAROLD⁹, LILLIE FLORENCE⁸ GRISE, MARGARET ACHIE⁷ MANN, ABEL⁶, GEORGE⁵, COLONEL JOHN JR.⁴, JOHN SR.³, GEORGE BERNARD², HANS¹) was born January 11, 1945. She married JEAN DENLINGER December 30, 1974.

Children of HAROLD WALKER and JEAN DENLINGER are:
i. BRAD¹¹ DENLINGER, b. October 31, 1978.
ii. HAROLD DENLINGER, b. July 08, 1981.

277. PHYLISS¹⁰ COOK (HELEN IRENE⁹ GRISE, RUBEN⁸, MARGARET ACHIE⁷ MANN, ABEL⁶, GEORGE⁵, COLONEL JOHN JR.⁴, JOHN SR.³, GEORGE BERNARD², HANS¹) was born October 03, 1931. She married JACK LINK September 11, 1951.

Children of PHYLISS COOK and JACK LINK are:
i. MARVIN¹¹ LINK, b. January 18, 1954.
ii. CHRISTINE LINK, b. March 30, 1955.
iii. GALE LINK, b. June 21, 1958.

278. HAROLD¹⁰ FOLKERTH (ETOILE⁹ GRISE, RUBEN⁸, MARGARET ACHIE⁷ MANN, ABEL⁶, GEORGE⁵, COLONEL JOHN JR.⁴, JOHN SR.³, GEORGE BERNARD², HANS¹) was born December 06, 1931. He married SANDRA LONG June 01, 1957.

Colonel John Mann Jr. His kith, his kin, his ancestors, his descendants.

Children of HAROLD FOLKERTH and SANDRA LONG are:
    i.   ANN[11] FOLKERTH.
    ii. REBECCA FOLKERTH, b. June 29, 1958.
    iii. HUGH FOLKERTH, b. November 1959.

279. PATRICK[10] GRISE (HARVEY DAVID[9], RUBEN[8], MARGARET ACHIE[7] MANN, ABEL[6], GEORGE[5], COLONEL JOHN JR.[4], JOHN SR.[3], GEORGE BERNARD[2], HANS[1]) was born November 30, 1951. He married TERESA ASHER December 29, 1972.

Children of PATRICK GRISE and TERESA ASHER are:
    i.   JENNIFER LYNN[11] GRISE, b. June 25, 1973.
    ii. KERRI MARIE GRISE, b. December 10, 1976.

280. SHERYL[10] GRISE (RICHARD[9], ELI C.[8], MARGARET ACHIE[7] MANN, ABEL[6], GEORGE[5], COLONEL JOHN JR.[4], JOHN SR.[3], GEORGE BERNARD[2], HANS[1]) was born January 13, 1952. She married GEORGE LARSON September 07, 1973.

Children of SHERYL GRISE and GEORGE LARSON are:
    i.   MIRANDA[11] LARSON, b. June 09, 1980.
    ii. GEORGIA ROCHELLE LARSON, b. August 17, 1987.

281. GAIL[10] GRISE (RICHARD[9], ELI C.[8], MARGARET ACHIE[7] MANN, ABEL[6], GEORGE[5], COLONEL JOHN JR.[4], JOHN SR.[3], GEORGE BERNARD[2], HANS[1]) was born June 23, 1953. She married JERRY ALAN SPICER May 22, 1976.

Child of GAIL GRISE and JERRY SPICER is:
    i.   KRISTIN SUZANNE[11] SPICER, b. August 04, 1981.

282. SANDRA[10] GRISE (RICHARD[9], ELI C.[8], MARGARET ACHIE[7] MANN, ABEL[6], GEORGE[5], COLONEL JOHN JR.[4], JOHN SR.[3], GEORGE BERNARD[2], HANS[1]) was born January 18, 1958. She married THOMAS SARVER December 22, 1979.

Children of SANDRA GRISE and THOMAS SARVER are:
    i.   ABIGAIL RAE[11] SARVER, b. July 02, 1981.
    ii. JOSEPH ELI SARVER, b. December 15, 1983.
    iii. KELSEY JANE SARVER, b. August 20, 1988.

283. DALE EVERETT[10] THOMPSON (RUTH[9] SHAFER, BERTHA MAE[8] MATTHEWS, ELIZABETH E.[7] MANN, ABEL[6], GEORGE[5], COLONEL JOHN JR.[4], JOHN SR.[3], GEORGE

BERNARD², HANS¹) was born December 03, 1920 in MIAMI COUNTY, OHIO. He married MARY AGNES PIERRON March 22, 1945 in MONTGOMERY COUNTY, OHIO.

Children of DALE THOMPSON and MARY PIERRON are:
364.   i.   MARILEE ANN¹¹ THOMPSON, b. May 10, 1946, DAYTON, OHIO.
365.   ii. ALBERT JOSEPH THOMPSON, b. September 01, 1947, MONTGOMERY COUNTY, OHIO.
366.   iii. MARGARET LOUISE THOMPSON, b. September 05, 1948, MONTGOMERY COUNTY, OHIO.

284.   DELMAR LEROY¹⁰ THOMPSON (RUTH⁹ SHAFER, BERTHA MAE⁸ MATTHEWS, ELIZABETH E.⁷ MANN, ABEL⁶, GEORGE⁵, COLONEL JOHN JR.⁴, JOHN SR.³, GEORGE BERNARD², HANS¹) was born March 28, 1922 in MIAMI COUNTY, OHIO. He married MARY LOUISE GRAGG October 30, 1942 in MIAMI COUNTY, OHIO.

Children of DELMAR THOMPSON and MARY GRAGG are:
       i.   DELOUISE KAY¹¹ THOMPSON, b. July 14, 1944, MIAMI COUNTY, OHIO.
       ii. SANDRA LEE THOMPSON, b. December 31, 1946, PIQUA, OHIO; d. December 11, 1963, SPRINGFIELD, OHIO.

285.   ROBERT LEE¹⁰ THOMPSON (RUTH⁹ SHAFER, BERTHA MAE⁸ MATTHEWS, ELIZABETH E.⁷ MANN, ABEL⁶, GEORGE⁵, COLONEL JOHN JR.⁴, JOHN SR.³, GEORGE BERNARD², HANS¹) was born January 28, 1924 in MIAMI COUNTY, OHIO. He married MARY ELIZABETH HOLDREN January 03, 1948 in MIAMI COUNTY, OHIO.

Child of ROBERT THOMPSON and MARY HOLDREN is:
       i.   TIMOTHY¹¹ THOMPSON, b. March 05, 1949, TROY, OHIO.

286.   BETTY LOU¹⁰ THOMPSON (RUTH⁹ SHAFER, BERTHA MAE⁸ MATTHEWS, ELIZABETH E.⁷ MANN, ABEL⁶, GEORGE⁵, COLONEL JOHN JR.⁴, JOHN SR.³, GEORGE BERNARD², HANS¹) was born January 28, 1924. She married LAWRENCE RAYMOND WARNER.

Children of BETTY THOMPSON and LAWRENCE WARNER are:
367.   i.   LARRY ALLEN¹¹ WARNER, b. October 13, 1947, PIQUA, OHIO.
       ii. NICKI WARNER, b. January 12, 1949, PIQUA, OHIO; m. DAVID WOOLF, June 29, 1969, DAYTON, OHIO.

287. JOSEPH DAVID[10] SHAFER *(JOSEPH DAVID[9], BERTHA MAE[8] MATTHEWS, ELIZABETH E.[7] MANN, ABEL[6], GEORGE[5], COLONEL JOHN JR.[4], JOHN SR.[3], GEORGE BERNARD[2], HANS[1])* was born February 01, 1956. He married SHARON LYNN ANDERSON July 19, 1980.

Children of JOSEPH SHAFER and SHARON ANDERSON are:
    i.   JENNIFER[11] SHAFER.
    ii. JUSTIN SHAFER, b. November 26, 1985.

288. MARILYN SUE[10] PEARSON *(RUTH[9] MATTHEWS, FORREST[8], ELIZABETH E.[7] MANN, ABEL[6], GEORGE[5], COLONEL JOHN JR.[4], JOHN SR.[3], GEORGE BERNARD[2], HANS[1])* was born 1946. She married LARRY DILLY.

Children of MARILYN PEARSON and LARRY DILLY are:
    i.   DOUGLAS[11] DILLY, b. June 30, 1971.
    ii. CHRISTOPHER DILLY, b. April 20, 1973.

289. LYNN[10] KELLER *(HELEN[9] MATTHEWS, FORREST[8], ELIZABETH E.[7] MANN, ABEL[6], GEORGE[5], COLONEL JOHN JR.[4], JOHN SR.[3], GEORGE BERNARD[2], HANS[1])* was born 1941. He married PENNY HATFIELD.

Children of LYNN KELLER and PENNY HATFIELD are:
    i.   DARIN[11] KELLER.
    ii. BRANDON KELLER.

Generation No. 9 of John Mann Sr.

290. ANGEL RENEE[11] MOON *(JOAN LOURIE[10] EARLS, PHYLLIS EILEEN[9] MANN, JOHN ALLEN SR.[8], DORSEY VIRGIL[7], LEWIS JACKSON[6], ISAAC[5], COLONEL JOHN JR.[4], JOHN SR.[3], GEORGE BERNARD[2], HANS[1])* was born July 08, 1977 in PIQUA, OHIO. She married (1) JONATHON THOMPSON, son of JOHN THOMPSON and GLENDA DOUGLAS. She married (2) TIMOTHY SCOTT FERRYMAN June 22, 1996, son of GARY FERRYMAN and JANE DAVIS.

Child of ANGEL MOON and JONATHON THOMPSON is:
- i.   MARRKUS JAY[12] THOMPSON, b. July 11, 1995.

Children of ANGEL MOON and TIMOTHY FERRYMAN are:
- i.   MORGAN FERRYMAN
- ii. MELEAH FERRYMAN

291. RONALD HILTON[11] TONEY *(LUCILLE KATHERINE[10] MANN, HARRY CHRIS[9], ISAAC ORAN[8], CHRISTIAN[7], ISAAC JR.[6], ISAAC[5], COLONEL JOHN JR.[4], JOHN SR.[3], GEORGE BERNARD[2], HANS[1])* was born May 08, 1952. He married RHONDA CARROLL June 02, 1979.

Children of RONALD TONEY and RHONDA CARROLL are:
- i.   ERIC[12] TONEY, b. November 07, 1980.
- ii. TARA TONEY, b. November 16, 1982.

292. CYNTHIA MARIE[11] TONEY *(LUCILLE KATHERINE[10] MANN, HARRY CHRIS[9], ISAAC ORAN[8], CHRISTIAN[7], ISAAC JR.[6], ISAAC[5], COLONEL JOHN JR.[4], JOHN SR.[3], GEORGE BERNARD[2], HANS[1])* was born March 29, 1955. She married TIM MARTIN November 17, 1973.

Children of CYNTHIA TONEY and TIM MARTIN are:
- i.   JASON EDWARD[12] MARTIN, b. April 23, 1975.
- ii. JAIME MARIE MARTIN, b. August 07, 1978.

293. SUSANNE CHRISTINE[11] TONEY *(LUCILLE KATHERINE[10] MANN, HARRY CHRIS[9], ISAAC ORAN[8], CHRISTIAN[7], ISAAC JR.[6], ISAAC[5], COLONEL JOHN JR.[4], JOHN SR.[3], GEORGE BERNARD[2], HANS[1])* was born January 01, 1958. She married DAVID VICE August 24, 1984.

Children of SUSANNE TONEY and DAVID VICE are:
- i.   ASHLEY SUSANNE[12] VICE, b. March 26, 1985.
- ii. BRANDON DAVID VICE, b. April 24, 1986.

294. MARK RICHARD[11] JONES *(STEPHEN D.[10], LANCE DARREL[9], EDITH A.[8] MANN, CHRISTIAN[7], ISAAC JR.[6], ISAAC[5], COLONEL JOHN JR.[4], JOHN SR.[3], GEORGE BERNARD[2], HANS[1])* was born February 09, 1967 *in* ELKHART, INDIANA.

Children of MARK RICHARD JONES are:
- i.   TRENTON[12] JONES, b. February 1988, ELKHART, INDIANA.
- ii. COURTNEY JONES, b. 1990, ELKHART, INDIANA.

295. PATRICK[11] SCHEETS *(CHERRIE LOU[10] MANN, STEWARD RAYMOND[9], HARLEY R.[8], CHRISTIAN[7], ISAAC JR.[6], ISAAC[5], COLONEL JOHN JR.[4], JOHN SR.[3], GEORGE BERNARD[2], HANS[1])* was born July 13, 1959 *in* ELKHART, INDIANA. He married KATHLEEN LORING May 25, 1985 *in* MISHAWAKA, INDIANA.

Children of PATRICK SCHEETS and KATHLEEN LORING are:
- i.   JULIE RENAE[12] SCHEETS, b. July 13, 1988, SOUTH BEND, INDIANA.
- ii. JONATHON PATRICK SCHEETS, b. January 09, 1990, SOUTH BEND INDIANA.

296. MICHAEL GARY[11] SHAUM *(GARY LOWELL[10], LUCILLE BERNICE[9] WALTER, RUTH LAPEARL[8] MANN, CHRISTIAN[7], ISAAC JR.[6], ISAAC[5], COLONEL JOHN JR.[4], JOHN SR.[3], GEORGE BERNARD[2], HANS[1])* was born November 23, 1970 *in* ELKHART, INDIANA. He married ANGELA RIVERA April 18, 1997 *in* ELKHART, INDIANA.

Child of MICHAEL SHAUM and ANGELA RIVERA is:
- i.   CASSIDY LYN RUBLE[12] SHAUM, b. April 25, 1997, SOUTH BEND, INDIANA.

297. ROBERT[11] JOHNSON *(CHALMER EDWARD[10], WELMA OPAL[9] TRICK, SAMANTHA[8] GRISE, MARGARET ACHIE[7] MANN, ABEL[6], GEORGE[5], COLONEL JOHN JR.[4], JOHN SR.[3], GEORGE BERNARD[2], HANS[1])* was born January 30, 1943. He married DEBORAH KAY COPPS.

Children of ROBERT JOHNSON and DEBORAH COPPS are:
- i.   ROBERT JR.[12] JOHNSON.
- ii. KERI KAY JOHNSON, b. 1974.

298. TIMOTHY RALPH[11] FESSLER *(ELSIE CORDA[10] JONES, PERRY[9], CORDA ACHIE[8] GRISE, MARGARET ACHIE[7] MANN, ABEL[6], GEORGE[5], COLONEL JOHN JR.[4], JOHN SR.[3], GEORGE BERNARD[2], HANS[1])* was born December 23, 1955. He married BRENDA K. FORSHA February 27, 1978.

Children of TIMOTHY FESSLER and BRENDA FORSHA are:
- i.   ANGELA[12] FESSLER, b. July 07, 1978.
- ii. JOSHUA FESSLER, b. March 04, 1980.

SR.[3], GEORGE BERNARD[2], HANS[1]) was born December 23, 1955. He married BRENDA K. FORSHA February 27, 1978.

Children of TIMOTHY FESSLER and BRENDA FORSHA are:
  i. ANGELA[12] FESSLER, b. July 07, 1978.
  ii. JOSHUA FESSLER, b. March 04, 1980.
  iii. MATHEW EDWARD FESSLER, b. July 14, 1981.

299. GREGORY ALAN[11] FESSLER (ELSIE CORDA[10] JONES, PERRY[9], CORDA ACHIE[8] GRISE, MARGARET ACHIE[7] MANN, ABEL[6], GEORGE[5], COLONEL JOHN JR.[4], JOHN SR.[3], GEORGE BERNARD[2], HANS[1]) was born April 17, 1957. He married MELODY ANN ESTEP November 01, 1976.

Children of GREGORY FESSLER and MELODY ESTEP are:
  i. CARRIE JO[12] FESSLER, b. April 27, 1977.
  ii. BRADLEY FESSLER, b. November 10, 1979.

300. CAROL LOUISE[11] FURNAS (THERM RODNEY[10], LAURA[9] JONES, CORDA ACHIE[8] GRISE, MARGARET ACHIE[7] MANN, ABEL[6], GEORGE[5], COLONEL JOHN JR.[4], JOHN SR.[3], GEORGE BERNARD[2], HANS[1]) was born April 04, 1949. She married PATRICK SCHIERMEYER.

Children of CAROL FURNAS and PATRICK SCHIERMEYER are:
  i. CHRISTINE[12] SCHIERMEYER, b. June 05, 1976.
  ii. ALICIA SCHIERMEYER, b. April 02, 1979.
  iii. CHARLES ANTHONY SCHIERMEYER, b. October 28, 1981.

301. RODNEY LEE[11] SAMPSON (HELEN MAE[10] FURNAS, LAURA[9] JONES, CORDA ACHIE[8] GRISE, MARGARET ACHIE[7] MANN, ABEL[6], GEORGE[5], COLONEL JOHN JR.[4], JOHN SR.[3], GEORGE BERNARD[2], HANS[1]) was born November 02, 1939. He married (1) PHYLLIS TOWER September 02, 1961. He married (2) CHARLOTTE WEAVER 1994.

Children of RODNEY SAMPSON and PHYLLIS TOWER are:
368. i. DANIEL LEE[12] SAMPSON, b. August 24, 1964.
  ii. SHERRI LYNN SAMPSON, b. July 28, 1970; m. TERRY WAYNE BARNES, March 21, 1993.

302. JAMES ALLEN[11] SAMPSON (HELEN MAE[10] FURNAS, LAURA[9] JONES, CORDA ACHIE[8] GRISE, MARGARET ACHIE[7] MANN, ABEL[6], GEORGE[5], COLONEL JOHN JR.[4],

JOHN SR.[3], GEORGE BERNARD[2], HANS[1]) was born June 23, 1941. He married DELORIS VARIAN January 27, 1962.

Children of JAMES SAMPSON and DELORIS VARIAN are:
369.   i.   DEBRA SUE[12] SAMPSON, b. August 16, 1962.
370.   ii. RANDY ALLEN SAMPSON, b. August 08, 1964.
371.   iii. DAVID BRYAN SAMPSON, b. November 11, 1965; d. April 13, 1994.

303. JEANETTE MARIE[11] SAMPSON (HELEN MAE[10] FURNAS, LAURA[9] JONES, CORDA ACHIE[8] GRISE, MARGARET ACHIE[7] MANN, ABEL[6], GEORGE[5], COLONEL JOHN JR.[4], JOHN SR.[3], GEORGE BERNARD[2], HANS[1]) was born March 25, 1947. She married MICHAEL BRYAN September 25, 1965.

Child of JEANETTE SAMPSON and MICHAEL BRYAN is:
372.   i.   JAMES MICHAEL[12] BRYAN, b. October 27, 1966.

304. STEVEN LEE[11] SAMPSON (HELEN MAE[10] FURNAS, LAURA[9] JONES, CORDA ACHIE[8] GRISE, MARGARET ACHIE[7] MANN, ABEL[6], GEORGE[5], COLONEL JOHN JR.[4], JOHN SR.[3], GEORGE BERNARD[2], HANS[1]) was born November 15, 1952. He married JUDY ANN BERNSDORF October 28, 1978.

Children of STEVEN SAMPSON and JUDY BERNSDORF are:
        i.   JOSEPH PAUL[12] SAMPSON, b. February 18, 1982.
        ii. JONATHON ROBERT SAMPSON, b. April 24, 1984.
        iii. THOMAS ALLEN SAMPSON, b. February 25, 1989.

305. JAMES[11] BUCHOLZ (JAMES ROGER[10], LORING[9], ESTHER ANN[8] GRISE, MARGARET ACHIE[7] MANN, ABEL[6], GEORGE[5], COLONEL JOHN JR.[4], JOHN SR.[3], GEORGE BERNARD[2], HANS[1]) was born September 23, 1954. He married ELLEN STEWART September 27, 1974.

Children of JAMES BUCHOLZ and ELLEN STEWART are:
        i.   NATHANIEL JAMES[12] BUCHOLZ, b. May 17, 1976.
        ii. NICHOLAS DAVID BUCHOLZ, b. October 29, 1978.
        iii. AMANDA DAVID BUCHOLZ, b. November 20, 1980.

306. KIM JOSEPH[11] BUCHOLZ (JAMES ROGER[10], LORING[9], ESTHER ANN[8] GRISE, MARGARET ACHIE[7] MANN, ABEL[6], GEORGE[5], COLONEL JOHN JR.[4], JOHN SR.[3],

GEORGE BERNARD[2], HANS[1]) was born March 13, 1957. He married SHARON WEBER April 22, 1978.

Children of KIM BUCHOLZ and SHARON WEBER are:
 i. JOHN OLIVER[12] BUCHOLZ, b. September 24, 1984.
 ii. SUSAN BUCHOLZ, b. September 26, 1989.

307. ELDON[11] BUCHOLZ (JAMES ROGER[10], LORING[9], ESTHER ANN[8] GRISE, MARGARET ACHIE[7] MANN, ABEL[6], GEORGE[5], COLONEL JOHN JR.[4], JOHN SR.[3], GEORGE BERNARD[2], HANS[1]) was born May 02, 1960. He married LISA MONTGOMERY May 03, 1980.

Children of ELDON BUCHOLZ and LISA MONTGOMERY are:
 i. ANDREA ELIZABETH[12] BUCHOLZ, b. December 15, 1984.
 ii. RYAN MICHAEL BUCHOLZ, b. October 13, 1989.

308. ELLEN ANN[11] BARANCIK (JOYCE IRENE[10] BUCHOLZ, LORING[9], ESTHER ANN[8] GRISE, MARGARET ACHIE[7] MANN, ABEL[6], GEORGE[5], COLONEL JOHN JR.[4], JOHN SR.[3], GEORGE BERNARD[2], HANS[1]) was born May 22, 1955. She married KENNETH R. WEISENBERGER October 14, 1978.

Children of ELLEN BARANCIK and KENNETH WEISENBERGER are:
 i. HEIDI ANN[12] WEISENBERGER, b. March 21, 1981.
 ii. KELLIE MARIE WEISENBERGER, b. April 22, 1983.

309. JEFFERY[11] BARANCIK (JOYCE IRENE[10] BUCHOLZ, LORING[9], ESTHER ANN[8] GRISE, MARGARET ACHIE[7] MANN, ABEL[6], GEORGE[5], COLONEL JOHN JR.[4], JOHN SR.[3], GEORGE BERNARD[2], HANS[1]) was born July 14, 1956. He married TERRY JO WILLIAMS June 07, 1980.

Children of JEFFERY BARANCIK and TERRY WILLIAMS are:
 i. TARA LYNN[12] BARANCIK, b. August 24, 1983.
 ii. CLAYTON JEFFERY BARANCIK, b. October 13, 1986.

310. CURTIS ANDREW[11] BARANCIK (JOYCE IRENE[10] BUCHOLZ, LORING[9], ESTHER ANN[8] GRISE, MARGARET ACHIE[7] MANN, ABEL[6], GEORGE[5], COLONEL JOHN JR.[4], JOHN SR.[3], GEORGE BERNARD[2], HANS[1]) was born January 15, 1958. He married SUSAN MARIE DUQUID February 16, 1980.

Children of CURTIS BARANCIK and SUSAN DUQUID are:
  i. JOSHUA CURTIS[12] BARANCIK, b. April 03, 1981.
  ii. CHRISTOPHER ANDREW BARANCIK, b. January 15, 1983.

311. JILL[11] BARANCIK (JOYCE IRENE[10] BUCHOLZ, LORING[9], ESTHER ANN[8] GRISE, MARGARET ACHIE[7] MANN, ABEL[6], GEORGE[5], COLONEL JOHN JR.[4], JOHN SR.[3], GEORGE BERNARD[2], HANS[1]) was born October 04, 1961. She married RICHARD LEWIS HANKINS February 23, 1979.

    Child of JILL BARANCIK and RICHARD HANKINS is:
      i. SHERRI[12] HANKINS, b. August 01, 1979.

312. TONY LEE[11] TUPICA (BARBARA[10] BUCHOLZ, LORING[9], ESTHER ANN[8] GRISE, MARGARET ACHIE[7] MANN, ABEL[6], GEORGE[5], COLONEL JOHN JR.[4], JOHN SR.[3], GEORGE BERNARD[2], HANS[1]) was born November 16, 1963. He married MICHELLE FABUS.

    Child of TONY TUPICA and MICHELLE FABUS is:
      i. MICHAEL LEE[12] TUPICA.

313. JODY LYNN[11] SMITH (GARY LYNN[10], HELEN IRENE[9] BUCHOLZ, ESTHER ANN[8] GRISE, MARGARET ACHIE[7] MANN, ABEL[6], GEORGE[5], COLONEL JOHN JR.[4], JOHN SR.[3], GEORGE BERNARD[2], HANS[1]) was born February 26, 1958. He married DEBORAH WEHNER March 24, 1979.

    Children of JODY SMITH and DEBORAH WEHNER are:
      i.   JESSICA LYNN[12] SMITH, b. March 23, 1981.
      ii. LORALEE GRACE SMITH, b. November 22, 1985.
      iii. JAKOB PAUL SMITH, b. August 24, 1987.

314. AUDREY[11] SMITH (GARY LYNN[10], HELEN IRENE[9] BUCHOLZ, ESTHER ANN[8] GRISE, MARGARET ACHIE[7] MANN, ABEL[6], GEORGE[5], COLONEL JOHN JR.[4], JOHN SR.[3], GEORGE BERNARD[2], HANS[1]) was born October 04, 1963. She married DAVID ANTHONY SOVIS September 13, 1986.

    Children of AUDREY SMITH and DAVID SOVIS are:
      i. ANTHONY DAVID[12] SOVIS, b. March 29, 1990.
      ii. STEPHEN JOSEPH SOVIS, b. June 03, 1991.

315. STEVEN KENT[11] KIENITZ (RUBY ELLEN[10] SMITH, HELEN IRENE[9] BUCHOLZ, ESTHER ANN[8] GRISE, MARGARET ACHIE[7] MANN, ABEL[6], GEORGE[5], COLONEL JOHN JR.[4], JOHN SR.[3], GEORGE BERNARD[2], HANS[1]) was born April 20, 1960. He married CLAUDIA GRIFFUS June 30, 1979.

Children of STEVEN KIENITZ and CLAUDIA GRIFFUS are:
 i. CAITLYN[12] KIENITZ, b. December 22, 1985.
 ii. ALEXANDER STEVEN KIENITZ, b. February 14, 1989.

316. SALLY JO[11] KIENITZ (RUBY ELLEN[10] SMITH, HELEN IRENE[9] BUCHOLZ, ESTHER ANN[8] GRISE, MARGARET ACHIE[7] MANN, ABEL[6], GEORGE[5], COLONEL JOHN JR.[4], JOHN SR.[3], GEORGE BERNARD[2], HANS[1]) was born July 25, 1963. She married CRAIG WINGLE November 26, 1983.

Children of SALLY KIENITZ and CRAIG WINGLE are:
 i. CHRISTOPHER SCOTT[12] WINGLE, b. March 01, 1986.
 ii. AMANDA JANE WINGLE, b. November 06, 1988.

317. ADAM TROY[11] KIENITZ (RUBY ELLEN[10] SMITH, HELEN IRENE[9] BUCHOLZ, ESTHER ANN[8] GRISE, MARGARET ACHIE[7] MANN, ABEL[6], GEORGE[5], COLONEL JOHN JR.[4], JOHN SR.[3], GEORGE BERNARD[2], HANS[1]) was born November 29, 1964. He married SHARON M. WOLFGRAM October 19, 1991.

Children of ADAM KIENITZ and SHARON WOLFGRAM are:
 i. KELLY LYNN[12] KIENITZ, b. June 30, 1993.
 ii. LINDSEY ELAINE KIENITZ, b. September 03, 1995.

318. JERRY TODD[11] KIENITZ (RUBY ELLEN[10] SMITH, HELEN IRENE[9] BUCHOLZ, ESTHER ANN[8] GRISE, MARGARET ACHIE[7] MANN, ABEL[6], GEORGE[5], COLONEL JOHN JR.[4], JOHN SR.[3], GEORGE BERNARD[2], HANS[1]) was born August 02, 1968. He married WENDY ELLEN ATHEY March 16, 1991.

Children of JERRY KIENITZ and WENDY ATHEY are:
 i. KERSTIE ROSE[12] KIENITZ, b. July 22, 1991.
 ii. GAGE TYLER KIENITZ, b. February 04, 1994.

319. NICHOLAS JACOB[11] SMITH (KENNETH WARD[10], HELEN IRENE[9] BUCHOLZ, ESTHER ANN[8] GRISE, MARGARET ACHIE[7] MANN, ABEL[6], GEORGE[5], COLONEL JOHN JR.[4], JOHN SR.[3], GEORGE BERNARD[2], HANS[1]) was born March 19, 1975. He married BRIDGET July 21, 1996.

Child of NICHOLAS SMITH and BRIDGET is:
    i.   KRYSENTHIA AUTUMN[12] SMITH, b. April 02, 1996.

320. ROBERT[11] BRANDT (GLENNA MAE[10] HILL, MARY BELL[9] BASHORE, LOVA CATHERINE[8] GRISE, MARGARET ACHIE[7] MANN, ABEL[6], GEORGE[5], COLONEL JOHN JR.[4], JOHN SR.[3], GEORGE BERNARD[2], HANS[1]) was born October 03, 1942. He married MARY HARTMAN August 01, 1964.

    Children of ROBERT BRANDT and MARY HARTMAN are:
    i.   KIMBERLY LYNN[12] BRANDT, b. October 21, 1970.
    ii. TAMARA SUE BRANDT, b. January 31, 1975.

321. MARY ANN[11] BRANDT (GLENNA MAE[10] HILL, MARY BELL[9] BASHORE, LOVA CATHERINE[8] GRISE, MARGARET ACHIE[7] MANN, ABEL[6], GEORGE[5], COLONEL JOHN JR.[4], JOHN SR.[3], GEORGE BERNARD[2], HANS[1]) was born July 28, 1944. She married CORNELIUS O'BRIEN August 25, 1963.

    Children of MARY BRANDT and CORNELIUS O'BRIEN are:
    i.   TIMOTHY[12] O'BRIEN, b. July 04, 1967; m. AMY HUBERT, May 18, 1991.
    ii. KEVIN PATRICK O'BRIEN, b. March 03, 1970; m. JILL METCALF, May 27, 1994.
    iii. JEFFERY JOSEPH O'BRIEN, b. April 28, 1972.

322. DONALD[11] BRANDT (GLENNA MAE[10] HILL, MARY BELL[9] BASHORE, LOVA CATHERINE[8] GRISE, MARGARET ACHIE[7] MANN, ABEL[6], GEORGE[5], COLONEL JOHN JR.[4], JOHN SR.[3], GEORGE BERNARD[2], HANS[1]) was born March 06, 1948. He married RHONA SUTTON April 30, 1988.

    Child of DONALD BRANDT and RHONA SUTTON is:
    i.   ASHLEY LORAINE[12] BRANDT, b. October 1989.

323. THOMAS JAMES[11] HILL (KENNETH[10], MARY BELL[9] BASHORE, LOVA CATHERINE[8] GRISE, MARGARET ACHIE[7] MANN, ABEL[6], GEORGE[5], COLONEL JOHN JR.[4], JOHN SR.[3], GEORGE BERNARD[2], HANS[1]) was born April 30, 1947. He married DARLENE FRANCIS March 05, 1966.

Children of THOMAS HILL and DARLENE FRANCIS are:
373.   i.   KAREN LYNN[12] HILL, b. July 10, 1967.
374.   ii. THOMAS LOWELL HILL, b. October 01, 1968.
        iii. NANCY KAY HILL, b. March 06, 1971.

324. CONNIE EILEEN[11] HILL (KENNETH[10], MARY BELL[9] BASHORE, LOVA CATHERINE[8] GRISE, MARGARET ACHIE[7] MANN, ABEL[6], GEORGE[5], COLONEL JOHN JR.[4], JOHN SR.[3], GEORGE BERNARD[2], HANS[1]) was born October 15, 1948. She married WILLIAM MCAFEE March 28, 1969.

    Child of CONNIE HILL and WILLIAM MCAFEE is:
        i.   SHAWN PATRICK[12] MCAFEE, b. March 08, 1973.

325. PHILLIP KIRK[11] BASHORE (WAYNE[10], JESSE E.[9], LOVA CATHERINE[8] GRISE, MARGARET ACHIE[7] MANN, ABEL[6], GEORGE[5], COLONEL JOHN JR.[4], JOHN SR.[3], GEORGE BERNARD[2], HANS[1]) was born May 20, 1961. He married JUANA ROSE MOUBRAY January 23, 1982 in MIAMI COUNTY, OHIO.

    Child of PHILLIP BASHORE and JUANA MOUBRAY is:
        i.   MEGAN J.[12] BASHORE.

326. JUDITH ANN[11] REDMAN (DALE E.[10], EDITH MARGARET[9] BASHORE, LOVA CATHERINE[8] GRISE, MARGARET ACHIE[7] MANN, ABEL[6], GEORGE[5], COLONEL JOHN JR.[4], JOHN SR.[3], GEORGE BERNARD[2], HANS[1]) was born August 13, 1944 in DARKE COUNTY, OHIO. She married GERALD PHILLIPS June 12, 1965 in OXFORD, MICHIGAN.

    Children of JUDITH REDMAN and GERALD PHILLIPS are:
        i.   JENNIFER LYNN[12] PHILLIPS, b. September 04, 1967; m. ERIC
             VERARDI, March 18, 1990.
        ii. GERALD LAREN PHILLIPS, b. October 16, 1971.
        iii. JOSHUA AARON PHILLIPS, b. December 14, 1974.

327. ONDA LEE[11] REDMAN (DALE E.[10], EDITH MARGARET[9] BASHORE, LOVA CATHERINE[8] GRISE, MARGARET ACHIE[7] MANN, ABEL[6], GEORGE[5], COLONEL JOHN JR.[4], JOHN SR.[3], GEORGE BERNARD[2], HANS[1]) was born December 30, 1946 in DARKE COUNTY, OHIO. She married (1) DOUG TRUEMAN December 05, 1964. She married (2) JERRY PATTERSON June 1970. She married (3) TERRY CLARK April 30, 1977.

Child of ONDA REDMAN and DOUG TRUEMAN is:
 i. TAMARA SUE[12] TRUEMAN, b. July 04, 1966, OXFORD, MICHIGAN;
   m. KIP FLOWERS, May 27, 1989.

Child of ONDA REDMAN and JERRY PATTERSON is:
 ii. WENDY MICHELLE[12] PATTERSON, b. August 18, 1970, OXFORD,
   MICHIGAN; m. PHILLIP FUGATE, March 02, 1990.

Child of ONDA REDMAN and TERRY CLARK is:
 iii. JEFFERY L.[12] CLARK, b. December 10, 1977.

328. BETTY LOU[11] REDMAN (DALE E.[10], EDITH MARGARET[9] BASHORE, LOVA CATHERINE[8] GRISE, MARGARET ACHIE[7] MANN, ABEL[6], GEORGE[5], COLONEL JOHN JR.[4], JOHN SR.[3], GEORGE BERNARD[2], HANS[1]) was born December 09, 1948 in DARKE COUNTY, OHIO. She married JOHN LASHER October 22, 1969 in OXFORD, MICHIGAN.

 Children of BETTY REDMAN and JOHN LASHER are:
 i. ELIZABETH ANN[12] LASHER, b. April 07, 1974, OXFORD,
   MICHIGAN.
 ii. JASON DAVID LASHER, b. September 15, 1978, OXFORD,
   MICHIGAN.
 iii. EMILY LOUISE LASHER, b. April 01, 1986.

329. ANITA KAY[11] REDMAN (DALE E.[10], EDITH MARGARET[9] BASHORE, LOVA CATHERINE[8] GRISE, MARGARET ACHIE[7] MANN, ABEL[6], GEORGE[5], COLONEL JOHN JR.[4], JOHN SR.[3], GEORGE BERNARD[2], HANS[1]) was born June 19, 1951 in DARKE COUNTY, OHIO. She married CLAUDE THAYER July 11, 1970 in OXFORD, MICHIGAN.

 Children of ANITA REDMAN and CLAUDE THAYER are:
 i. CHAD DALE[12] THAYER, b. July 12, 1971, MARYLAND.
 ii. KIMBERLY JO THAYER, b. January 31, 1973, OXFORD, MICHIGAN.
 iii. JEREMY MATTHEW THAYER, b. August 24, 1975, OXFORD,
   MICHIGAN.

330. RITA MAY[11] REDMAN (DALE E.[10], EDITH MARGARET[9] BASHORE, LOVA CATHERINE[8] GRISE, MARGARET ACHIE[7] MANN, ABEL[6], GEORGE[5], COLONEL JOHN JR.[4], JOHN SR.[3], GEORGE BERNARD[2], HANS[1]) was born June 19, 1951 in DARKE COUNTY, OHIO. She married (1) TERRY HORTON January 16, 1971 in OXFORD,

MICHIGAN. She married (2) DONALD VINCENT LIGHTNER May 19, 1978 in TUSCON, ARIZONA.

Children of RITA REDMAN and DONALD LIGHTNER are:
  i.   MELISSA MICHELLE[12] LIGHTNER, b. July 19, 1979, TUSCON, ARIZONA.
  ii. ELIZABETH NICOLE LIGHTNER, b. November 19, 1980, TUSCON, ARIZONA.

331.   STEPHEN RAY[11] REDMAN (NORMAN[10], EDITH MARGARET[9] BASHORE, LOVA CATHERINE[8] GRISE, MARGARET ACHIE[7] MANN, ABEL[6], GEORGE[5], COLONEL JOHN JR.[4], JOHN SR.[3], GEORGE BERNARD[2], HANS[1]) was born November 04, 1948 in GREENVILLE, OHIO. He married MARGARET SEILER June 23, 1973.

Children of STEPHEN REDMAN and MARGARET SEILER are:
  i.   NATHAN RAY[12] REDMAN, b. May 09, 1978.
  ii. CHRISTOPHER REDMAN, b. February 11, 1982.

332.   ALICE REGINA[11] REDMAN (NORMAN[10], EDITH MARGARET[9] BASHORE, LOVA CATHERINE[8] GRISE, MARGARET ACHIE[7] MANN, ABEL[6], GEORGE[5], COLONEL JOHN JR.[4], JOHN SR.[3], GEORGE BERNARD[2], HANS[1]) was born October 21, 1953 in DARKE COUNTY, OHIO. She married MICHAEL HOGG June 26, 1982 in GREENVILLE, OHIO.

Child of ALICE REDMAN and MICHAEL HOGG is:
  i.   WHITNEY NOEL[12] HOGG, b. December 22, 1983, DAYTON, OHIO.

333.   JANE ANN[11] THIEBEAU (NANCY JANE[10] REDMAN, EDITH MARGARET[9] BASHORE, LOVA CATHERINE[8] GRISE, MARGARET ACHIE[7] MANN, ABEL[6], GEORGE[5], COLONEL JOHN JR.[4], JOHN SR.[3], GEORGE BERNARD[2], HANS[1]) was born January 30, 1959 in GREENVILLE, OHIO. She married GREG VOGEL August 07, 1976 in VERSAILLES, OHIO.

Children of JANE THIEBEAU and GREG VOGEL are:
  i.   CHRISTY[12] VOGEL, b. November 05, 1980.
  ii. RYAN VOGEL, b. July 09, 1984.

334.   JOHN PAUL WILLIAM[11] THIEBEAU (NANCY JANE[10] REDMAN, EDITH MARGARET[9] BASHORE, LOVA CATHERINE[8] GRISE, MARGARET ACHIE[7] MANN, ABEL[6], GEORGE[5], COLONEL JOHN JR.[4], JOHN SR.[3], GEORGE BERNARD[2], HANS[1]) was born August

27, 1963 in GREENVILLE, OHIO. He married DONNA BELL PALMER November 22, 1980 in GENEVA, INDIANA.

Children of JOHN THIEBEAU and DONNA PALMER are:
    i.   JENNIFER[12] THIEBEAU, b. December 01, 1981.
    ii. NICOLAS THIEBEAU, b. August 06, 1986.

335. CHRISTINA MARIE[11] THIEBEAU (NANCY JANE[10] REDMAN, EDITH MARGARET[9] BASHORE, LOVA CATHERINE[8] GRISE, MARGARET ACHIE[7] MANN, ABEL[6], GEORGE[5], COLONEL JOHN JR.[4], JOHN SR.[3], GEORGE BERNARD[2], HANS[1]) was born July 24, 1964 in GREENVILLE, OHIO. She married MICHAEL BERGMAN August 25, 1985.

Children of CHRISTINA THIEBEAU and MICHAEL BERGMAN are:
    i.   DEREK[12] BERGMAN, b. December 12, 1987.
    ii. ARIELLE BERGMAN, b. August 30, 1990.

336. KATHERINE LOUISE[11] THIEBEAU (NANCY JANE[10] REDMAN, EDITH MARGARET[9] BASHORE, LOVA CATHERINE[8] GRISE, MARGARET ACHIE[7] MANN, ABEL[6], GEORGE[5], COLONEL JOHN JR.[4], JOHN SR.[3], GEORGE BERNARD[2], HANS[1]) was born September 26, 1965 in DARKE COUNTY, OHIO. She married DOUG SCHILLING January 07, 1984 in DARKE COUNTY, OHIO.

Children of KATHERINE THIEBEAU and DOUG SCHILLING are:
    i.   JOSHUA CHRISTOPHER[12] SCHILLING, b. March 07, 1983, GREENVILLE, OHIO.
    ii. KENNETH SCHILLING, b. October 05, 1984.
    iii. JUSTIN SCHILLING, b. October 07, 1986.

337. STEVEN[11] STROBEL (LEWIS[10], IZORA VIOLA[9] BASHORE, LOVA CATHERINE[8] GRISE, MARGARET ACHIE[7] MANN, ABEL[6], GEORGE[5], COLONEL JOHN JR.[4], JOHN SR.[3], GEORGE BERNARD[2], HANS[1]) was born May 07, 1957. He married MARCIA MEIER June 06, 1981.

Children of STEVEN STROBEL and MARCIA MEIER are:
    i.   MEGAN ELIZABETH[12] STROBEL, b. May 29, 1983.
    ii. KRISTEN HEATHER STROBEL, b. January 13, 1985.
    iii. MATTHEW MICHAEL STROBEL, b. February 23, 1987.

338. JOYCE[11] BEAVER (FLORENCE[10] STROBEL, IZORA VIOLA[9] BASHORE, LOVA CATHERINE[8] GRISE, MARGARET ACHIE[7] MANN, ABEL[6], GEORGE[5], COLONEL JOHN

JR.[4], JOHN SR.[3], GEORGE BERNARD[2], HANS[1]) was born December 13, 1948. He married (1) MRS. BEAVER. He married (2) SHARON SHAW December 27, 1968.

Children of JOYCE BEAVER and MRS. BEAVER are:
  i.   SCHUYLER LEWIS[12] BEAVER, b. December 26, 1979.
  ii. JUSTIN RAY BEAVER, b. September 04, 1984.

Child of JOYCE BEAVER and SHARON SHAW is:
  iii. MICHELLE LYNN[12] BEAVER, b. November 03, 1970.

339. CHERYL[11] BEAVER (FLORENCE[10] STROBEL, IZORA VIOLA[9] BASHORE, LOVA CATHERINE[8] GRISE, MARGARET ACHIE[7] MANN, ABEL[6], GEORGE[5], COLONEL JOHN JR.[4], JOHN SR.[3], GEORGE BERNARD[2], HANS[1]) was born December 13, 1949. She married BEN BARNETT May 01, 1971.

Children of CHERYL BEAVER and BEN BARNETT are:
  i.   ERIC DAVID[12] BARNETT, b. February 25, 1980.
  ii. KYLE JAMES BARNETT, b. February 18, 1982.

340. ANNA LOUISE[11] HAMILTON (MARY LOUISE[10] STROBEL, IZORA VIOLA[9] BASHORE, LOVA CATHERINE[8] GRISE, MARGARET ACHIE[7] MANN, ABEL[6], GEORGE[5], COLONEL JOHN JR.[4], JOHN SR.[3], GEORGE BERNARD[2], HANS[1]) was born March 15, 1952. She married DENNIS HUDELSON March 10, 1974.

Children of ANNA HAMILTON and DENNIS HUDELSON are:
  i.   ANGELA MARIE[12] HUDELSON, b. April 14, 1978.
  ii. MELISSA ANN HUDELSON, b. June 04, 1982.

341. DUANE[11] HAMILTON (MARY LOUISE[10] STROBEL, IZORA VIOLA[9] BASHORE, LOVA CATHERINE[8] GRISE, MARGARET ACHIE[7] MANN, ABEL[6], GEORGE[5], COLONEL JOHN JR.[4], JOHN SR.[3], GEORGE BERNARD[2], HANS[1]) was born December 22, 1954. He married (1) ELIZABETH GALPIN 1978. He married (2) DEBBIE GREENWOOD October 15, 1983.

Children of DUANE HAMILTON and DEBBIE GREENWOOD are:
  i.   ANDREW LEE[12] HAMILTON, b. April 03, 1984.
  ii. AUSTIN TYLER HAMILTON, b. July 04, 1985.
  iii. BRYCE JACOB HAMILTON, b. February 08, 1988.
  iv. CLAIRE MACKENZIE HAMILTON, b. December 15, 1995.

342. BRUCE CHARLES[11] STROBEL (CARL RICHARD[10], IZORA VIOLA[9] BASHORE, LOVA CATHERINE[8] GRISE, MARGARET ACHIE[7] MANN, ABEL[6], GEORGE[5], COLONEL JOHN JR.[4], JOHN SR.[3], GEORGE BERNARD[2], HANS[1]) was born March 10, 1973. He married ANGELA WHIPP September 18, 1993.

   Child of BRUCE STROBEL and ANGELA WHIPP is:
      i. NICHOLLE DAWN[12] STROBEL, b. October 18, 1994, TROY, OHIO.

343. CARLA ANN[11] STROBEL (CARL RICHARD[10], IZORA VIOLA[9] BASHORE, LOVA CATHERINE[8] GRISE, MARGARET ACHIE[7] MANN, ABEL[6], GEORGE[5], COLONEL JOHN JR.[4], JOHN SR.[3], GEORGE BERNARD[2], HANS[1]) was born March 15, 1974. She married SHANE KENWORTHY May 02, 1992.

   Children of CARLA STROBEL and SHANE KENWORTHY are:
      i.   JOSHUA DAVID[12] KENWORTHY, b. June 10, 1992.
      ii. CELESTE MARIE KENWORTHY, b. December 01, 1994.
      iii. SHANIA CARLENE KENWORTHY, b. November 29, 1996.

344. LEE ANN MARIE[11] STROBEL (LUTHER[10], IZORA VIOLA[9] BASHORE, LOVA CATHERINE[8] GRISE, MARGARET ACHIE[7] MANN, ABEL[6], GEORGE[5], COLONEL JOHN JR.[4], JOHN SR.[3], GEORGE BERNARD[2], HANS[1]) was born March 19, 1967. She married CHARLES HEITKAMP June 30, 1990 in NORTH STAR, OHIO.

   Children of LEE STROBEL and CHARLES HEITKAMP are:
      i.   KATHERYN MARIE[12] HEITKAMP, b. May 03, 1991.
      ii. ANDREW HEITKAMP, b. January 10, 1995.

345. SHERRY[11] HORNER (H. DEAN[10], VERTIE ALWILDA[9] BASHORE, LOVA CATHERINE[8] GRISE, MARGARET ACHIE[7] MANN, ABEL[6], GEORGE[5], COLONEL JOHN JR.[4], JOHN SR.[3], GEORGE BERNARD[2], HANS[1]) was born March 11, 1961. She married DAVID TODD.

   Children of SHERRY HORNER and DAVID TODD are:
      i.   SARA MARIE[12] TODD, b. January 06, 1980.
      ii. JONATHON VINCENT TODD, b. October 21, 1982.

346. SCOTT[11] HORNER (H. DEAN[10], VERTIE ALWILDA[9] BASHORE, LOVA CATHERINE[8] GRISE, MARGARET ACHIE[7] MANN, ABEL[6], GEORGE[5], COLONEL JOHN JR.[4], JOHN SR.[3], GEORGE BERNARD[2], HANS[1]) was born March 11, 1961. He married STACY.

Child of SCOTT HORNER and STACY is:
    i. WILLIAM LEE[12] HORNER, b. May 08, 1992.

347. LAVON[11] WRIGHT REED (DONNA[10] HORNER, VERTIE ALWILDA[9] BASHORE, LOVA CATHERINE[8] GRISE, MARGARET ACHIE[7] MANN, ABEL[6], GEORGE[5], COLONEL JOHN JR.[4], JOHN SR.[3], GEORGE BERNARD[2], HANS[1]) was born August 31, 1959. He married (1) ANN KREMER. He married (2) LISA LONG.

Children of LAVON WRIGHT REED and ANN KREMER are:
    i. WENDY MARIE[12] REED, b. January 03, 1978.
    ii. ANTHONY ROBERT REED, b. March 31, 1979.

Child of LAVON WRIGHT REED and LISA LONG is:
    iii. BENJAMIN JOSEPH[12] REED, b. October 13, 1981.

348. REX[11] WRIGHT REED (DONNA[10] HORNER, VERTIE ALWILDA[9] BASHORE, LOVA CATHERINE[8] GRISE, MARGARET ACHIE[7] MANN, ABEL[6], GEORGE[5], COLONEL JOHN JR.[4], JOHN SR.[3], GEORGE BERNARD[2], HANS[1]) was born March 14, 1961. He married (1) RHONDA MAGATO. He married (2) CARLA PRICE.

Child of REX WRIGHT REED and RHONDA MAGATO is:
    i. JEFFERY ALAN[12] REED, b. October 12, 1979.

Child of REX WRIGHT REED and CARLA PRICE is:
    ii. ASHLEY NICOLE[12] REED, b. March 15, 1983.

349. DEBORAH[11] REED (DONNA[10] HORNER, VERTIE ALWILDA[9] BASHORE, LOVA CATHERINE[8] GRISE, MARGARET ACHIE[7] MANN, ABEL[6], GEORGE[5], COLONEL JOHN JR.[4], JOHN SR.[3], GEORGE BERNARD[2], HANS[1]) was born February 22, 1965. She married LARRY BARGER 1986.

Children of DEBORAH REED and LARRY BARGER are:
    i. WILLIAM JOSEPH[12] BARGER, b. March 26, 1987.
    ii. ELIZABETH ROCHELLE BARGER, b. February 22, 1990.

350. CYNTHIA LYNN[11] BASHORE (SAMUEL WILLIAM[10], JOHN MARTIN[9], LOVA CATHERINE[8] GRISE, MARGARET ACHIE[7] MANN, ABEL[6], GEORGE[5], COLONEL JOHN JR.[4], JOHN SR.[3], GEORGE BERNARD[2], HANS[1]) was born October 20, 1967 in

GREENVILLE, OHIO. She married STEVEN M. SHOENLEBEN November 16, 1991 *in* GREENVILLE, OHIO.

    Children of CYNTHIA BASHORE *and* STEVEN SHOENLEBEN *are:*
        i. BETH ANN[12] SHOENLEBEN, b. September 03, 1993, MIAMI COUNTY, OHIO.
        ii. BROOKE MARIE SHOENLEBEN, b. April 13, 1996, MIAMI COUNTY, OHIO.

351. TERRY LEE[11] BASHORE *(SAMUEL WILLIAM[10], JOHN MARTIN[9], LOVA CATHERINE[8] GRISE, MARGARET ACHIE[7] MANN, ABEL[6], GEORGE[5], COLONEL JOHN JR.[4], JOHN SR.[3], GEORGE BERNARD[2], HANS[1])* was born July 25, 1969. He married DEBORAH SUE MILLER November 03, 1989.

    Children of TERRY BASHORE *and* DEBORAH MILLER *are:*
        i. DUSTIN MICHAEL[12] BASHORE, b. April 25, 1990, GREENVILLE, OHIO.
        ii. CODY LEE BASHORE, b. October 22, 1991, MIAMI COUNTY, OHIO.

352. MELISSA[11] BASHORE *(KENNETH[10], ORTHA SAMUEL[9], LOVA CATHERINE[8] GRISE, MARGARET ACHIE[7] MANN, ABEL[6], GEORGE[5], COLONEL JOHN JR.[4], JOHN SR.[3], GEORGE BERNARD[2], HANS[1])* was born October 08, 1966. She married RUE EDWIN BOWMAN December 19, 1987.

    Children of MELISSA BASHORE *and* RUE BOWMAN *are:*
        i. MICHAEL EDWARD[12] BOWMAN, b. November 1991, GREENVILLE, OHIO.
        ii. JACOB WILLIAM BOWMAN, b. June 22, 1993.

353. ANITA DARLENE[11] BASHORE *(HARRY[10], ORTHA SAMUEL[9], LOVA CATHERINE[8] GRISE, MARGARET ACHIE[7] MANN, ABEL[6], GEORGE[5], COLONEL JOHN JR.[4], JOHN SR.[3], GEORGE BERNARD[2], HANS[1])* was born December 27, 1969. She married (2) RALPH MEADOWS September 1993.

    Child of ANITA DARLENE BASHORE *is:*
        i. ANNA RENEE[12] BASHORE, b. March 22, 1991.

    Child of ANITA BASHORE *and* RALPH MEADOWS *is:*
        ii. SHELBY LEE[12] MEADOWS, b. July 02, 1996.

354. DURINDA[11] ROGERS *(NOVA[10] RHOADES, DOROTHY CATHERINE[9] BASHORE, LOVA CATHERINE[8] GRISE, MARGARET ACHIE[7] MANN, ABEL[6], GEORGE[5], COLONEL JOHN JR.[4], JOHN SR.[3], GEORGE BERNARD[2], HANS[1])* was born March 20, 1961. She married (1) HAROLD SIMMERMAN. She married (2) RICHARD CANAN April 19, 1980.

Child of DURINDA ROGERS and HAROLD SIMMERMAN is:
    i.   JEFFERY[12] SIMMERMAN, b. December 10, 1985.

Child of DURINDA ROGERS and RICHARD CANAN is:
    ii. BRADLEY THOMAS[12] CANAN, b. March 20, 1961.

355. KIMBERLY ANN[11] UNGER *(NINA[10] RHOADES, DOROTHY CATHERINE[9] BASHORE, LOVA CATHERINE[8] GRISE, MARGARET ACHIE[7] MANN, ABEL[6], GEORGE[5], COLONEL JOHN JR.[4], JOHN SR.[3], GEORGE BERNARD[2], HANS[1])* was born March 31, 1967. She married ROBERT SCOTT STICKLEY July 22, 1989.

Child of KIMBERLY UNGER and ROBERT STICKLEY is:
    i.   CLAYTON SCOTT[12] STICKLEY, b. November 10, 1994, DAYTON, OHIO.

356. CRAIG DUANE[11] UNGER *(NINA[10] RHOADES, DOROTHY CATHERINE[9] BASHORE, LOVA CATHERINE[8] GRISE, MARGARET ACHIE[7] MANN, ABEL[6], GEORGE[5], COLONEL JOHN JR.[4], JOHN SR.[3], GEORGE BERNARD[2], HANS[1])* was born January 16, 1969. He married TRACI BENZ February 18, 1995.

Child of CRAIG UNGER and TRACI BENZ is:
    i.   ALLISON TAYLOR[12] UNGER, b. April 09, 1996, DAYTON, OHIO.

357. KENNETH LEE[11] SMITH *(KENNETH LEO[10], ETHEL LEOTA[9] TROUTWINE, LAURA JANE[8] GRISE, MARGARET ACHIE[7] MANN, ABEL[6], GEORGE[5], COLONEL JOHN JR.[4], JOHN SR.[3], GEORGE BERNARD[2], HANS[1])* was born April 24, 1942. He married CHARLYNE RAE CLYLOR June 12, 1965.

Children of KENNETH SMITH and CHARLYNE CLYLOR are:
    i.   ELIZABETH ANNE[12] SMITH, b. November 29, 1967, TROY, OHIO;
         m. ROSS JAMES BARRY, October 24, 1992.
    ii. KIMBERLY LYNN SMITH, b. December 05, 1969, DAYTON, OHIO;
         m. HONDO LOUIS IMWALLE, June 20, 1992.

358. JAMES ALLAN[11] SMITH *(KENNETH LEO*[10]*, ETHEL LEOTA*[9] *TROUTWINE, LAURA JANE*[8] *GRISE, MARGARET ACHIE*[7] *MANN, ABEL*[6]*, GEORGE*[5]*, COLONEL JOHN JR.*[4]*, JOHN SR.*[3]*, GEORGE BERNARD*[2]*, HANS*[1] *)* was born July 05, 1944 in PIQUA, OHIO. He married (1) NANCY KURTZ January 23, 1965. He married (2) KATHY JO PAGETT June 15, 1974.

Child of JAMES SMITH and NANCY KURTZ is:
i. JULIE SMITH[12], b. August 09, 1966.

Children of JAMES SMITH and KATHY PAGETT are:
ii. TELCIE JO[12] SMITH, b. April 27, 1981, XENIA, OHIO.
iii. JAMES TRENTON SMITH, b. March 05, 1986, XENIA, OHIO.

359. ANNE M.[11] MILLER *(LOWELL*[10]*, TOILEY*[9] *WALKER, LILLIE FLORENCE*[8] *GRISE, MARGARET ACHIE*[7] *MANN, ABEL*[6]*, GEORGE*[5]*, COLONEL JOHN JR.*[4]*, JOHN SR.*[3]*, GEORGE BERNARD*[2]*, HANS*[1] *)* was born December 10, 1943. She married DAVID SCHELL.

Children of ANNE MILLER and DAVID SCHELL are:
i. STEVEN[12] SCHELL.
ii. PAUL SCHELL.

360. DENNIS WAYNE[11] MILLER *(LOWELL*[10]*, TOILEY*[9] *WALKER, LILLIE FLORENCE*[8] *GRISE, MARGARET ACHIE*[7] *MANN, ABEL*[6]*, GEORGE*[5]*, COLONEL JOHN JR.*[4]*, JOHN SR.*[3]*, GEORGE BERNARD*[2]*, HANS*[1] *)* was born February 05, 1945. He married BRENDA.

Children of DENNIS MILLER and BRENDA are:
i. KEITH[12] MILLER.
ii. CRAIG MILLER.
iii. SCOTT MILLER.

361. BETH J.[11] MILLER *(LOWELL*[10]*, TOILEY*[9] *WALKER, LILLIE FLORENCE*[8] *GRISE, MARGARET ACHIE*[7] *MANN, ABEL*[6]*, GEORGE*[5]*, COLONEL JOHN JR.*[4]*, JOHN SR.*[3]*, GEORGE BERNARD*[2]*, HANS*[1] *)* was born March 19, 1951. She married RICHARD WILMOTH.

Children of BETH MILLER and RICHARD WILMOTH are:
i. LAURA[12] WILMOTH.
ii. RHONDA WILMOTH.

362. MARTIN[11] CROMES (PAUL[10], LOUISE[9] WALKER, LILLIE FLORENCE[8] GRISE, MARGARET ACHIE[7] MANN, ABEL[6], GEORGE[5], COLONEL JOHN JR.[4], JOHN SR.[3], GEORGE BERNARD[2], HANS[1]) was born September 24, 1960. He married VALERIE BUSBAMKISH August 1983.

Children of MARTIN CROMES and VALERIE BUSBAMKISH are:
    i.   ADAM[12] CROMES.
   ii. BRADLEY LEWIS CROMES, b. May 16, 1984.

363. MICHAEL[11] CROMES (MARION[10], LOUISE[9] WALKER, LILLIE FLORENCE[8] GRISE, MARGARET ACHIE[7] MANN, ABEL[6], GEORGE[5], COLONEL JOHN JR.[4], JOHN SR.[3], GEORGE BERNARD[2], HANS[1]) was born February 12, 1959. He married RENEE MAYSE.

Children of MICHAEL CROMES and RENEE MAYSE are:
    i.   RICHARD[12] CROMES.
   ii. MICHELLE CROMES.

364. MARILEE ANN[11] THOMPSON (DALE EVERETT[10], RUTH[9] SHAFER, BERTHA MAE[8] MATTHEWS, ELIZABETH E.[7] MANN, ABEL[6], GEORGE[5], COLONEL JOHN JR.[4], JOHN SR.[3], GEORGE BERNARD[2], HANS[1]) was born May 10, 1946 in DAYTON, OHIO. She married EDWIN W. PENCE January 21, 1967.

Children of MARILEE THOMPSON and EDWIN PENCE are:
    i.   JEANNINE ANN[12] PENCE, b. January 01, 1969, DAYTON, OHIO.
   ii. CHRISTOPHER EDWIN PENCE, b. November 23, 1970, DAYTON, OHIO.

365. ALBERT JOSEPH[11] THOMPSON (DALE EVERETT[10], RUTH[9] SHAFER, BERTHA MAE[8] MATTHEWS, ELIZABETH E.[7] MANN, ABEL[6], GEORGE[5], COLONEL JOHN JR.[4], JOHN SR.[3], GEORGE BERNARD[2], HANS[1]) was born September 01, 1947 in MONTGOMERY COUNTY, OHIO. He married LINDA SUE LAWSON June 19, 1971.

Children of ALBERT THOMPSON and LINDA LAWSON are:
    i.   JAMES DALE[12] THOMPSON, b. June 05, 1973, XENIA, OHIO.
   ii. STEVEN JOSEPH THOMPSON, b. January 04, 1976, XENIA, OHIO.

366. MARGARET LOUISE[11] THOMPSON (DALE EVERETT[10], RUTH[9] SHAFER, BERTHA MAE[8] MATTHEWS, ELIZABETH E.[7] MANN, ABEL[6], GEORGE[5], COLONEL JOHN JR.[4],

JOHN SR.[3], GEORGE BERNARD[2], HANS[1]) was born September 05, 1948 in MONTGOMERY COUNTY, OHIO. She married (1) JOHN R. PHILLIPS May 26, 1969. She married (2) JOSEPH MICHAEL HAUGH October 06, 1973.

Child of MARGARET THOMPSON and JOHN PHILLIPS is:
    i.   JENNIFER MARIE[12] PHILLIPS, b. December 17, 1969, XENIA, OHIO.

Child of MARGARET THOMPSON and JOSEPH HAUGH is:
    ii.   JOSEPH MICHAEL[12] HAUGH, b. April 07, 1976, XENIA, OHIO.

367.   LARRY ALLEN[11] WARNER (BETTY LOU[10] THOMPSON, RUTH[9] SHAFER, BERTHA MAE[8] MATTHEWS, ELIZABETH E.[7] MANN, ABEL[6], GEORGE[5], COLONEL JOHN JR.[4], JOHN SR.[3], GEORGE BERNARD[2], HANS[1]) was born October 13, 1947 in PIQUA, OHIO. He married SUE SINEY October 22, 1967 in KETTERING, OHIO.

Children of LARRY WARNER and SUE SINEY are:
    i.   TODD PATRICK[12] WARNER, b. January 26, 1968, KETTERING, OHIO.
    ii.   TRACY LYNN WARNER, b. March 18, 1972, KETTERING, OHIO.

Generation No. 10 of John Mann Sr.

368. DANIEL LEE[12] SAMPSON (RODNEY LEE[11], HELEN MAE[10] FURNAS, LAURA[9] JONES, CORDA ACHIE[8] GRISE, MARGARET ACHIE[7] MANN, ABEL[6], GEORGE[5], COLONEL JOHN JR.[4], JOHN SR.[3], GEORGE BERNARD[2], HANS[1]) was born August 24, 1964. He married LYNN NOLAN.

   Child of DANIEL SAMPSON and LYNN NOLAN is:
      i.   DANIEL LEE JR.[13] SAMPSON, b. August 11, 1984.

369. DEBRA SUE[12] SAMPSON (JAMES ALLEN[11], HELEN MAE[10] FURNAS, LAURA[9] JONES, CORDA ACHIE[8] GRISE, MARGARET ACHIE[7] MANN, ABEL[6], GEORGE[5], COLONEL JOHN JR.[4], JOHN SR.[3], GEORGE BERNARD[2], HANS[1]) was born August 16, 1962. She married MICHAEL A. THOMPSON March 27, 1982.

   Children of DEBRA SAMPSON and MICHAEL THOMPSON are:
      i.   HEATHER MARIE[13] THOMPSON, b. July 12, 1983.
      ii. JAMES JUDSON THOMPSON, b. April 27, 1989.

370. RANDY ALLEN[12] SAMPSON (JAMES ALLEN[11], HELEN MAE[10] FURNAS, LAURA[9] JONES, CORDA ACHIE[8] GRISE, MARGARET ACHIE[7] MANN, ABEL[6], GEORGE[5], COLONEL JOHN JR.[4], JOHN SR.[3], GEORGE BERNARD[2], HANS[1]) was born August 08, 1964. He married KAREN BURGESS.

   Child of RANDY SAMPSON and KAREN BURGESS is:
      i.   BRIAN ALLEN[13] SAMPSON, b. November 22, 1987.

371. DAVID BRYAN[12] SAMPSON (JAMES ALLEN[11], HELEN MAE[10] FURNAS, LAURA[9] JONES, CORDA ACHIE[8] GRISE, MARGARET ACHIE[7] MANN, ABEL[6], GEORGE[5], COLONEL JOHN JR.[4], JOHN SR.[3], GEORGE BERNARD[2], HANS[1]) was born November 11, 1965, and died April 13, 1994. He married ROBIN REINKE January 26, 1985.

   Child of DAVID SAMPSON and ROBIN REINKE is:
      i.   STACI LYNN[13] SAMPSON, b. June 05, 1985.

372. JAMES MICHAEL[12] BRYAN (JEANETTE MARIE[11] SAMPSON, HELEN MAE[10] FURNAS, LAURA[9] JONES, CORDA ACHIE[8] GRISE, MARGARET ACHIE[7] MANN, ABEL[6],

GEORGE[5], COLONEL JOHN JR.[4], JOHN SR.[3], GEORGE BERNARD[2], HANS[1]) was born October 27, 1966. He married KARMEL L. RITTER.

Child of JAMES BRYAN and KARMEL RITTER is:
    i. KYLE LEE[13] BRYAN, b. March 16, 1989.

373. KAREN LYNN[12] HILL (THOMAS JAMES[11], KENNETH[10], MARY BELL[9] BASHORE, LOVA CATHERINE[8] GRISE, MARGARET ACHIE[7] MANN, ABEL[6], GEORGE[5], COLONEL JOHN JR.[4], JOHN SR.[3], GEORGE BERNARD[2], HANS[1]) was born July 10, 1967. She married STEVEN B. OVERHOLSER June 27, 1992 in DARKE COUNTY, OHIO.

Child of KAREN HILL and STEVEN OVERHOLSER is:
    i. TYLER[13] OVERHOLSER, b. June 15, 1995, DARKE COUNTY, OHIO.

374. THOMAS LOWELL[12] HILL (THOMAS JAMES[11], KENNETH[10], MARY BELL[9] BASHORE, LOVA CATHERINE[8] GRISE, MARGARET ACHIE[7] MANN, ABEL[6], GEORGE[5], COLONEL JOHN JR.[4], JOHN SR.[3], GEORGE BERNARD[2], HANS[1]) was born October 01, 1968. He married (1) CAROLYN SUE BOWMAN December 12, 1987 in GETTYSBURG, OHIO. He married (2) AMANDA MONNIN September 06, 1993.

Children of THOMAS HILL and CAROLYN BOWMAN are:
    i. MEGAN SUE[13] HILL, b. March 28, 1989, GREENVILLE, OHIO.
    ii. NATHANIEL THOMAS HILL, b. June 10, 1991, GREENVILLE, OHIO.

Child of THOMAS HILL and AMANDA MONNIN is:
    iii. EMILY[13] HILL, b. July 19, 1994.

Colonel John Mann Jr. His kith, his kin, his ancestors, his descendants.

Sources for chapter 8 are:

1. George Adam Mann 1734-1821, A Family on Four Frontiers. By Dorothy Knoff.
2. International Genealogical Society (IGS) Surname Index, 1992 and 1993 Ancestral File. By The Church of Jesus Christ Latter-Day Saints.
3. The New River Early Settlement by Patricia Givens Johnson.
4. Oliver Battreall Family History.
5. The Scrapbook of Mrs. Charles Sinks, containing two articles by Dr. Asa Coleman, printed in the Troy Times. This scrapbook is in the possession of the Hayner House in Troy, Ohio.
6. A Brief of Wills and Marriages, in Montgomery and Fincastle Counties, Virginia., by Ann Lowery Worrell.
7. A History of Miami County, Ohio 1807-1953. By the Miami County Sesquicentennial Historical Committee.
8. Montgomery County, Virginia, circa 1790. By Netti Schreiner-Yantis.
9. Index to the Grave Records of Servicemen of the War of 1812, State of Ohio. Compiled by the Ohio Society, United States Daughters of 1812.
10. Genealogical and Biographical Record of Miami County, Ohio. Published in 1900 by Lewis and Company.
11. Roster of Ohio Soldiers in the War of 1812 by the Adjutant General of Ohio.
12. Probate Court Register of Marriages, Montgomery County, Virginia.
13. DAR Magazine April 1954.
14. Marriage Records of Shelby County, Ohio. Volume 1 and 2. Compiled by Barbara Adams and Gene Mozely.
15. Probate Court, Miami and Shelby County, Ohio Marriage Records.
16. The History of Miami County, Ohio. By W.H. Beers and Company. Published 1880.
17. 1816 Federal Tax List for Miami County, Ohio.
18. Virginia Valley Records. By John W. Wayland, Genealogical Publishing Company.
19. First Families of Darke County, Ohio by the Darke County Genealogical Society.
20. Indian Blood, Finding Your Native American Ancestor. By Richard Pangburn.
21. Shelby County Indiana Health Department records.
22. Census Records for Miami and Shelby County Ohio.

23. *Early Settlers of Montgomery County, Ohio Genealogical Abstracts from Common Pleas Court Records, Civil and Probate,* by Shirley Kelley Mikesell.
24. *Miami County, Ohio Land Patent Records*
25. *A Name & Source Description Index to Persons in the Ohio Counties Montgomery and Greene 1796-1810.* By the Celebration '96 Bicentennial Committee.
26. *Memoirs of the Miami Valley, Volume I* by Robert O. Law Company 1919.
27. *Birth Records, Shelby County, Ohio, Book 1* by Mrs. Vera G. Taglieber.
28. *Montgomery County, Virginia Will Book 1 1786-1809* by Netti Schreiner-Yantis.
29. *Darke County, Ohio Marriages 1851-1898* by the Darke County Genealogical Society.
30. *Turtle Creek Presbyterian Church Register of Communicants.* November 25, 192?
31. *1900 Census Gratiot County, Michigan.*
32. *Early Miami County, Ohio, Guardianship Records.*
33. *Cemetery Inscriptions of Newberry Township, Miami County, Ohio.* by Joseph H. Bosserman, Sr.
34. *Records of the Peak Mountain Church, Rockingham County, Virginia.*
35. *Darke County, Ohio Marriages 1899-1911* by Doris R. Aultman.
36. *Cemetery Inscriptions, Darke County, Ohio Volume 1* by Mrs. Don Short and Mrs. Dale Bowers.
37. *Cemetery Inscriptions, Darke County, Ohio Volumes II and IV* by Anita Short and Ruth Bowers.
38. *Oran Christian Church 125th Anniversary Homecoming Bulletin* August 18, 1957.
39. *Montgomery County Virginia Marriage Bonds, Microfilm Reel #38.*
40. *Sidney Journal,* Sidney, Ohio, newspaper article dated September 7, 1894, entitled "Old Pioneers."
41. *Shelby County Democrat,* Sidney, Ohio, newspaper article dated 1932 or 1935 entitled "Oran's Christian Church has had an interesting History...
42. *Memorial Records of Shelby County, Ohio 1819-1975.* Complied by Barbara Adams and Gene Mozely.
43. *Sidney Daily News,* Sidney, Ohio, newspaper article dated December 26, 1989 entitled "Early Farm Life in Shelby County, outlined".
44. *Early History of Ft. Loramie, Sesquintcentennial, 1837-1987.* Published by the Fort Loramie Historical Society.
45. *Annuals of St. Michaels Parish, 1907.* By Pigot.
46. *Military History of Ohio.* By H. H. Hardsey.

47. *History of Shelby County, Ohio and Representative Citizens by A. B. C. Hitchcock, Sidney, Ohio.*

48. *Shelbyville City Directories, Shelbyville, Indiana 1891-1899.*

49. *Union City Times, Union City, Ohio, newspaper article entitled "W. Mann visiting relatives in Sidney, Ohio and Union City, Indiana."*

50. *Sidney Daily News, Sidney, Ohio, newspaper article dated November 2, 1989 entitled "Lifelong resident recalls busy town of Dawson."*

51. *Sidney Daily News, Sidney, Ohio, newspaper article dated December 21, 1988 entitled "Oran was one of the oldest settlements.*

52. *Early Adventures on the Western Waters by Mary B. Kegley.*

53. *Centennial History of Troy, Piqua and Miami County, Ohio and Representative Citizens, 1919.*

54. *Sidney Daily News, Sidney, Ohio, newspaper article dated December 23, 1989 entitled "Early Settlers found land of Indians, Bears.*

55. *The Fallen Heros of the Civil War, Shelby County's Roll of Honor by Barbara Adams.*

56. *Sidney Daily News, Sidney, Ohio, newspaper article dated December 27, 1989 entitled "Mann Grant, Mt. Jefferson Church and an Early canal scene."*

57. *Sidney Journal, Sidney, Ohio, newspaper article dated September 7, 1894, entitled "Early History & Old Pioneers."*

58. *History of Shelby County Ohio, reprint, Shelby County Historical Society, 1968.*

59. Will or Estate	Location	Date or Number
Lewis S Austin	(1)	A1815
Catherine Williams Mann	(1)	A1618
Elizabeth Shell Mann	(2)	March 15, 1858
Isaac Mann	(2)	September 1860
Colonel John Mann	(1)	A78
John Allen Mann, Sr.	(2)	July 14, 1981
Lewis Jackson Mann	(3)	12712
William Skillen	(1)	A317
Elizabeth Louella Mann Yount	(3)	21040

(1) *Probate Court Shelby County, Ohio*
(2) *Probate Court Miami County, Ohio*
(3) *Probate Court Darke County, Ohio*

60. <u>Death Certificate</u>   <u>Location</u>   <u>Died</u>

    Abel Mann   (3)   October 23, 1907
    Dorsey V. Mann   (4)   July 14, 1940
    Ester Mann   (3)   January 27, 1892
    John A. Mann, Sr   (2)   May 7, 1985
    Lewis Jackson Mann   (3)   March 12, 1919
    Martha Tyler Mann   (3)   October 6, 1918
    Nellie L. Herron Mann   (2)   November 16, 1994
    Eugene C Schwaiger, Jr.   (4)   June 14, 1977

(1) Shelby County, Ohio
(2) Miami County, Ohio
(3) Darke County, Ohio
(4) Montgomery County, Ohio

Colonel John Mann Jr. His kith, his kin, his ancestors, his descendants.

61. _Obituaries_

Obituaries	_Newspaper_	_Date_
Harry Bangs	(5)	May 17, 1984
Ellen V. Mann Bangs	(5)	(3)
Andrew J. Mann	(1)	October 14, 1929
Charley Mann	(3)	1872
Dorcay O. Mann	(3)	1946
George S. Mann	(3)	1945
James Mann	(3)	1924
John A. Mann, Sr.	(3 & 4)	May 8, 1985
John L. Mann	(1)	June 18, 1946
John W. Mann	(3)	1928
Joseph Mann	(3)	1923
Lewis Jackson Mann	(3)	1919
Martha Jane Mann	(1)	December 30, 1925
Martha Tyler Mann	(3)	1918
Mary C. Spade Mann	(3)	
Mary Jane Moyer Mann	(2)	July 12, 1940
Mattie Mann	(1)	July 25, 1936
Nellie L. Mann	(3&4)	November 16, 1994
Sarah Jane Mann	(1)	July 26, 1920
Stephan B. Mann	(1)	January 29, 1914
William S. Mann	(1)	August 25, 1911
Richard S. Shannon	(2)	August 13, 1998

(1) Shelbyville Democrat, Shelbyville, Indiana
(2) Sidney Daily News, Sidney, Ohio
(3) Unknown
(4) Piqua Daily Call, Piqua, Ohio
(5) Dayton Daily News, Dayton, Ohio.

Colonel John Mann Jr. His kith, his kin, his ancestors, his descendants.

Lewis and Martha Mann

Kinship Report of Hans Mann

Name	Relationship with HANS MANN

Name	Relationship with HANS MANN
ABBOTT, MR.	Husband of the 6th great-granddaughter
ALBERT, JEANETTE	Wife of the 6th great-grandson
ALDERSON, THOMAS H.	Husband of the 3rd great-granddaughter
ALEXANDER, ARMILDA	Wife of the 2nd great-grandson
ALLISON, ANN E.	3rd great-granddaughter
ALLISON, ARMILDA	3rd great-granddaughter
ALLISON, DAVID GRAY	Husband of the 2nd great-granddaughter
ALLISON, EMANUEL	3rd great-grandson
ALLISON, JACOB	3rd great-grandson
ALLISON, JAMES	Husband of the 2nd great-granddaughter
ALLISON, JAMES	3rd great-grandson
ALLISON, JOHN	3rd great-grandson
ALLISON, JOHN A.	3rd great-grandson
ALLISON, LUCRETIA	3rd great-granddaughter
ALLISON, MARGARET	3rd great-granddaughter
ALLISON, MARION	3rd great-grandson
ALLISON, MARY	3rd great-granddaughter
ALLISON, MARY E.	3rd great-granddaughter
ALLISON, NATHANIEL	3rd great-grandson

ALLISON, RACHAEL F.	3rd great-granddaughter
ALLISON, REUBEN	3rd great-grandson
ALLISON, SALLY	3rd great-granddaughter
ALLISON, SALLY A.	3rd great-granddaughter
ALLISON, SUSANNA	3rd great-granddaughter
ALMA	Wife of the 6th great-grandson
ANDERSON, MARY ETTA	Wife of the 5th great-grandson
ANDERSON, SHARON LYNN	Wife of the 7th great-grandson
ANNA	Wife of the 6th great-grandson
ANNA MARIA (MARY)	Wife of the grandson
ANNE C.	Wife of the 5th great-grandson
APPLE, CLARENCE	6th great-grandson
APPLE, HENRY	Husband of the 5th great-granddaughter
APPLE, MARTHA	6th great-granddaughter
APPLE, ORVILLE	6th great-grandson
APPLE, RALPH	6th great-grandson
ARMSTRONG, BETTY	Wife of the 6th great-grandson
ARMSTRONG, LOUETTA	Wife of the 4th great-grandson
ARNETTE, LILLIE MAY	Wife of the 5th great-grandson
ASHER, TERESA	Wife of the 7th great-grandson
ATHEY, WENDY ELLEN	Wife of the 8th great-grandson
AUSTIN, CATHERINE	4th great-granddaughter
AUSTIN, ISAAC	4th great-grandson
AUSTIN, JESSE	4th great-grandson
AUSTIN, JOSEPH	4th great-grandson
AUSTIN, LEWIS S.	Husband of the 3rd great-granddaughter
AUSTIN, LUCINDA	4th great-granddaughter
AUSTIN, MARGARET	4th great-granddaughter
AUSTIN, POLLY	Wife of the 2nd great-grandson
AUSTIN, SAMUEL	4th great-grandson
BAIL, MARGARET	Wife of the 7th great-grandson
BAJOK, ANTONINETTE (ANN)	Wife of the 7th great-grandson
BAKER, ROBERT	Husband of the 6th great-granddaughter
BAKER, VIRGINIA	7th great-granddaughter
BALDWIN, ELIGE	Husband of the 5th great-granddaughter
BALDWIN, ERNEST	6th great-grandson
BALDWIN, MIDGE	6th great-granddaughter
BALDWIN, PERRY J.	Husband of the 6th great-granddaughter
BALDWIN, RICHARD	6th great-grandson
BALLARD, BALDWIN	Husband of the 3rd great-granddaughter
BALLARD, ELIZABETH	Wife of the 3rd great-grandson
BALLARD, HARRIET	Wife of the 3rd great-grandson
BALLARD, HUGH	Husband of the 3rd great-granddaughter

BALLARD, JAMES	Husband of the 3rd great-granddaughter
BALLARD, MILLIE	Wife of the 2nd great-grandson
BALLARD, NANCY	Wife of the 3rd great-grandson
BANGS, HARRY	Husband of the 5th great-granddaughter
BANGS, JANE MARIE	6th great-granddaughter
BANKER, MAX	7th great-grandson
BANKER, STANLEY	Husband of the 6th great-granddaughter
BANKER, STANLEY JR.	7th great-grandson
BANNING, JOSEPHINE	Wife of the 4th great-grandson
BANNING, MARY	Wife of the 4th great-grandson
BARANCIK, ANDREW	Husband of the 7th great-granddaughter
BARANCIK, CHRISTOPHER A.	9th great-grandson
BARANCIK, CLAYTON JEFFERY	9th great-grandson
BARANCIK, CURTIS ANDREW	8th great-grandson
BARANCIK, DAVID MARK	8th great-grandson
BARANCIK, ELLEN ANN	8th great-granddaughter
BARANCIK, JEFFERY	8th great-grandson
BARANCIK, JILL	8th great-granddaughter
BARANCIK, JOSHUA CURTIS	9th great-grandson
BARANCIK, SHEILA MARIE	8th great-granddaughter
BARANCIK, TARA LYNN	9th great-granddaughter
BARGER, ELIZABETH ROCHELLE	9th great-granddaughter
BARGER, LARRY	Husband of the 8th great-granddaughter
BARGER, WILLIAM JOSEPH	9th great-grandson
BARLOW, MARY A.	Wife of the 3rd great-grandson
BARNES, TERRY WAYNE	Husband of the 9th great-granddaughter
BARNETT, BEN	Husband of the 8th great-granddaughter
BARNETT, EDNA	Wife of the 7th great-grandson
BARNETT, ERIC DAVID	9th great-grandson
BARNETT, JOHN	Husband of the 3rd great-granddaughter
BARNETT, KYLE JAMES	9th great-grandson
BARRY, ROSS JAMES	Husband of the 9th great-granddaughter
BARTON, ELIZABETH	Wife of the 2nd great-grandson
BASHORE, ALYSSIA ANN	8th great-granddaughter
BASHORE, AMBER RENEE	8th great-granddaughter
BASHORE, ANISSA JANE	8th great-granddaughter
BASHORE, ANITA DARLENE	8th great-granddaughter
BASHORE, ANTHONY WAYNE	8th great-grandson
BASHORE, BERTHA EMMA	6th great-granddaughter
BASHORE, BONNIE JEAN	8th great-granddaughter
BASHORE, BRIAN SCOTT	8th great-grandson
BASHORE, CODY LEE	9th great-grandson
BASHORE, CYNTHIA LYNN	8th great-granddaughter

BASHORE, DALE ALLEN	8th great-grandson
BASHORE, DEBORAH ARLENE	7th great-granddaughter
BASHORE, DONALD JAMES	7th great-grandson
BASHORE, DOROTHY CATHERINE	6th great-granddaughter
BASHORE, DUSTIN MICHAEL	9th great-grandson
BASHORE, EDITH MARGARET	6th great-granddaughter
BASHORE, HARMON WALTER	6th great-grandson
BASHORE, HARRY	7th great-grandson
BASHORE, ISAAC C.	6th great-grandson
BASHORE, IZORA VIOLA	6th great-granddaughter
BASHORE, JESSE E.	6th great-grandson
BASHORE, JOHN MARTIN	6th great-grandson
BASHORE, KATHERINE	7th great-granddaughter
BASHORE, KENNETH	7th great-grandson
BASHORE, LARRY JOE	7th great-grandson
BASHORE, MARY BELL	6th great-granddaughter
BASHORE, MEGAN J.	9th great-granddaughter
BASHORE, MELISSA	8th great-granddaughter
BASHORE, OLIVE MAY	6th great-granddaughter
BASHORE, ORTHA SAMUEL	6th great-grandson
BASHORE, PHILLIP KIRK	8th great-grandson
BASHORE, PHYLLIS JOAN	7th great-granddaughter
BASHORE, RICHARD ADDISON	8th great-grandson
BASHORE, RICHARD LEE	7th great-grandson
BASHORE, SAMUEL MARTIN	Husband of the 5th great-granddaughter
BASHORE, SAMUEL WILLIAM	7th great-grandson
BASHORE, SANDRA K.	8th great-granddaughter
BASHORE, SHARRON MARIE	8th great-granddaughter
BASHORE, SHAWN FREDRIC	8th great-grandson
BASHORE, TERRY LEE	8th great-grandson
BASHORE, VERTIE ALWILDA	6th great-granddaughter
BASHORE, WAYNE	7th great-grandson
BASTELA, KATHERINE	Wife of the 6th great-grandson
BATES, KEVIN	Husband of the 8th great-granddaughter
BATTREALL, LAURAHOMA	3rd great-granddaughter
BATTREL, ANDREW	2nd great-grandson
BATTREL, ANNA	3rd great-granddaughter
BATTREL, CATHERINE	3rd great-granddaughter
BATTREL, ELIZABETH	3rd great-granddaughter
BATTREL, ELIZABETH	2nd great-granddaughter
BATTREL, JACOB	2nd great-grandson
BATTREL, JOHN	Husband of the great-granddaughter
BATTREL, JOHN W.	2nd great-grandson

BATTREL, JOSEPH	2nd great-grandson
BATTREL, MARY	3rd great-granddaughter
BATTREL, MARY	2nd great-granddaughter
BATTREL, SAMUEL	3rd great-grandson
BATTREL, SUSANNAH	2nd great-granddaughter
BATTREL, WILLIAM	2nd great-grandson
BEAVER, CHERYL	8th great-granddaughter
BEAVER, JOYCE	8th great-grandson
BEAVER, JUSTIN RAY	9th great-grandson
BEAVER, MICHELLE LYNN	9th great-granddaughter
BEAVER, MRS.	Wife of the 8th great-grandson
BEAVER, PAUL	Husband of the 7th great-granddaughter
BEAVER, SCHUYLER LEWIS	9th great-grandson
BECKY	Wife of the 8th great-grandson
BEISNER, BETTY	Wife of the 7th great-grandson
BENZ, TRACI	Wife of the 8th great-grandson
BERGMAN, ARIELLE	9th great-granddaughter
BERGMAN, DEREK	9th great-grandson
BERGMAN, MICHAEL	Husband of the 8th great-granddaughter
BERNHART, EMMA L.	Wife of the 7th great-grandson
BERNSDORF, JUDY ANN	Wife of the 8th great-grandson
BERRY, RACHAEL	Wife of the great-grandson
BIGELOW, ROBERT	Husband of the 6th great-granddaughter
BLACK, BERTHA	5th great-granddaughter
BLACK, ONDA	5th great-granddaughter
BLACK, PERRY A.	Husband of the 4th great-granddaughter
BLAKE, SARAH	Wife of the 4th great-grandson
BLIGHT, MARY	Wife of the 8th great-grandson
BLUME, ALBERT	Husband of the 4th great-granddaughter
BOGGS, BETTY	Wife of the 7th great-grandson
BOGUE, SARAH JANE	Wife of the 7th great-grandson
BOSSERMAN, FERN	Wife of the 5th great-grandson
BOWEN, GLEN CLIFTON	Husband of the 5th great-granddaughter
BOWEN, HERBERT F.	6th great-grandson
BOWEN, THOMAS LEE	7th great-grandson
BOWIE, MARY	Wife of the 3rd great-grandson
BOWLES, BILLIE	7th great-grandchild
BOWLES, R. SHELBY	Husband of the 6th great-granddaughter
BOWLES, ROBERT	7th great-grandson
BOWMAN, CAROLYN SUE	Wife of the 9th great-grandson
BOWMAN, JACOB WILLIAM	9th great-grandson
BOWMAN, MICHAEL EDWARD	9th great-grandson
BOWMAN, RUE EDWIN	Husband of the 8th great-granddaughter

BOYCE, ALLEN W.	Husband of the 3rd great-granddaughter
BRAMLETTE, BETTY SUE	Wife of the 8th great-grandson
BRADLEY, MAVEN LEE	9th great-grandson
BRANDT, ASHLEY LORAINE	9th great-granddaughter
BRANDT, DONALD	8th great-grandson
BRANDT, HILDA	Wife of the 6th great-grandson
BRANDT, KIMBERLY LYNN	9th great-granddaughter
BRANDT, MARY ANN	8th great-granddaughter
BRANDT, ROBERT	Husband of the 7th great-granddaughter
BRANDT, ROBERT	8th great-grandson
BRANDT, TAMARA SUE	9th great-granddaughter
BRATTAIN, LAURA LOUISE	Wife of the 5th great-grandson
BRENDA	Wife of the 8th great-grandson
BRIDGET	Wife of the 8th great-grandson
BRILL, KAREN PEARL	Wife of the 7th great-grandson
BRISON, ELIZA CONNER	Wife of the 3rd great-grandson
BROCKER, NANCY E.	Wife of the 3rd great-grandson
BROWN, BARRY M.	Husband of the 7th great-granddaughter
BROWN, BRADY ARTHUR	8th great-grandson
BROWN, CASEY ANN	8th great-granddaughter
BROWN, EARL	Husband of the 5th great-granddaughter
BROWN, MARY A.	Wife of the 3rd great-grandson
BROWN, RUBY	Wife of the 6th great-grandson
BRUMBAUGH, MARLENE	Wife of the 6th great-grandson
BRUMFIELD, C.F.	Husband of the 6th great-granddaughter
BRUNNER, TONY	Husband of the 5th great-granddaughter
BRYAN, JAMES MICHAEL	9th great-grandson
BRYAN, KYLE LEE	10th great-grandson
BRYAN, MICHAEL	Husband of the 8th great-granddaughter
BUCHANNON KITURAH	Wife of the 2nd great-grandson
BUCHOLZ, AMANDA DAVID	9th great-granddaughter
BUCHOLZ, ANDREA E.	9th great-granddaughter
BUCHOLZ, BARBARA	7th great-granddaughter
BUCHOLZ, ELDON	8th great-grandson
BUCHOLZ, GROVER	6th great-grandson
BUCHOLZ, GROVER JR.	7th great-grandson
BUCHOLZ, HELEN IRENE	6th great-granddaughter
BUCHOLZ, HERMAN	6th great-grandson
BUCHOLZ, JAMES	8th great-grandson
BUCHOLZ, JAMES	8th great-grandson
BUCHOLZ, JAMES ROGER	7th great-grandson
BUCHOLZ, JANICE	8th great-granddaughter
BUCHOLZ, JEANETTE	8th great-granddaughter

BUCHOLZ, JEFFERY	8th great-grandson
BUCHOLZ, JOHN	8th great-grandson
BUCHOLZ, JOHN OLIVER	9th great-grandson
BUCHOLZ, JOSEPH	Husband of the 5th great-granddaughter
BUCHOLZ, JOSEPH	8th great-grandson
BUCHOLZ, JOYCE IRENE	7th great-granddaughter
BUCHOLZ, JULIE	8th great-granddaughter
BUCHOLZ, KELLY	8th great-grandson
BUCHOLZ, KIM JOSEPH	8th great-grandson
BUCHOLZ, LEON GERALD	8th great-grandson
BUCHOLZ, LORING	6th great-grandson
BUCHOLZ, LOVA	6th great-granddaughter
BUCHOLZ, NATHANIEL J.	9th great-grandson
BUCHOLZ, NICHOLAS DAVID	9th great-grandson
BUCHOLZ, RYAN MICHAEL	9th great-grandson
BUCHOLZ, SUSAN	9th great-granddaughter
BUCHOLZ, TOILA	6th great-granddaughter
BURGESS, KAREN	Wife of the 9th great-grandson
BURKETT, ESTHER	Wife of the 3rd great-grandson
BUSBAMKISH, VALERIE	Wife of the 8th great-grandson
BUTT, BARBARY ANN	4th great-granddaughter
BUTT, CATHERINE	4th great-granddaughter
BUTT, CLEMENT	5th great-grandson
BUTT, EDWARD	5th great-grandson
BUTT, ELLEN	4th great-granddaughter
BUTT, FLORA	5th great-granddaughter
BUTT, GEORGE	Husband of the 3rd great-granddaughter
BUTT, JACOB J.	4th great-grandson
BUTT, JOHN M.	4th great-grandson
BUTT, JOHN M.	5th great-grandson
BUTT, MARY JANE	4th great-grandson
BUTT, NATHAN	5th great-grandson
BUTT, RACHAEL	5th great-granddaughter
BUTT, RACHEL A.	4th great-granddaughter
BUTT, SARAH	4th great-granddaughter
BUTT, THOMAS	4th great-grandson
BUTT, WILLIAM	5th great-grandson
CAIN, IONA P.	Wife of the 5th great-grandson
CAINE, SAMUEL	Husband of the 5th great-granddaughter
CAMPBELL, GEORGE M.	Husband of the 3rd great-granddaughter
CANAN, BRADLEY THOMAS	9th great-grandson
CANAN, RICHARD	Husband of the 8th great-granddaughter
CANNON, MATILDA LAVINA	Wife of the 4th great-grandson

CARLBERG, HELSHMAN	8th great-grandson
CARLBERG, IRVING REINGHARD	Husband of the 6th great-granddaughter
CARLBERG, LEONARD R.	7th great-grandson
CARLBERG, NANCY	7th great-granddaughter
CARLBERG, NORMAN	7th great-grandson
CARLBERG, SCOTT	8th great-grandson
CARLBERG, WILLIAM	8th great-grandson
CARROLL, RHONDA	Wife of the 8th great-grandson
CASHMAN, ADA B.	Wife of the 5th great-grandson
CASSADAY, DAVID	4th great-grandson
CASSADAY, JOHN	Husband of the 3rd great-granddaughter
CASSADAY, ORA B.	4th great-granddaughter
CASSADAY, SARAH E.	4th great-granddaughter
CASSADAY, WILLIAM	4th great-grandson
CHANEY, LEDA	Wife of the 7th great-grandson
CHAPMAN, ROBERTA DIANE	Wife of the 7th great-grandson
CHARPIOT, CLARA M.	Wife of the 5th great-grandson
CHRISMAN, ROBERT	Husband of the 6th great-granddaughter
CHRISTIAN, DOUG	Husband of the 7th great-granddaughter
CHRISTINA	Wife of the 7th great-grandson
CLARK, CYNTHIA ANN	Wife of the 6th great-grandson
CLARK, JEFFERY L.	9th great-grandson
CLARK, LUCY	Wife of the 5th great-grandson
CLARK, NANCY	Wife of the 3rd great-grandson
CLARK, TERRY	Husband of the 8th great-granddaughter
CLARK, VIRGIE	Wife of the 6th great-grandson
CLAWSON, BEVERLY	8th great-granddaughter
CLAWSON, CECIL ELSWORTH	6th great-grandson
CLAWSON, CHARLES EDWARD	6th great-grandson
CLAWSON, CORA	5th great-granddaughter
CLAWSON, ELFA MARCELLA	6th great-granddaughter
CLAWSON, ELIZA	Wife of the 3rd great-grandson
CLAWSON, ELLA (EMMA ELLEN)	5th great-granddaughter
CLAWSON, FRANK SILVESTER	6th great-grandson
CLAWSON, FRANK WILLIAM	5th great-grandson
CLAWSON, FREDERICK	8th great-grandson
CLAWSON, FREDERICK A.	5th great-grandson
CLAWSON, GARY	8th great-grandson
CLAWSON, GERTRUDE E.	5th great-granddaughter
CLAWSON, HELEN	6th great-granddaughter
CLAWSON, JAMES ELLIS	5th great-grandson
CLAWSON, LUCILLE MAE	6th great-granddaughter
CLAWSON, LUCINDA	Wife of the 3rd great-grandson

CLAWSON, MARY	Wife of the 3rd great-grandson
CLAWSON, MAURICE F.	7th great-grandson
CLAWSON, NATHAN	5th great-grandson
CLAWSON, OPAL FRANCES	6th great-granddaughter
CLAWSON, PEARL MARIE	6th great-granddaughter
CLAWSON, RACHEL ANN	6th great-granddaughter
CLAWSON, RALPH F.	6th great-grandson
CLAWSON, RICHARD	8th great-grandson
CLAWSON, RICHARD	7th great-grandson
CLAWSON, SARAH J.	Wife of the 3rd great-grandson
CLAWSON, SARAH JANE	5th great-granddaughter
CLAWSON, VERNISHES EMORY	6th great-grandson
CLAWSON, WALDO	6th great-grandson
CLAWSON, WILLIAM G.	Husband of the 4th great-granddaughter
CLAWSON, WILLIAM PETER	6th great-grandson
CLAWSON, WILMA IRENE	6th great-granddaughter
CLAYTON, MR.	Husband of the 5th great-granddaughter
CLYLOR, CHARLYNE RAE	Wife of the 8th great-grandson
COATE, WILLIAM	Husband of the 5th great-granddaughter
COLLIER, ADELAIDE	Wife of the 6th great-grandson
COMPTON, PEGGY SUE	Wife of the 7th great-grandson
COOK, CARL	Husband of the 6th great-granddaughter
COOK, FRANK	Husband of the 4th great-granddaughter
COOK, PHYLISS	7th great-granddaughter
COOK, SUSAN	Wife of the 3rd great-grandson
COOPER, AUDREY ALBERTA	6th great-granddaughter
COOPER, DOROTHY	5th great-granddaughter
COOPER, EDWARD DODD	5th great-grandson
COOPER, ELIZABETH BLUME	5th great-granddaughter
COOPER, HARRY	Husband of the 5th great-granddaughter
COOPER, MARY BELL	6th great-granddaughter
COOPER, MARY LOUISE	5th great-granddaughter
COOPER, MARY VIRGINIA	6th great-granddaughter
COOPER, RUTH LEY	6th great-granddaughter
COOPER, WILLIAM ANDREW	Husband of the 4th great-granddaughter
COOPER, WILLIAM MOSS	5th great-grandson
COPPS, DEBORAH KAY	Wife of the 8th great-grandson
COVAULT, JAMES	Husband of the 6th great-granddaughter
COVAULT, SANDRA	7th great-granddaughter
COVULT, CLARENCE CLYDE	Husband of the 6th great-granddaughter
COVULT, LOIS V.	7th great-granddaughter

CRAWFORD, CARL STEPHEN	Husband of the 7th great-granddaughter
CRAWFORD, HELEN	Wife of the 7th great-grandson
CREMEANS, CORA ADAMS	Wife of the 7th great-grandson
CRENSHAW, JOHN ALLEN	Husband of the 5th great-granddaughter
CRESS, BERT SAMUEL	5th great-grandson
CRESS, BLANCHE	5th great-granddaughter
CRESS, CAROLYN	6th great-grandchild
CRESS, CHARLES FORREST	5th great-grandson
CRESS, CLARA	5th great-granddaughter
CRESS, CLARENCE C.	5th great-grandson
CRESS, DESSIE MAE	5th great-granddaughter
CRESS, DEWEY	5th great-grandson
CRESS, EDNA R.	5th great-granddaughter
CRESS, EDWIN	5th great-grandson
CRESS, ERNEST	5th great-grandson
CRESS, ESTELLA B.	5th great-granddaughter
CRESS, GEORGE	Husband of the 3rd great-granddaughter
CRESS, HELEN C.	5th great-granddaughter
CRESS, HENRY	4th great-grandson
CRESS, HORATIO GATES	4th great-grandson
CRESS, JACK	6th great-grandson
CRESS, JANICE	6th great-granddaughter
CRESS, JUNE	6th great-granddaughter
CRESS, MARJORIE JEAN	6th great-granddaughter
CRESS, MARVIN	6th great-grandson
CRESS, MARV	6th great-granddaughter
CRESS, MARV E.	5th great-granddaughter
CRESS, MARV JANE	4th great-granddaughter
CRESS, MORRIS	6th great-grandson
CRESS, NAOMI	6th great-grandchild
CRESS, ROBERT DAVIS	4th great-grandson
CRESS, RUTH	6th great-granddaughter
CRESS, VIRGIL	6th great-grandson
CRESS, WALTER E.	5th great-grandson
CRESS, ZELMA	6th great-granddaughter
CRICK, HARVEY JR.	Husband of the 7th great-granddaughter
CRICK, JOANNE	8th great-granddaughter
CRICK, NANCY	8th great-granddaughter
CRICK, SUSAN	8th great-granddaughter
CRIDEL, DOROTHY	Wife of the 7th great-grandson
CRINER, LIZZIE	Wife of the 3rd great-grandson
CRIPE, VIRGINIA	Wife of the 6th great-grandson

CROMER, MR.	Husband of the 2nd great-granddaughter
CROMES, ADAM	9th great-grandson
CROMES, BENNY	7th great-grandson
CROMES, BRADLEY LEWIS	9th great-grandson
CROMES, CHARLES	8th great-grandson
CROMES, CHRISTOPHER STEVEN	8th great-grandson
CROMES, DANIEL KEVIN	8th great-grandson
CROMES, DANNY	7th great-grandson
CROMES, DAVID	8th great-grandson
CROMES, DEBRA	8th great-granddaughter
CROMES, DELBERT	7th great-grandson
CROMES, DENISE NICOLE	8th great-granddaughter
CROMES, DOUGLAS	8th great-grandson
CROMES, JANE ANNA	8th great-granddaughter
CROMES, JEFFERY	8th great-grandson
CROMES, KAREN LYNN	8th great-granddaughter
CROMES, KENDRA	8th great-granddaughter
CROMES, LYNETTE	8th great-granddaughter
CROMES, MARION	7th great-grandson
CROMES, MARTIN	Husband of the 6th great-granddaughter
CROMES, MARTIN	8th great-grandson
CROMES, MATTHEW L.	8th great-grandson
CROMES, MELISSA	8th great-granddaughter
CROMES, MICHAEL	8th great-grandson
CROMES, MICHELLE	9th great-granddaughter
CROMES, PAUL	7th great-grandson
CROMES, RICHARD	9th great-grandson
CROMES, TAWANA ELAINE	8th great-granddaughter
CROMES, WANDA	7th great-granddaughter
CROSE, ELIZABETH CATHERINE	Wife of the 3rd great-grandson
CROSS, NORA MAY	Wife of the 5th great-grandson
CULLERS, SHIRLEY	Wife of the 8th great-grandson
CUMMINGS, JOHN	Husband of the 3rd great-granddaughter
CUMMINGS, WILLIAM	Husband of the 2nd great-granddaughter
CURTIS, EMMA	Wife of the 4th great-grandson
CUSTER, SUSANNAH	Wife of the 2nd great-grandson
DAY, KELLY JR. BRUCE	6th great-grandson
DAY, KELLY SR. BRUCE	Husband of the 5th great-granddaughter
DEBBIE	Wife of the 7th great-grandson
DECKER, KATHY	Wife of the 8th great-grandson
DEETER, OTTO JIM	Husband of the 6th great-granddaughter

DEETER, RALPH	Husband of the 7th great-granddaughter
DENLINGER, BRAD	8th great-grandson
DENLINGER, HAROLD	8th great-grandson
DENLINGER, JEAN	Husband of the 7th great-granddaughter
DENNARD, BERNIE R.	Husband of the 6th great-granddaughter
DENNETT, ANGELINE	Wife of the 2nd great-grandson
DERSHEM, JULIA ANN	Wife of the 6th great-grandson
DEWITT, JACOB	Husband of the 2nd great-granddaughter
DIETZ, LORI ANN	8th great-granddaughter
DIETZ, MR.	Husband of the 7th great-granddaughter
DILLY, CHRISTOPHER	8th great-grandson
DILLY, DOUGLAS	8th great-grandson
DILLY, LARRY	Husband of the 7th great-granddaughter
DONNA	Wife of the 8th great-grandson
DOROTHY	Wife of the 5th great-grandson
DUDLEY, RUSSELL	Husband of the 6th great-granddaughter
DUGAN, ALBERT VIRGIL	5th great-grandson
DUGAN, BABY	5th great-grandchild
DUGAN, CHARLES C.	5th great-grandson
DUGAN, DORA B.	5th great-granddaughter
DUGAN, EUGENIA MARIE	6th great-granddaughter
DUGAN, GEORGE RUSSELL	5th great-grandson
DUGAN, GILBERT	5th great-grandson
DUGAN, HERBERT	6th great-grandson
DUGAN, IRENE	6th great-granddaughter
DUGAN, JAMES CHAMBERS	Husband of the 4th great-granddaughter
DUGAN, LILLIAN	5th great-granddaughter
DUGAN, MABEL ERNESTINE	6th great-granddaughter
DUGAN, MARQEUERITE	6th great-granddaughter
DUGAN, MYRTLE	6th great-granddaughter
DUGAN, ROBERT CORNIELUIS	6th great-grandson
DUGAN, ROY A.	5th great-grandson
DUNBAR, SARAH	Wife of the 3rd great-grandson
DUNCAN, ELIZA	Wife of the 3rd great-grandson
DUQUID, SUSAN MARIE	Wife of the 8th great-grandson
EARLS, HARRY E.	Husband of the 6th great-granddaughter
EARLS, JASON WAYNE	8th great-grandson
EARLS, JOAN LOURIE	7th great-granddaughter
EARLS, JOSEPH EDWARD	7th great-grandson
EARLS, RYAN JOSEPH	8th great-grandson
EARLS, SUSAN ELAINE	7th great-granddaughter

EARLYWINE, ELIZABETH	Wife of the 2nd great-grandson
ELEANOR	Wife of the 2nd great-grandson
ELIZABETH	Wife of the great-grandson
ELIZABETH J.	Wife of the 4th great-grandson
ELLIS, JOEL	Husband of the 2nd great-granddaughter
ELLISON (ALLISON), LUCINDA	Wife of the 2nd great-grandson
ELLISON, SAMUEL G.	Husband of the 3rd great-granddaughter
ELLISON, SUSAN	Wife of the 3rd great-grandson
ELLISON, WILLIAM JR.	Husband of the 7th great-granddaughter
ELSTUN, MR.	Husband of the 4th great-granddaughter
ENSMINGER, LOUISE	Wife of the 7th great-grandson
ERWIN, BERNICE IRENE	6th great-granddaughter
ERWIN, CATHERINE JANE	4th great-granddaughter
ERWIN, CECIL CHESLEY	6th great-grandson
ERWIN, EDNA ADELINE	6th great-granddaughter
ERWIN, EDNA MAY	6th great-granddaughter
ERWIN, ELSIE ELLEN	6th great-granddaughter
ERWIN, GEORGINA ALICE	6th great-granddaughter
ERWIN, HAROLD WORTH	6th great-grandson
ERWIN, HAROLD WRIGHT	6th great-grandson
ERWIN, HECTOR FELIX	5th great-grandson
ERWIN, ISAAC HORTON	4th great-grandson
ERWIN, JESSIE GRACE	6th great-granddaughter
ERWIN, JOHN	Husband of the 3rd great-granddaughter
ERWIN, JOSEPHINE	5th great-granddaughter
ERWIN, PHOEBE	5th great-granddaughter
ERWIN, SPENCER GAIL	6th great-grandson
ERWIN, THOMAS E.	5th great-grandson
ERWIN, VIRETTA	5th great-granddaughter
ERWIN, WILLIS ISAAC	6th great-grandson
ESTEP, MELODY ANN	Wife of the 8th great-grandson
EURY, JOANNE	Wife of the 7th great-grandson
FABUS, MICHELLE	Wife of the 8th great-grandson
FAEHR, VIOLET	Wife of the 7th great-grandson
FALKNOR, CATHERINE	6th great-granddaughter
FALKNOR, EARL	Husband of the 5th great-granddaughter
FALKNOR, JEAN	6th great-granddaughter
FALKNOR, LEONA MAGGIE	Wife of the 5th great-grandson
FANCHER, DONALD	7th great-grandson
FANCHER, LEONARD	Husband of the 6th great-granddaughter
FANCHER, PATTY	8th great-granddaughter

FANCHER, RALPH	8th great-grandson
FANCHER, ROBERT	7th great-grandson
FARLEY, JOHN	Husband of the 7th great-granddaughter
FAVORITE, JAMES	Husband of the 7th great-granddaughter
FAVORITE, JAMES	8th great-grandson
FAVORITE, JULIA	8th great-granddaughter
FAVORITE, RANDY	8th great-grandson
FERRYMAN, TIMOTHY SCOTT	Husband of the 8th great-granddaughter
FESSLER, ANGELA	9th great-granddaughter
FESSLER, BERTHA	Wife of the 5th great-grandson
FESSLER, BRADLEY	9th great-grandson
FESSLER, CARRIE JO	9th great-granddaughter
FESSLER, CLARENCE	Husband of the 7th great-granddaughter
FESSLER, GREGORY ALAN	8th great-grandson
FESSLER, JOSHUA	9th great-grandson
FESSLER, MATHEW EDWARD	9th great-grandson
FESSLER, TIMOTHY RALPH	8th great-grandson
FESSLER, WILLIAM JOE	8th great-grandson
FETTER (PUTERBAUGH), MARGARET	Wife of the 3rd great-grandson
FINE, WALTER	Husband of the 5th great-granddaughter
FISHER, MR.	Husband of the 5th great-granddaughter
FLEGAL, MARGORIE	Wife of the 6th great-grandson
FLEMING, ABEL	Husband of the 4th great-granddaughter
FLEMING, ABEL	Husband of the 3rd great-granddaughter
FLEMING, THEODORE	5th great-grandson
FLICKENGER, DENNIS	Husband of the 7th great-granddaughter
FLICKENGER, MICHAEL ALLEN	8th great-grandson
FLICKENGER, TRAY ANDREW	8th great-grandson
FLINN, POLLY	Wife of the great-grandson
FLOWERS, KIP	Husband of the 9th great-granddaughter
FOLKERTH, ANN	8th great-granddaughter
FOLKERTH, HAROLD	Husband of the 6th great-granddaughter
FOLKERTH, HAROLD	7th great-grandson
FOLKERTH, HUGHM	8th great-grandson
FOLKERTH, REBECCA	8th great-granddaughter
FORD, JOHN	Husband of the 3rd great-granddaughter
FORREST, DALE	Husband of the 7th great-granddaughter
FORREST, JOHN	8th great-grandson
FORREST, NICHOLAS	8th great-grandson
FORSHA, BRENDA K.	Wife of the 8th great-grandson
FOSTER, LLOYD	Husband of the 6th great-granddaughter

FOX, FRANCIS MARION	Husband of the 4th great-granddaughter
FOX, GRANT	5th great-grandson
FOX, RUTH	6th great-granddaughter
FOX, TREVA	6th great-granddaughter
FRANCESE, TANIA JANE	Wife of the 7th great-grandson
FRANCIS, DARLENE	Wife of the 8th great-grandson
FREEMAN, GAYLE	Wife of the 7th great-grandson
FREES, MELISSA	8th great-granddaughter
FREES, MR.	Husband of the 7th great-granddaughter
FREES, SANDRA	8th great-granddaughter
FRIEND, DAVID	8th great-grandson
FRIEND, DEBBIE	8th great-granddaughter
FRIEND, MARK	8th great-grandson
FRIEND, RITA	8th great-granddaughter
FRIEND, ROGER	Husband of the 7th great-granddaughter
FROGGE, CLAYTON	Husband of the 6th great-granddaughter
FROGGE, SANDRA KAY	7th great-grandson
FROGGE, SARA ANN	7th great-granddaughter
FUGATE, PHILLIP	Husband of the 9th great-granddaughter
FURMAN, ELLEN	Wife of the 4th great-grandson
FURNAS, CAROL LOUISE	8th great-granddaughter
FURNAS, HELEN MAE	7th great-granddaughter
FURNAS, RUSSELL	Husband of the 6th great-granddaughter
FURNAS, RUSSELL EDWARD	8th great-grandson
FURNAS, THERM RODNEY	7th great-grandson
GALPIN, ELIZABETH	Wife of the 8th great-grandson
GEISSER, ANNA MARGRETHA	Daughter-in-law
GIBSON, ADAM	Husband of the 3rd great-granddaughter
GIBSON, MR.	Husband of the 2nd great-granddaughter
GIBSON, WILSON	Husband of the 3rd great-granddaughter
GILBERT, HORACE LEE	Husband of the 4th great-granddaughter
GIRTON, THOMPSON	Husband of the 3rd great-granddaughter
GLENNA	Wife of the 5th great-grandson
GOINGS, HANNAH	Wife of the 4th great-grandson
GOLDEN, MARY E.	Wife of the 2nd great-grandson
GOLDNER, MARK W.	Husband of the 8th great-granddaughter
GOMBERT, MR.	Husband of the 8th great-granddaughter
GORDON, RUTH	Wife of the 6th great-grandson
GORMAN, LOVA	Wife of the 6th great-grandson
GRAGG, MARY LOUISE	Wife of the 7th great-grandson
GRAVES, OSCAR	Husband of the 6th great-granddaughter
GREEN, ANDREW PAUL	8th great-grandson

GREEN, DORCAS O.	Wife of the 5th great-grandson
GREEN, FLOYD	Husband of the 7th great-granddaughter
GREEN, JENNIFER RENEE	8th great-granddaughter
GREEN, MATTHEW	Husband of the 5th great-granddaughter
GREENWOOD, DEBBIE	Wife of the 8th great-grandson
GRIFFEY, BESSIE CLARINA	6th great-granddaughter
GRIFFEY, EVERETT FRANKLIN	6th great-grandson
GRIFFEY, IDA MAE	6th great-granddaughter
GRIFFEY, JAMES C.	6th great-grandson
GRIFFEY, WALTER	Husband of the 5th great-granddaughter
GRIFFIN, THOMAS	Husband of the 7th great-granddaughter
GRIFFITH, ROY	Husband of the 5th great-granddaughter
GRIFFUS, CLAUDIA	Wife of the 8th great-grandson
GRISE, ALMA	5th great-granddaughter
GRISE, CARL	6th great-grandson
GRISE, CORA	5th great-granddaughter
GRISE, CORDA ACHIE	5th great-granddaughter
GRISE, CORDELIA	6th great-granddaughter
GRISE, EARL	5th great-grandson
GRISE, ELI C.	5th great-grandson
GRISE, ESTHER ANN	5th great-granddaughter
GRISE, ETOILE	6th great-granddaughter
GRISE, GAIL	7th great-granddaughter
GRISE, GROVER	5th great-grandson
GRISE, HARVEY DAVID	6th great-grandson
GRISE, HELEN IRENE	6th great-granddaughter
GRISE, JENNIFER LYNN	8th great-granddaughter
GRISE, KERRI MARIE	8th great-granddaughter
GRISE, LAURA JANE	5th great-granddaughter
GRISE, LILLIE FLORENCE	5th great-granddaughter
GRISE, LOVA CATHERINE	5th great-granddaughter
GRISE, MARION	6th great-grandson
GRISE, MYRON	6th great-grandson
GRISE, NORMA	6th great-granddaughter
GRISE, PATRICK	7th great-grandson
GRISE, PETER SANGLETON	Husband of the 4th great-granddaughter
GRISE, RICHARD	6th great-grandson
GRISE, ROBERT	6th great-grandson
GRISE, RUBEN	5th great-grandson
GRISE, SAMANTHA	5th great-granddaughter

GRISE, SANDRA	7th great-granddaughter
GRISE, SHERYL	7th great-granddaughter
GROFF, JUDY	Wife of the 7th great-grandson
HAFER, SHARON	Wife of the 7th great-grandson
HAGAN, GREGORY ALAN	8th great-grandson
HAGAN, JEFFREY	Husband of the 7th great-granddaughter
HAGAN, KASEY	8th great-granddaughter
HAGAN, MELODY LYNN	8th great-granddaughter
HALE, MICHAEL	Husband of the 3rd great-granddaughter
HALL, REUBEN	Husband of the 2nd great-granddaughter
HALSTEAD, EMILY A.	Wife of the 3rd great-grandson
HALSTEAD, JOHN	Husband of the 2nd great-granddaughter
HALSTEAD, RHODA	Wife of the 3rd great-grandson
HALSTEAD, SARAH	Wife of the 3rd great-grandson
HAM, BRICE W.	Husband of the 3rd great-granddaughter
HAM, CARRIE	4th great-granddaughter
HAM, CHLOE	4th great-granddaughter
HAM, JAMES L.	4th great-grandson
HAM, JESSIE B.	4th great-grandchild
HAMILTON, ANDREW LEE	9th great-grandson
HAMILTON, ANNA LOUISE	8th great-granddaughter
HAMILTON, AUSTIN TYLER	9th great-grandson
HAMILTON, BRYCE JACOB	9th great-grandson
HAMILTON, CLAIRE MACKENZIE	9th great-granddaughter
HAMILTON, DUANE	8th great-grandson
HAMILTON, ELDEAN	Husband of the 7th great-granddaughter
HANCOCK, MR.	Husband of the 5th great-granddaughter
HANKINS, RICHARD LEWIS	Husband of the 8th great-granddaughter
HANKINS, SHERRI	9th great-granddaughter
HARLACHER, ELMER	Husband of the 4th great-granddaughter
HARLACHER, LETHA	5th great-granddaughter
HARSHBARGER, MINNIE C.	Wife of the 4th great-grandson
HARSHBERGER, CATHERINE	Wife of the 3rd great-grandson
HARTMAN, MARY	Wife of the 8th great-grandson
HARVEY, HENRY	Husband of the 3rd great-granddaughter
HARVEY, LORENZO	Husband of the 3rd great-granddaughter
HARVEY, MILLIE	Wife of the 2nd great-grandson
HARVEY, MR.	Husband of the 2nd great-granddaughter
HARVEY, NANCY	Wife of the 2nd great-grandson
HARVEY, SARAH	Wife of the 3rd great-grandson
HATFIELD, ANDREW	Husband of the great-granddaughter
HATFIELD, PENNY	Wife of the 7th great-grandson

HAUGH, JOSEPH MICHAEL   9th great-grandson
HAWYER, GEORGE W.   Husband of the 3rd great-granddaughter
HAZELBAKER, ANDREW   Husband of the 3rd great-granddaughter
HAZELBAKER, ANDREW JACKSON   Husband of the 4th great-granddaughter
HAZELBAKER, DANIEL   Husband of the 3rd great-granddaughter
HECATHORN, OPAL   Wife of the 6th great-grandson
HEISEL, FLORENCE M.   Wife of the 6th great-grandson
HEISEY, ANNA   Wife of the 6th great-grandson
HEITKAMP, ANDREW   9th great-grandson
HEITKAMP, CHARLES   Husband of the 8th great-granddaughter
HEITKAMP, KATHERYN MARIE   9th great-granddaughter
HELEN   Wife of the 6th great-grandson
HELLER, HENRIETTA   Wife of the 4th great-grandson
HELMKE, LYNN ADELE   Wife of the 8th great-grandson
HERMAN, MARIA ELIZABETH   Wife of the grandson
HERMAN, PETER (HANCE)   Husband of the granddaughter
HERRON, NELLIE LOURIE   Wife of the 5th great-grandson
HESSE, IDA MARIA   Wife of the 4th great-grandson
HESTER, MR.   Husband of the 5th great-granddaughter
HETZLER, GEORGE   Husband of the 4th great-granddaughter
HILE, THEDA   Wife of the 7th great-grandson
HILL, CONNIE EILEEN   8th great-granddaughter
HILL, EMILY   10th great-granddaughter
HILL, GARY EUGENE   8th great-grandson
HILL, GLENNA MAE   7th great-granddaughter
HILL, KAREN LYNN   9th great-granddaughter
HILL, KENNETH   7th great-grandson
HILL, MEGAN SUE   10th great-granddaughter
HILL, NANCY KAY   9th great-granddaughter
HILL, NATHANIEL THOMAS   10th great-grandson
HILL, THOMAS   Husband of the 6th great-granddaughter
HILL, THOMAS JAMES   8th great-grandson
HILL, THOMAS LOWELL   9th great-grandson
HINDS, SARAH JANE (JENNIE)   Wife of the 4th great-grandson
HINGE, SHIRLEY   Wife of the 6th great-grandson
HISSONG, HELEN   Wife of the 6th great-grandson
HITE, CARL   Husband of the 5th great-granddaughter

HOGG, MICHAEL	Husband of the 8th great-granddaughter
HOGG, WHITNEY NOEL	9th great-granddaughter
HOLDREN, MARY ELIZABETH	Wife of the 7th great-grandson
HOLDREN, ROGER	Husband of the 7th great-granddaughter
HOLDREN, ROGER	8th great-grandson
HOLDREN, TOMMIE RAY	8th great-grandson
HOLE, CORDELLA BELLE	6th great-granddaughter
HOLE, HAZEL ESTHER	6th great-granddaughter
HOLE, JOHN LEWIS	6th great-grandson
HOLE, LARKEN	Husband of the 5th great-granddaughter
HOLEBEK, GEORGEANNA	Wife of the 7th great-grandson
HONEYMAN, MARGARET	Wife of the 5th great-grandson
HORNER, DAVID	8th great-grandson
HORNER, DONNA	7th great-granddaughter
HORNER, H. DEAN	7th great-grandson
HORNER, HARRY	Husband of the 6th great-granddaughter
HORNER, HERMAN	7th great-grandson
HORNER, SCOTT	8th great-grandson
HORNER, SHERRY	8th great-granddaughter
HORNER, THEODORE B.	Husband of the 4th great-granddaughter
HORNER, WILLIAM LEE	9th great-grandson
HORTON, ISAAC HOMER	5th great-grandson
HORTON, TERRY	Husband of the 8th great-granddaughter
HOUCHINS, JOHN	Husband of the 3rd great-granddaughter
HOUSE, MARY ANN	Wife of the 3rd great-grandson
HOUSER, MR.	Husband of the 6th great-granddaughter
HOWELL, SUSAN	Wife of the 6th great-grandson
HUBERT, AMY	Wife of the 9th great-grandson
HUDELSON, ANGELA MARIE	9th great-granddaughter
HUDELSON, DENNIS	Husband of the 8th great-granddaughter
HUDELSON, MELISSA ANN	9th great-granddaughter
HUGHES, GRETCHEN MARIE	Wife of the 7th great-grandson
HUGHES, LUCINDA T.	Wife of the 3rd great-grandson
HUMPHREYS, MR.	Husband of the 8th great-granddaughter
HUMPHREYS, NANCY W.	Wife of the 2nd great-grandson
HUNT, CHARLES	5th great-grandson
HUNT, ELIZABETH	5th great-granddaughter
HUNT, JERRY	5th great-grandson
HUNT, JOHN E.	5th great-grandson
HUNT, JOSEPH	Husband of the 4th great-granddaughter
HUNT, LENOX	5th great-grandson
HUNT, MINNIE	5th great-granddaughter
HUNT, WILLIAM	5th great-grandson

HUNTER, GLADYS   *Wife of the 5th great-grandson*
IMWALLE, HONDO LOUIS   *Husband of the 9th great-granddaughter*
INDERRIEDEN, MR.   *Husband of the 6th great-granddaughter*
IRVIN, RACHAEL   *Wife of the great-grandson*
IRWIN (ERWINE), REBECCA JANE   *Wife of the 3rd great-grandson*
ISHMAEL, ARMILDA   *4th great-granddaughter*
ISHMAEL, BENJAMIN L.   *Husband of the 3rd great-granddaughter*
ISHMAEL, JOSEPHUS   *4th great-grandchild*
ISHMAEL, MILDRED   *4th great-granddaughter*
ISHMAEL, OLIVER   *4th great-grandson*
JANE   *Wife of the 4th great-grandson*
JEFFERS, LOUNIE SUE   *Wife of the 7th great-grandson*
JENKINS, LYDIA   *Wife of the great-grandson*
JENNIFER   *Wife of the 8th great-grandson*
JENSEN, ANDREW LOUIS   *8th great-grandson*
JENSEN, AARON PARKER   *8th great-grandson*
JENSEN, KENNETH ANDREW   *Husband of the 7th great-granddaughter*
JOHNS, RACHAEL ARENA   *Wife of the great-grandson*
JOHNSON, ANDREA S.   *8th great-granddaughter*
JOHNSON, CAROLL   *8th great-grandson*
JOHNSON, CHALMER EDWARD   *7th great-grandson*
JOHNSON, CHARLES DALE   *7th great-grandson*
JOHNSON, GARY   *8th great-grandson*
JOHNSON, JACK   *7th great-grandson*
JOHNSON, JAMES L.   *Husband of the 6th great-granddaughter*
JOHNSON, JAY   *7th great-grandson*
JOHNSON, JAYNIE   *8th great-granddaughter*
JOHNSON, JENA   *8th great-granddaughter*
JOHNSON, JOANN   *8th great-granddaughter*
JOHNSON, KELLIE H.   *8th great-granddaughter*
JOHNSON, KERI KAY   *9th great-granddaughter*
JOHNSON, MAC   *7th great-grandson*
JOHNSON, PENNY   *8th great-granddaughter*
JOHNSON, PHYLLIS   *7th great-granddaughter*
JOHNSON, ROBERT   *8th great-grandson*
JOHNSON, ROBERT JR.   *9th great-grandson*
JOHNSON, RONNIE   *8th great-grandson*
JOHNSON, RUBY   *7th great-granddaughter*
JOHNSON, STEPHANIE   *8th great-granddaughter*
JOHNSON, STEVE   *8th great-grandson*
JOHNSON, VALERIE D.   *8th great-granddaughter*

JOHNSTON, ROSALYN MARIE   Wife of the 6th great-grandson
JONES, BARBERRY   Wife of the great-grandson
JONES, CAROL   7th great-granddaughter
JONES, CHERRIE J.   8th great-granddaughter
JONES, DIANA SUE   7th great-granddaughter
JONES, DONALD R.   6th great-grandson
JONES, DOROTHY GLADYS   6th great-granddaughter
JONES, EDWARD   7th great-grandson
JONES, ELIZABETH   Wife of the great-grandson
JONES, ELSIE CORDA   7th great-granddaughter
JONES, ERNEST E.   6th great-grandson
JONES, EUGENE   Husband of the 5th great-granddaughter
JONES, ICENA J.   8th great-granddaughter
JONES, JACK   7th great-grandson
JONES, JOHN E.   7th great-grandson
JONES, KATHIE   7th great-granddaughter
JONES, KATHRYN   Wife of the 4th great-grandson
JONES, LANCE DARREL   6th great-grandson
JONES, LAURA   6th great-granddaughter
JONES, LINDA KATHLEEN   7th great-granddaughter
JONES, LOMA IRENE   6th great-granddaughter
JONES, MARGORIE   7th great-granddaughter
JONES, MARK RICHARD   8th great-granddaughter
JONES, PAUL E.   6th great-grandson
JONES, PERRY   6th great-grandson
JONES, RACHEL   7th great-granddaughter
JONES, ROBERT LANCE   8th great-grandson
JONES, ROBIN   8th great-granddaughter
JONES, RONALD   7th great-grandson
JONES, RUTH ANN   7th great-granddaughter
JONES, SALLY ANN   7th great-granddaughter
JONES, SARA JANE   7th great-granddaughter
JONES, STEPHEN D.   7th great-grandson
JONES, TOMMIE J.   8th great-grandson
JONES, WALTER   Husband of the 5th great-granddaughter
KALASHIAN, ALICE   Wife of the 7th great-grandson
KASPRAZAK, HARRY K.   Husband of the 7th great-granddaughter
KASPRAZAK, HEATHER RENEE   8th great-granddaughter
KASPRAZAK, JASON TODD   8th great-grandson
KEAGLE, THOMAS   Husband of the 6th great-granddaughter
KEATON, CYNTHIA   Wife of the 3rd great-grandson
KEATON, JANE   Wife of the 3rd great-grandson
KEATON, LUCY   Wife of the 2nd great-grandson

KELLER, BRANDON	8th great-grandson
KELLER, DARIN	8th great-grandson
KELLER, LYNN	7th great-grandson
KELLER, MELVIN	Husband of the 6th great-granddaughter
KELLY, DONALD	6th great-grandson
KELLY, DUANE	6th great-grandson
KELLY, EDITH	Wife of the 7th great-grandson
KELLY, JOSEPH	Husband of the 5th great-granddaughter
KELLY, MAX	6th great-grandson
KENWORTHY, CELESTE MARIE	9th great-granddaughter
KENWORTHY, JOSHUA DAVID	9th great-grandson
KENWORTHY, SHANE	Husband of the 8th great-granddaughter
KENWORTHY, SHANIA CARLENE	9th great-granddaughter
KESSINGER, MARY	Wife of the great-grandson
KESSLER, CARL WILLIAM	Husband of the 6th great-granddaughter
KESSLER, DOLLIE	Wife of the 5th great-grandson
KESSLER, MICHAEL MADISON	Husband of the 4th great-granddaughter
KESSLER, THOMAS	7th great-grandson
KIDDER, ELIZABETH	Wife of the 7th great-grandson
KIENITZ, ADAM TROY	8th great-grandson
KIENITZ, ALAN JAY	8th great-grandson
KIENITZ, ALEXANDER STEVEN	9th great-grandson
KIENITZ, CAITLYN	9th great-granddaughter
KIENITZ, GAGE TYLER	9th great-grandson
KIENITZ, GERALD	Husband of the 7th great-granddaughter
KIENITZ, JERRY TODD	8th great-grandson
KIENITZ, KELLY LYNN	9th great-granddaughter
KIENITZ, KERSTIE ROSE	9th great-granddaughter
KIENITZ, LINDSEY ELAINE	9th great-granddaughter
KIENITZ, PATRICK GERALD	8th great-grandson
KIENITZ, SALLY JO	8th great-granddaughter
KIENITZ, STEVEN KENT	8th great-grandson
KING, DWIGHT	Husband of the 6th great-granddaughter
KING, MARY ELLEN	Wife of the 4th great-grandson
KINNY, ROBERT	Husband of the 6th great-granddaughter
KIRBY, ANN	Wife of the 7th great-grandson
KISNER, ELIZABETH	Wife of the 6th great-grandson
KITE, DAVID	Husband of the 2nd great-granddaughter
KNIGHT, ELLA	Wife of the 4th great-grandson
KNOFF, ELIZABETH ANN	6th great-granddaughter
KNOFF, GERALD E.	Husband of the 5th great-granddaughter
KNOFF, SARA LOUISE	6th great-granddaughter

KNOFF, WILLIAM COOPER	6th great-grandson
KNOUFF, ARTHUR BURDETTE	Husband of the 6th great-granddaughter
KONZ, CHARLES	7th great-grandson
KONZ, DEBRA	8th great-granddaughter
KONZ, DONALD	7th great-grandson
KONZ, MARVIN	7th great-grandson
KONZ, MICHAEL	8th great-grandson
KONZ, RICHARD	Husband of the 6th great-granddaughter
KONZ, RITA	7th great-granddaughter
KONZ, TAMMIE	8th great-granddaughter
KORRECKI, AMY	8th great-granddaughter
KORRECKI, BONNIE	8th great-granddaughter
KORRECKI, CINDY	8th great-granddaughter
KORRECKI, DIANE	8th great-granddaughter
KORRECKI, DON	Husband of the 7th great-granddaughter
KREMER, ANN	Wife of the 8th great-grandson
KUHLMAN, MYRTLE P.	Wife of the 7th great-grandson
KULP, DEBORAH	7th great-granddaughter
KULP, DIANE	7th great-granddaughter
KULP, MICHAEL	Husband of the 6th great-granddaughter
KULP, PATRICK	7th great-grandson
KURTZ, NANCY	Wife of the 8th great-grandson
KUSSMAN, MARTHA	Wife of the 6th great-grandson
LANE, WILLIAM CLYDE	Husband of the 8th great-granddaughter
LARSON, GEORGE	Husband of the 7th great-granddaughter
LARSON, GEORGIA ROCHELLE	8th great-granddaughter
LARSON, MIRANDA	8th great-granddaughter
LASHER, ELIZABETH ANN	9th great-granddaughter
LASHER, EMILY LOUISE	9th great-granddaughter
LASHER, JASON DAVID	9th great-grandson
LASHER, JOHN	Husband of the 8th great-granddaughter
LAWSON, LINDA SUE	Wife of the 8th great-grandson
LEIS, SOPHIA ADALINE	Wife of the 5th great-grandson
LEMASTER, ANGELA KAY	Wife of the 8th great-grandson
LEONARD, CORA ALICE	Wife of the 4th great-grandson
LESHER, ROBERT RAY	Husband of the 5th great-granddaughter
LEY, LILLIAN RUTH	Wife of the 5th great-grandson
LIGHTNER, DONALD VINCENT	Husband of the 8th great-granddaughter
LIGHTNER, ELIZABETH NICOLE	9th great-granddaughter
LIGHTNER, MELISSA MICHELLE	9th great-granddaughter
LINDQUIST, MARY	Wife of the 6th great-grandson

LINK, CHRISTINE	8th great-grandson
LINK, GALE	8th great-grandchild
LINK, JACK	Husband of the 7th great-granddaughter
LINK, MARVIN	8th great-grandson
LINVILLE, EARL BERNARD	Husband of the 6th great-granddaughter
LONG, CHARLES	Husband of the 5th great-granddaughter
LONG, LISA	Wife of the 8th great-grandson
LONG, RICHARD	6th great-grandson
LONG, SANDRA	Wife of the 7th great-grandson
LONG, VIRGIL	6th great-grandson
LORING, KATHLEEN	Wife of the 8th great-grandson
LOUNSBURG, CLIFFORD	Husband of the 5th great-granddaughter
LOUNSBURG, GERALD	6th great-grandson
LOUNSBURG, ROLAND	6th great-grandson
LOUNSBURG, VERNA	6th great-granddaughter
LOVEJOY, SHEILA KAY	Wife of the 7th great-grandson
MACHELAN, GEORGE W.	Husband of the 3rd great-granddaughter
MADDRY, WILLIAM	Husband of the great-granddaughter
MADDY, JACKSON	Husband of the 3rd great-granddaughter
MADDY, JOHN C.	Husband of the 2nd great-granddaughter
MADDY, MARY	Wife of the great-grandson
MAGATO, RHONDA	Wife of the 8th great-grandson
MAGGIE	Wife of the 5th great-grandson
MAHAN, WILLIAM O.	Husband of the 5th great-granddaughter
MANIX, TISH	Wife of the 7th great-grandson
MANN, (TWIN)	5th great-grandchild
MANN, (TWIN)	5th great-grandchild
MANN, ABEL	3rd great-grandson
MANN, ABRAHAM L.	4th great-granddaughter
MANN, ADAM	2nd great-grandson
MANN, ADAM	Great-grandson
MANN, ADAM	2nd great-grandson
MANN, ADDISON	4th great-grandson
MANN, ALBERT	3rd great-grandson
MANN, ALEXANDER	3rd great-grandson
MANN, ALICE MAE	6th great-granddaughter
MANN, ALLEN M.	4th great-grandson
MANN, ALONZO LEE	4th great-grandson
MANN, AMANDA	3rd great-granddaughter

MANN, AMELIA A.	3rd great-granddaughter
MANN, AMOS	2nd great-grandson
MANN, ANDREW	3rd great-grandson
MANN, ANDREW J.	4th great-grandson
MANN, ANDREW JACKSON	4th great-grandson
MANN, ANGELINE	3rd great-granddaughter
MANN, ANN E.	4th great-granddaughter
MANN, ANNA	4th great-granddaughter
MANN, ANNA MARIA	Granddaughter
MANN, ANNIE	3rd great-granddaughter
MANN, ANNIE	4th great-granddaughter
MANN, ANNIE H.	4th great-granddaughter
MANN, ANNV	2nd great-granddaughter
MANN, ARCHIBALD	3rd great-grandson
MANN, ARLA LOGAN	5th great-grandchild
MANN, ARMILDA	4th great-granddaughter
MANN, ARMILDA J.	4th great-granddaughter
MANN, ARTHUR A.	5th great-grandson
MANN, ASA A.	4th great-grandson
MANN, AUSTIN	3rd great-grandson
MANN, AUSTIN	3rd great-grandson
MANN, AUSTIN	4th great-grandson
MANN, BABY	5th great-grandchild
MANN, BABY BOY	4th great-grandson
MANN, BABY BOY	5th great-grandson
MANN, BABY BOY	5th great-grandson
MANN, BABY BOY	5th great-grandson
MANN, BABY BOY	5th great-grandson
MANN, BABY BOY	7th great-grandson
MANN, BABY BOY	6th great-grandson
MANN, BABY GIRL	5th great-granddaughter
MANN, BARBARA J.	3rd great-granddaughter
MANN, BENJAMIN F.	3rd great-grandson
MANN, BERTHA ALVILDA	4th great-granddaughter
MANN, BERTHA JAUNITA	5th great-granddaughter
MANN< BERTHA L.	5th great-grandaughter
MANN, BETTY JEANNE	6th great-granddaughter
MANN, BEVERLY JANE	6th great-granddaughter
MANN, BLUFORD	3rd great-grandson
MANN, BRENDA LEE	7th great-granddaughter
MANN, CAROLINE	2nd great-grandson
MANN, CAROLINE	3rd great-granddaughter
MANN, CAROLYN DIANE	7th great-granddaughter

MANN, CATARINA	Granddaughter
MANN, CATHERINE	2nd great-granddaughter
MANN, CATHERINE	3rd great-granddaughter
MANN, CATRIN	Daughter
MANN, CELESTIA A.	4th great-granddaughter
MANN, CELIA	3rd great-granddaughter
MANN, CHARLENE	6th great-granddaughter
MANN, CHARLES	2nd great-grandson
MANN, CHARLES	3rd great-grandson
MANN, CHARLES	Great-grandson
MANN, CHARLES	2nd great-grandson
MANN, CHARLES	3rd great-grandson
MANN, CHARLES	3rd great-grandson
MANN, CHARLES	4th great-grandson
MANN, CHARLES	4th great-grandson
MANN, CHARLES	6th great-grandson
MANN, CHARLES (GEORG CARL)	Grandson
MANN, CHARLES E.	4th great-grandson
MANN, CHARLES FRANK	5th great-grandson
MANN, CHARLES H.	3rd great-grandson
MANN, CHARLES L.	5th great-grandson
MANN, CHARLES M.	4th great-granddaughter
MANN, CHARLOTTE	6th great-granddaughter
MANN, CHERRIE LOU	7th great-granddaughter
MANN, CHLOE	2nd great-granddaughter
MANN, CHRISTIAN	4th great-grandson
MANN, CHRISTOPHER	3rd great-grandson
MANN, CLARA	3rd great-granddaughter
MANN, CLARA	5th great-granddaughter
MANN, CLARK	6th great-grandson
MANN, CLEMENTINA	3rd great-granddaughter
MANN, CLEMMENT ELZIE	4th great-grandson
MANN, CLIFFORD HERMAN	5th great-grandson
MANN, CLIFTON	3rd great-grandson
MANN, COLONEL JOHN JR.	**Great-grandson**
MANN, CORA ETTA	5th great-granddaughter
MANN, CYNTHIA	3rd great-granddaughter
MANN, CYNTHIA	3rd great-granddaughter
MANN, CYNTHIA ANN	2nd great-granddaughter
MANN, DAISY	5th great-granddaughter
MANN, DANIEL A.	3rd great-grandson
MANN, DARLADEEN	6th great-granddaughter
MANN, DAVID	Great-grandson

MANN, DAVID	2nd great-grandson
MANN, DAVID	2nd great-grandson
MANN, DAVID	3rd great-grandson
MANN, DAVID	4th great-grandson
MANN, DAVID	5th great-grandson
MANN, DAVID LEWIS	2nd great-grandson
MANN, DAVID LEWIS JR.	3rd great-grandson
MANN, DEBRA LYNN	7th great-granddaughter
MANN, DELILAH	3rd great-granddaughter
MANN, DORSEY VIRGIL	4th great-grandson
MANN, DRUSILA	3rd great-granddaughter
MANN, DULCINA MARGARET	5th great-granddaughter
MANN, EDGAR H.	4th great-grandson
MANN, EDITH	6th great-granddaughter
MANN, EDITH A.	5th great-granddaughter
MANN, EDWARD LOUIS JR.	7th great-grandson
MANN, EDWARD LOUIS SR.	6th great-grandson
MANN, ELI	3rd great-grandson
MANN, ELIAS	3rd great-grandson
MANN, ELIAS	3rd great-grandson
MANN, ELIZA	3rd great-granddaughter
MANN, ELIZA	3rd great-granddaughter
MANN, ELIZA J.	3rd great-granddaughter
MANN, ELIZA JANE	3rd great-grandson
MANN, ELIZA MELISSA	4th great-granddaughter
MANN, ELIZABETH	Wife of the 3rd great-grandson
MANN, ELIZABETH	3rd great-granddaughter
MANN, ELIZABETH	3rd great-granddaughter
MANN, ELIZABETH	Great-granddaughter
MANN, ELIZABETH	2nd great-granddaughter
MANN, ELIZABETH	Great-granddaughter
MANN, ELIZABETH	Great-granddaughter
MANN, ELIZABETH	2nd great-granddaughter
MANN, ELIZABETH	2nd great-grandson
MANN, ELIZABETH	3rd great-granddaughter
MANN, ELIZABETH	3rd great-grandson
MANN, ELIZABETH	3rd great-granddaughter
MANN, ELIZABETH ANN	3rd great-granddaughter
MANN, ELIZABETH E.	3rd great-granddaughter
MANN, ELIZABETH E.	4th great-granddaughter
MANN, ELIZABETH LOUELLA	4th great-granddaughter
MANN, ELIZABETH MARIE (BETSY)	8th great-granddaughter
MANN, ELLA EUNICE	5th great-granddaughter

MANN, ELLEN	3rd great-granddaughter
MANN, ELLEN VIOLA	5th great-granddaughter
MANN, ELMER	5th great-grandson
MANN, EMANUEL	2nd great-grandson
MANN, EMIL RAYMOND	5th great-grandson
MANN, EMILY	3rd great-granddaughter
MANN, EMMA	4th great-granddaughter
MANN, EMMA	5th great-granddaughter
MANN, EMMA DAISY MAY	5th great-granddaughter
MANN, EPHRIAM B.	3rd great-grandson
MANN, EPHRIAM B.	4th great-grandson
MANN, ESTELLA LEE	5th great-granddaughter
MANN, ESTELLA MAY	4th great-granddaughter
MANN, ETHELDA	6th great-granddaughter
MANN, EZIEKIEL	3rd great-grandson
MANN, FANNY	2nd great-granddaughter
MANN, FLORENCE	6th great-granddaughter
MANN, FLOYD	3rd great-grandson
MANN, FRANCIS	3rd great-grandson
MANN, FRANK	5th great-grandson
MANN, FRANK JEFFERSON	5th great-grandson
MANN, FRED E.	4th great-grandson
MANN, GARRET	3rd great-grandson
MANN, GEORGE	2nd great-grandson
MANN, GEORGE	Great-grandson
MANN, GEORGE	Great-grandson
MANN, GEORGE	2nd great-grandson
MANN, GEORGE (CUNRADT)	Grandson
MANN, GEORGE A.	3rd great-grandson
MANN, GEORGE ADAM	Grandson
MANN, GEORGE BERNARD	Son
MANN, GEORGE BERNARD	Grandson
MANN, GEORGE CONRAD	Great-grandson
MANN, GEORGE E.	3rd great-grandson
MANN, GEORGE HENRY HANSON	4th great-grandson
MANN, GEORGE IVAN	5th great-grandson
MANN, GEORGE SIMEON	4th great-grandson
MANN, GEORGE T.	5th great-grandson
MANN, GEORGE WILLIAM	3rd great-grandson
MANN, GEORGE W.	4th great-grandson
MANN, GEORGIA	5th great-granddaughter
MANN, GERALD BUD	6th great-grandson
MANN, GLENAMA E.	5th great-granddaughter
MANN, GRANVILLE	3rd great-grandson

MANN, HANS	Self	
MANN, HARLEY R.	5th great-grandson	
MANN, HAROLD	6th great-grandson	
MANN, HAROLD CHRIS	6th great-grandson	
MANN, HAROLD CHRIS III	8th great-grandson	
MANN, HAROLD CHRIS JR.	7th great-grandson	
MANN, HARRIET JANE	3rd great-granddaughter	
MANN, HARRY CHRIS	6th great-grandson	
MANN, HARRY CHRIS JR.	7th great-grandson	
MANN, HAZEL IRENE	5th great-granddaughter	
MANN, HELEN	6th great-granddaughter	
MANN, HELEN	5th great-granddaughter	
MANN, HENDERSON	4th great-grandson	
MANN, HENDLEY	3rd great-grandson	
MANN, HENRY	2nd great-grandson	
MANN, HENRY	Great-grandson	
MANN, HENRY	2nd great-grandson	
MANN, HENRY	2nd great-grandson	
MANN, HENRY	2nd great-grandson	
MANN, HENRY ALBERT	4th great-grandson	
MANN, HENRY CLAY	3rd great-grandson	
MANN, HENRY GEORGE	3rd great-grandson	
MANN, HERMAN R.	4th great-grandson	
MANN, HOLTON	3rd great-grandson	
MANN, HORACE	4th great-grandson	
MANN, HULDA (HULDY)	3rd great-granddaughter	
MANN, HULDA JANE	4th great-granddaughter	
MANN, IRA IRVIN	5th great-grandson	
MANN, ISAAC	2nd great-grandson	
MANN, ISAAC	2nd great-grandson	
MANN, ISAAC	2nd great-grandson	
MANN, ISAAC C.	4th great-grandson	
MANN, ISAAC JR.	3rd great-grandson	
MANN, ISAAC ORAN	5th great-grandson	
MANN, ISAAC ORVIS	4th great-grandson	
MANN, JACK	3rd great-grandson	
MANN, JACKSON	Husband of the 3rd great-granddaughter	
MANN, JACOB	3rd great-grandson	
MANN, JACOB	Great-grandson	
MANN, JACOB	2nd great-grandson	
MANN, (JOHN)JACOB	Grandson	
MANN, JACOB	Great-grandson	

MANN, JACOB	2nd great-grandson
MANN, JACOB	Great-grandson
MANN, JACOB	2nd great-grandson
MANN, JACOB	2nd great-grandson
MANN, JACOB	3rd great-grandson
MANN, JACOB	4th great-grandson
MANN, JACOB MARION	4th great-grandson
MANN, JACOB S.	5th great-grandson
MANN, JACOB W.	4th great-grandson
MANN, JAMES	2nd great-grandson
MANN, JAMES	2nd great-grandson
MANN, JAMES J.	2nd great-grandson
MANN, JAMES L.	3rd great-grandson
MANN, JAMES M.	4th great-grandson
MANN, JAMES OLIVER	3rd great-grandson
MANN, JAMES PRICE	4th great-grandson
MANN, JANE	2nd great-granddaughter
MANN, JEPTHA	3rd great-grandson
MANN, JERRY CLARENCE	5th great-grandson
MANN, JOHN	2nd great-grandson
MANN, JOHN	3rd great-grandson
MANN, JOHN	2nd great-grandson
MANN, JOHN	2nd great-grandson
MANN, JOHN	Great-grandson
MANN, JOHN	2nd great-grandson
MANN, JOHN	2nd great-grandson
MANN, JOHN	2nd great-grandson
MANN, JOHN	2nd great-grandson
MANN, JOHN	3rd great-grandson
MANN, JOHN	3rd great-grandson
MANN, JOHN	4th great-grandson
MANN, JOHN ALLEN	4th great-grandson
MANN, JOHN ALLEN JR.	6th great-grandson
MANN, JOHN ALLEN SR.	5th great-grandson
MANN, JOHN D.	4th great-grandson
MANN, JOHN EZRA (JACK)	5th great-grandson
MANN, JOHN F.	3rd great-grandson
MANN, JOHN GEORGE	Great-grandson
MANN, JOHN JR.	2nd great-grandson
MANN, JOHN L.	5th great-grandson
MANN, JOHN SR.	Grandson
MANN, JOHN SR.	Great-grandson
MANN, JOHN T.	3rd great-grandson

MANN, JOHN W.	3rd great-grandson
MANN, JOHN W.	4th great-grandson
MANN, JOHN WALTER	5th great-grandson
MANN, JOHN WESLEY	4th great-grandson
MANN, JOHN WILLIAM	4th great-grandson
MANN, JOSEPH	2nd great-grandson
MANN, JOSEPH ALLEN	7th great-grandson
MANN, JOSEPH M.	5th great-grandson
MANN, JULIA A.	3rd great-granddaughter
MANN, JULIA EATHEL	5th great-granddaughter
MANN, KAREN	7th great-granddaughter
MANN, KARLIEN RAE	8th great-granddaughter
MANN, KATHLEEN	7th great-granddaughter
MANN, KATHY JEAN	7th great-granddaughter
MANN, KENNETH	5th great-grandson
MANN, KENNETH LEROY	6th great-grandson
MANN, KILEY	5th great-grandchild
MANN, KILLIAN	3rd great-grandson
MANN, KIMBERLY ANN	7th great-granddaughter
MANN, KIMBERLY ANN	8th great-granddaughter
MANN, LACIE RODENSIA	5th great-granddaughter
MANN, LAURA	4th great-granddaughter
MANN, LAURA ANN	5th great-granddaughter
MANN, LAURA MAY	5th great-granddaughter
MANN, LAURY L.	3rd great-granddaughter
MANN, LEAH	3rd great-granddaughter
MANN, LENOX SULTIER	5th great-grandson
MANN, LEONARD	5th great-grandson
MANN, LEROY RUSSEL	6th great-grandson
MANN, LESTER LEROY	5th great-grandson
MANN, LETHA	3rd great-granddaughter
MANN, LEWIS	3rd great-grandson
MANN, LEWIS A.	4th great-grandson
MANN, LEWIS ALFORD	5th great-grandson
MANN, LEWIS JACKSON	3rd great-grandson
MANN, LIBBY M.	4th great-granddaughter
MANN, LILLIAN TENNESSEE	5th great-granddaughter
MANN, LLOYD B	5th great-grandson
MANN, LOUIS EDWARD	4th great-grandson
MANN, LOUISA	3rd great-granddaughter

MANN, LOUISA E.	5th great-granddaughter
MANN, LOUISA J.	5th great-granddaughter
MANN, LUCIEN T.	3rd great-grandchild
MANN, LUCILLE	6th great-granddaughter
MANN, LUCILLE KATHERINE	7th great-granddaughter
MANN, LUCINDA	3rd great-granddaughter
MANN, LUCY	3rd great-granddaughter
MANN, LUZERNE	3rd great-granddaughter
MANN, LYDIA	2nd great-granddaughter
MANN, LYDIA J.	4th great-granddaughter
MANN, MADISON	3rd great-grandson
MANN, MAGDALENE	Great-granddaughter
MANN, MAHALA	3rd great-granddaughter
MANN, MAHATHLIN	3rd great-granddaughter
MANN, MALINDA	3rd great-granddaughter
MANN, MALINDA	2nd great-granddaughter
MANN, MARGARET	2nd great-granddaughter
MANN, MARGARET ACHIE	4th great-granddaughter
MANN, MARGARET ELEN	3rd great-granddaughter
MANN, MARGARET ELSIE	5th great-granddaughter
MANN, MARIA MARGRETHA	Granddaughter
MANN, MARIA T.	5th great-granddaughter
MANN, MARINDA	3rd great-granddaughter
MANN, MARJORIE MARIE	7th great-granddaughter
MANN, MARSHA MARIE	7th great-granddaughter
MANN, MARTHA	3rd great-granddaughter
MANN, MARTHA	6th great-granddaughter
MANN, MARTHA A.	4th great-granddaughter
MANN, MARY	3rd great-granddaughter
MANN, MARY	Great-granddaughter
MANN, MARY	2nd great-granddaughter
MANN, MARY	3rd great-granddaughter
MANN, MARY (MISSOURI) BELLE	4th great-granddaughter
MANN, MARY A	3rd great-granddaughter
MANN, MARY ANN	3rd great-granddaughter
MANN, MARY C.	3rd great-granddaughter

MANN, MARY D.	5th great-granddaughter
MANN, MARY E.	3rd great-granddaughter
MANN, MARY ELIZABETH	4th great-granddaughter
MANN, MARY IDA	5th great-granddaughter
MANN, MARY J.	3rd great-granddaughter
MANN, MARY M.	5th great-granddaughter
MANN, MARY MARGARET A.	4th great-granddaughter
MANN, MARY MARIE	7th great-granddaughter
MANN, MARY OLIVE	3rd great-granddaughter
MANN, MELVINA	3rd great-granddaughter
MANN, MICHAEL	2nd great-grandson
MANN, MICHAEL	3rd great-grandson
MANN, MICHAEL	4th great-grandson
MANN, MICHAEL	5th great-grandson
MANN, MICHAEL	7th great-grandson
MANN, MICHAEL P.	3rd great-grandson
MANN, MICKEY	6th great-grandchild
MANN, MILDRED PEGGY	6th great-granddaughter
MANN, MILLIE	3rd great-granddaughter
MANN, MILLY	3rd great-granddaughter
MANN, MILTON	4th great-grandson
MANN, MINNIE	5th great-granddaughter
MANN, MINOR	3rd great-grandchild
MANN, MOLLY	2nd great-granddaughter
MANN, MORRIS	3rd great-grandson
MANN, MORTON	4th great-grandson
MANN, MOSES	2nd great-grandson
MANN, NANCY	2nd great-granddaughter
MANN, NANCY A.	5th great-granddaughter
MANN, NANCY J.	5th great-granddaughter
MANN, NANCY O.	4th great-granddaughter
MANN, OPHER ALLEN	5th great-grandson
MANN, ORA ABEL	5th great-grandson
MANN, ORA LOREN	5th great-grandson
MANN, ORENA B.	5th great-granddaughter
MANN, ORIN	4th great-grandson
MANN, ORTHA	4th great-grandson
MANN, OSCAR	4th great-grandson
MANN, OVERTON	3rd great-grandson
MANN, PAMELA ANNETTE	7th great-granddaughter
MANN, PEARL ETHEL	5th great-granddaughter
MANN, PETER	Great-grandson
MANN, PHOEBE C.	5th great-granddaughter

MANN, PHYLLIS EILEEN	6th great-granddaughter	
MANN, POLLY	3rd great-granddaughter	
MANN, POLLY	Wife of the 3rd great-grandson	
MANN, POLLY	3rd great-granddaughter	
MANN, POLLY	2nd great-granddaughter	
MANN, PRESTON L.	3rd great-grandson	
MANN, PRISCILLA	Great-granddaughter	
MANN, PRISCILLA	2nd great-granddaughter	
MANN, RACHAEL	3rd great-granddaughter	
MANN, RACHAEL ANN	4th great-granddaughter	
MANN, RACHAEL CAROLINE	4th great-granddaughter	
MANN, RALPH	6th great-grandson	
MANN, RAYMOND	6th great-grandson	
MANN, RENIE	3rd great-granddaughter	
MANN, REUBEN D.	3rd great-grandson	
MANN, RHODA	3rd great-granddaughter	
MANN, RHODA	2nd great-grandson	
MANN, RHODA J.	3rd great-granddaughter	
MANN, RICHARD BUDDY	6th great-grandson	
MANN, RICIE	3rd great-granddaughter	
MANN, ROBERT	5th great-grandson	
MANN, ROBERT	6th great-grandson	
MANN, ROBERT EUGENE	6th great-grandson	
MANN, ROBERT MILTON	4th great-grandson	
MANN, ROSA	5th great-granddaughter	
MANN, ROY	5th great-grandson	
MANN, ROY RUSSELL	5th great-grandson	
MANN, ROY WILLIAM	5th great-grandson	
MANN, RUSSELL	3rd great-grandson	
MANN, RUTH	5th great-granddaughter	
MANN, RUTH	3rd great-granddaughter	
MANN, RUTH LAPEARL	5th great-granddaughter	
MANN, SAMANTHA	3rd great-granddaughter	
MANN, SAMSON	3rd great-grandson	
MANN, SAMUEL	2nd great-grandson	
MANN, SAMUEL K.	3rd great-grandson	
MANN, SARA	7th great-granddaughter	
MANN, SARAH	3rd great-granddaughter	
MANN, SARAH	2nd great-granddaughter	

MANN, SARAH	3rd great-granddaughter
MANN, SARAH (SALLY)	2nd great-granddaughter
MANN, SARAH A.	3rd great-granddaughter
MANN, SARAH EVALINE	3rd great-granddaughter
MANN, SARE IDA O.	5th great-granddaughter
MANN, SHAYNA RACHELLE	8th great-granddaughter
MANN, SHERRI KAY	7th great-granddaughter
MANN, SQUIRE	3rd great-grandson
MANN, STANLEY	5th great-grandson
MANN, STEPHEN	4th great-grandson
MANN, STEWARD RAYMOND	6th great-grandson
MANN, STEWARD RAYMOND	6th great-grandson
MANN, SUSAN	3rd great-granddaughter
MANN, SUSAN	2nd great-granddaughter
MANN, SUSAN	3rd great-granddaughter
MANN, SUSAN LEE	7th great-granddaughter
MANN, SUSANNAH	3rd great-granddaughter
MANN, TERRY	6th great-grandson
MANN, THEODORE	4th great-grandson
MANN, THOMAS	3rd great-grandson
MANN, TIMOTHY ALLEN	7th great-grandson
MANN, VIRGIL HENRY	5th great-grandson
MANN, VIRGINIA	4th great-granddaughter
MANN, WARD	3rd great-grandson
MANN, WILLAM HENRY	3rd great-grandson
MANN, WILLIAM	3rd great-grandson
MANN, WILLIAM	2nd great-grandson
MANN, WILLIAM	3rd great-grandson
MANN, WILLIAM	2nd great-grandson
MANN, WILLIAM	3rd great-grandson
MANN, WILLIAM	4th great-grandson
MANN, WILLIAM	4th great-grandson
MANN, WILLIAM BARTON CUNNINGHAM	3rd great-grandson
MANN, WILLIAM BRYAN	5th great-grandson
MANN, WILLIAM GEORGE	6th great-grandson
MANN, WILLIAM GEORGE JR.	7th great-grandson
MANN, WILLIAM H.	3rd great-grandson
MANN, WILLIAM H. HARRISON	3rd great-grandson
MANN, WILLIAM P.	4th great-grandson
MANN, WILLIAM PERRY	5th great-grandson
MANN, WILLIS AUSTIN	5th great-grandson

MANN, WILLIS O.	4th great-grandson
MANN, WILLIS R.	3rd great-grandson
MANN, WOODSON	3rd great-grandson
MARIA	Wife of the grandson
MARIA ANNA MARGRETHA	Daughter-in-law
MARKER, DORA MARGARET	Wife of the 4th great-grandson
MARKS, MAVERNE MARIE	Wife of the 7th great-grandson
MARTIN, CHARLES F.	Husband of the 6th great-granddaughter
MARTIN, JAIME MARIE	9th great-granddaughter
MARTIN, JASON EDWARD	9th great-grandson
MARTIN, LEVI	Husband of the 4th great-granddaughter
MARTIN, TIM	Husband of the 8th great-granddaughter
MATTHEWS, BERTHA MAE	5th great-granddaughter
MATTHEWS, CLARENCE	6th great-grandson
MATTHEWS, DAVID	Husband of the 4th great-granddaughter
MATTHEWS, FORREST	5th great-grandson
MATTHEWS, HELEN	6th great-granddaughter
MATTHEWS, JOHN H.	5th great-grandson
MATTHEWS, MARIBEL	6th great-granddaughter
MATTHEWS, RUTH	6th great-granddaughter
MAY	Wife of the 5th great-grandson
MAYSE, RENEE	Wife of the 8th great-grandson
MCAFEE, SHAWN PATRICK	9th great-grandson
MCAFEE, WILLIAM	Husband of the 8th great-granddaughter
MCCORKLE, JOHN	Husband of the 3rd great-granddaughter
MCCULLOUGH, HELEN	Wife of the 5th great-grandson
MCDANIEL, CATHERINE	Wife of the great-grandson
MCGARRY, DANIEL	7th great-grandson
MCGARRY, JULIE	7th great-granddaughter
MCGARRY, ROBERT	Husband of the 6th great-granddaughter
MCGARRY, ROBERT	7th great-grandson
MCGARRY, ROGER	7th great-grandson
MCKAY, CLARA	Wife of the 6th great-grandson
MEADOWS, RALPH	Husband of the 8th great-granddaughter
MEADOWS, SHELBY LEE	9th great-granddaughter
MEEKER, CATHERINE	Wife of the 7th great-grandson
MEIER, MARCIA	Wife of the 8th great-grandson
MENDENHALL, ELIZABETH J.	3rd great-granddaughter
MENDENHALL, GOLDIE	Wife of the 6th great-grandson
MENDENHALL, JOSEPH	Husband of the 2nd great-granddaughter
MERRIETT, BLANCHE	Wife of the 6th great-grandson
MERRITT, WILLIAM	Husband of the 2nd great-granddaughter

METCALF, JILL	Wife of the 9th great-grandson
MIDDY, RUTH	Wife of the 7th great-grandson
MILDRED	Wife of the 6th great-grandson
MILLER, ALICE	7th great-granddaughter
MILLER, ANDREW MICHAEL	8th great-grandson
MILLER, ANNE M.	8th great-granddaughter
MILLER, BARBARA	Wife of the grandson
MILLER, BETH J.	8th great-granddaughter
MILLER, CRAIG	9th great-grandson
MILLER, DEBORAH SUE	Wife of the 8th great-grandson
MILLER, DENNIS WAYNE	8th great-grandson
MILLER, DOROTHY	7th great-granddaughter
MILLER, EARL	Husband of the 6th great-granddaughter
MILLER, ELLA LUCILLE	Wife of the 5th great-grandson
MILLER, ERVIN	Husband of the 3rd great-granddaughter
MILLER, GARY	Husband of the 7th great-granddaughter
MILLER, GARY ALLEN JR.	8th great-grandson
MILLER, GEORGE	Husband of the 3rd great-granddaughter
MILLER, JOHN	Husband of the 3rd great-granddaughter
MILLER, JUANITA	7th great-granddaughter
MILLER, JUDITH LYNN	7th great-granddaughter
MILLER, KEITH	9th great-grandson
MILLER, LOWELL	7th great-grandson
MILLER, MARY DEE	7th great-granddaughter
MILLER, MARY F.	Wife of the 3rd great-grandson
MILLER, PAUL LINK	Husband of the 6th great-granddaughter
MILLER, PAUL LINK	7th great-grandson
MILLER, PETER LINK	7th great-grandson
MILLER, POLLY	Wife of the 3rd great-grandson
MILLER, RUBY	7th great-granddaughter
MILLER, SCOTT	9th great-grandson
MINGER, DOROTHY	Wife of the 7th great-grandson
MITCHELL, NANCY	Wife of the 3rd great-grandson
MOHLER, JAMES	Husband of the 3rd great-granddaughter
MONNIN, AMANDA	Wife of the 9th great-grandson
MONTGOMERY, LISA	Wife of the 8th great-grandson
MOON, ANGEL RENEE	8th great-granddaughter
MOON, JAY ALLEN	Husband of the 7th great-granddaughter
MOORE, HARRIET L.	Wife of the 4th great-grandson
MORDAN, LYMON	Husband of the 6th great-granddaughter
MORRIS, JANE	Wife of the 2nd great-grandson
MORROW, MATILDA A.	Wife of the 3rd great-grandson
MOTHMILLER, CHRISTINE	8th great-granddaughter

MOTHMILLER, ROBERT	Husband of the 7th great-granddaughter
MOTTINGER, JAN	Wife of the 8th great-grandson
MOUBRAY, JUANA ROSE	Wife of the 8th great-grandson
MOWERY, CANDRA M.	Wife of the 7th great-grandson
MOYER, BARBARA	5th great-granddaughter
MOYER, ELIZABETH (BETSY)	Wife of the great-grandson
MOYER, HENRY	Husband of the 4th great-granddaughter
MOYER, IDA	5th great-granddaughter
MOYER, JACOB	5th great-grandson
MOYER, LEVI	5th great-grandson
MOYER, MARY JANE (MOLLY)	Wife of the 4th great-grandson
MOYER, MAUD	6th great-granddaughter
MOYER, SARAH	Wife of the 4th great-grandson
MOYER, WILLIAM H.	5th great-grandson
MUNS, DARLENE	Wife of the 7th great-grandson
MYERS, ORVILLE GLENN	Husband of the 6th great-granddaughter
NETZLEY, ALBERT WILLIAM	5th great-grandson
NETZLEY, ELI	Husband of the 4th great-granddaughter
NETZLEY, EVA DOT	5th great-granddaughter
NETZLEY, FAY	5th great-granddaughter
NETZLEY, HARRY	5th great-grandson
NETZLEY, RAY	5th great-grandson
NIESLEY, SUSAN	Wife of the 5th great-grandson
NOLAN, LYNN	Wife of the 9th great-grandson
NOLLEY, JOYCE	Wife of the 7th great-grandson
NORTHRUP, DEBRA	Wife of the 8th great-grandson
O'BRIEN, CORNELIUS	Husband of the 8th great-granddaughter
O'BRIEN, JEFFERY JOSEPH	9th great-grandson
O'BRIEN, KEVIN PATRICK	9th great-grandson
O'BRIEN, TIMOTHY	9th great-grandson
ODA, LANDON	Husband of the 6th great-granddaughter
OLDENBERG, DEBORAH A.	Wife of the 7th great-grandson
OSBORNE, PATRICIA ANN	Wife of the 7th great-grandson
OVERHOLSER, STEVEN B.	Husband of the 9th great-granddaughter
OVERHOLSER, TYLER	10th great-grandson
PAGETT, KATHY JO	Wife of the 8th great-grandson
PALASZEKI, LORETTA ANN	Wife of the 7th great-grandson
PALMER, DONNA BELL	Wife of the 8th great-grandson

PALMER, WARREN KEITH JR.	Husband of the 7th great-granddaughter
PARRISH, MATTIE	Wife of the 4th great-grandson
PARTHENA	Wife of the 2nd great-grandson
PASTORI, ANNETTE	8th great-grandson
PASTORI, CHARLES	Husband of the 7th great-granddaughter
PASTORI, LINDA	8th great-granddaughter
PATTERSON, JERRY	Husband of the 8th great-granddaughter
PATTERSON, WENDY MICHELLE	9th great-granddaughter
PAULINE G.	Wife of the 5th great-grandson
PEARSON, FLORETTA	Wife of the 5th great-grandson
PEARSON, HAROLD	Husband of the 6th great-granddaughter
PEARSON, MARGARET (PEGGY)	Wife of the 2nd great-grandson
PEARSON, MARILYN SUE	7th great-granddaughter
PENCE, CHRISTOPHER EDWIN	9th great-grandson
PENCE, EDWIN W.	Husband of the 8th great-granddaughter
PENCE, JEANNINE ANN	9th great-granddaughter
PENROD, JUSTICE	Husband of the 5th great-granddaughter
PENROD, MELINDA R.	Wife of the 4th great-grandson
PETERS, ZONA LOUISE	Wife of the 7th great-grandson
PEYTON, ELIZABETH	Wife of the 2nd great-grandson
PEYTON, MARY	Wife of the 2nd great-grandson
PHILLIPS, GEORGEANNA	Wife of the 4th great-grandson
PHILLIPS, GERALD	Husband of the 8th great-granddaughter
PHILLIPS, GERALD LAREN	9th great-grandson
PHILLIPS, JENNIFER LYNN	9th great-granddaughter
PHILLIPS, JENNIFER MARIE	9th great-grandson
PHILLIPS, JOHN R.	Husband of the 8th great-granddaughter
PHILLIPS, JOSHUA AARON	9th great-grandson
PHILLIPS, MARTHA JANE	Wife of the 4th great-grandson
PIERPORT, CAROLE	8th great-granddaughter
PIERPORT, DENISE	8th great-granddaughter
PIERPORT, GEORGE	8th great-grandson
PIERPORT, MARY	8th great-granddaughter
PIERPORT, MIKE	Husband of the 7th great-granddaughter
PIERPORT, PAMELA	8th great-granddaughter
PIERRON, MARY AGNES	Wife of the 7th great-grandson
PIKE, RALPH	Husband of the 8th great-granddaughter
PLUMMER, GEORGE	4th great-grandson
PLUMMER, HULDAH	4th great-granddaughter
PLUMMER, JOSEPH	Husband of the 3rd great-granddaughter
PLUMMER, JOSEPH	4th great-grandson
PLUMMER, MARY	4th great-granddaughter

POTVIN, ARTHUR	Husband of the 6th great-granddaughter
POUGE, ROBERT	Husband of the 8th great-granddaughter
POWERS, NANCY P.	Wife of the 3rd great-grandson
PRICE, CARLA	Wife of the 8th great-grandson
PRICE, SUSANNAH	Wife of the grandson
QUATE, JEFFERY ALLEN	7th great-grandson
QUATE, JESSICA LEE	8th great-granddaughter
QUATE, LEE JR.	Husband of the 6th great-granddaughter
QUATE, MARGARET ANN (PEGGY)	8th great-granddaughter
QUATE, NICOLE MARIE	8th great-granddaughter
QUATE, RANDALL LEE	7th great-grandson
QUATE, SARA ANN	8th great-granddaughter
QUATE, VANESSA JEANNE	7th great-granddaughter
RAINES, MARY	Wife of the 3rd great-grandson
RASK, LARRY RACK	7th great-grandson
RASK, LINDA RACK	7th great-granddaughter
RASK, RACK	Husband of the 6th great-granddaughter
RASOR, C. LLOYD	Husband of the 5th great-granddaughter
REDMAN, ALICE REGINA	8th great-granddaughter
REDMAN, ANITA KAY	8th great-granddaughter
REDMAN, BETTY LOU	8th great-granddaughter
REDMAN, CHRISTOPHER	9th great-grandson
REDMAN, DALE E.	7th great-grandson
REDMAN, JUDITH ANN	8th great-granddaughter
REDMAN, NANCY JANE	7th great-granddaughter
REDMAN, NATHAN RAY	9th great-granddaughter
REDMAN, NORMAN	7th great-grandson
REDMAN, ONDA LEE	8th great-granddaughter
REDMAN, RITA MAY	8th great-granddaughter
REDMAN, STEPHEN RAY	8th great-grandson
REDMAN, WILLIE E.	Husband of the 6th great-granddaughter
REED, ANTHONY ROBERT	9th great-grandson
REED, ASHLEY NICOLE	9th great-granddaughter
REED, BENJAMIN JOSEPH	9th great-grandson
REED, DEBORAH	8th great-granddaughter
REED, JEFFERY ALAN	9th great-grandson
REED, JUDITH ANN	Wife of the 7th great-grandson
REED, ROBERT	Husband of the 7th great-granddaughter
REED, WENDY MARIE	9th great-granddaughter
REINKE, ROBIN	Wife of the 9th great-grandson
RHOADES, DUANE	7th great-grandson
RHOADES, IVAN	Husband of the 6th great-granddaughter
RHOADES, NINA	7th great-granddaughter
RHOADES, NOVA	7th great-granddaughter

RIDER, HETTIE BELLE	Wife of the 6th great-grandson
RIENDEAU, BRIAN	8th great-grandson
RIENDEAU, CHRISTA	8th great-granddaughter
RIENDEAU, D. J.	Husband of the 7th great-granddaughter
RIFFE, CATHERINE	Wife of the 3rd great-grandson
RIFFELL, ALICE FAYE	7th great-granddaughter
RIFFELL, AOUDA F.	Wife of the 6th great-grandson
RIFFELL, JANET	Wife of the 7th great-grandson
RILEY, WILLARD	Husband of the 5th great-granddaughter
RIPPEY, MATHEW R.	Husband of the 4th great-granddaughter
RITTER, J. L.	Husband of the 6th great-granddaughter
RITTER, KARMEL L.	Wife of the 9th great-grandson
RIVERA, ANGELA	Wife of the 8th great-grandson
ROBBINS, DIANA	Wife of the 7th great-grandson
ROBERTS, EUGENE EARL	Husband of the 6th great-granddaughter
ROBERTS, KELLY	7th great-grandson
ROBIN	Wife of the 8th great-grandson
ROBNETT, BILLIE	Wife of the 5th great-grandson
ROGERS, ALLEN	Husband of the 7th great-granddaughter
ROGERS, CHAD	8th great-grandson
ROGERS, DURINDA	8th great-granddaughter
ROGERS, GENE	7th great-grandson
ROGERS, JAIME	8th great-granddaughter
ROGERS, MONTE	7th great-grandson
ROGERS, MR.	Husband of the 6th great-granddaughter
ROGERS, ROBERT	Husband of the 7th great-granddaughter
ROGERS, SHELLY KAY	8th great-granddaughter
ROOT, ARTHUR	Husband of the 6th great-granddaughter
ROSS, KATHERINE CLARINA	7th great-granddaughter
ROSS, KIMBERLY ELLEN	8th great-granddaughter
ROSS, LARRY THOMAS	7th great-grandson
ROSS, LAURA ANN	8th great-granddaughter
ROSS, SUSAN	Wife of the 4th great-grandson
ROSS, WILLIAM ARTHUR	7th great-grandson
ROSS, WILLIAM T.	Husband of the 6th great-granddaughter
ROSZEL, MR.	Husband of the 8th great-granddaughter
ROWAN, GEORGE	Husband of the 5th great-granddaughter
ROWE, DOUGLAS	8th great-grandson
ROWE, JEFFERY S.	8th great-grandson

SAMPSON, BRIAN ALLEN	10th great-grandson
SAMPSON, DANIEL LEE	9th great-grandson
SAMPSON, DANIEL LEE JR.	10th great-grandson
SAMPSON, DAVID BRYAN	9th great-grandson
SAMPSON, DEBRA SUE	9th great-granddaughter
SAMPSON, JAMES ALLEN	8th great-grandson
SAMPSON, JEANETTE MARIE	8th great-granddaughter
SAMPSON, JONATHON ROBERT	9th great-grandson
SAMPSON, JOSEPH PAUL	9th great-grandson
SAMPSON, LEO	Husband of the 7th great-granddaughter
SAMPSON, RANDY ALLEN	9th great-grandson
SAMPSON, RODNEY LEE	8th great-grandson
SAMPSON, SHERRI LYNN	9th great-granddaughter
SAMPSON, STACI LYNN	10th great-granddaughter
SAMPSON, STEVEN LEE	8th great-grandson
SAMPSON, THOMAS ALLEN	9th great-grandson
SAMS, BECKY	8th great-granddaughter
SAMS, KATHY	8th great-granddaughter
SAMS, VICKY	8th great-granddaughter
SAMS, WILLIAM	Husband of the 7th great-granddaughter
SARAH C.	Wife of the 3rd great-grandson
SARVER, ABIGAIL RAE	8th great-granddaughter
SARVER, JOSEPH ELI	8th great-grandson
SARVER, KELSEY JANE	8th great-granddaughter
SARVER, THOMAS	Husband of the 7th great-granddaughter
SCHEETS, JOHN R.	Husband of the 7th great-granddaughter
SCHEETS, JON	8th great-grandson
SCHEETS, JONATHON PATRICK	9th great-grandson
SCHEETS, JULIE RENAE	9th great-granddaughter
SCHEETS, LORI	8th great-granddaughter
SCHEETS, PATRICK	8th great-grandson
SCHELL, DAVID	Husband of the 8th great-granddaughter
SCHELL, PAUL	9th great-grandson
SCHELL, STEVEN	9th great-grandson
SCHIERMEYER, ALICIA	9th great-granddaughter
SCHIERMEYER, CHARLES ANTHONY	9th great-grandson
SCHIERMEYER, CHRISTINE	9th great-granddaughter

SCHIERMEYER, PATRICK	Husband of the 8th great-granddaughter
SCHILLING, DOUG	Husband of the 8th great-granddaughter
SCHILLING, JOSHUA CHRISTOPHER	9th great-grandson
SCHILLING, JUSTIN	9th great-grandson
SCHILLING, KENNETH	9th great-grandson
SCHIMMEL, BETTY	Wife of the 7th great-grandson
SCHNEIDER, DAVID	Husband of the 7th great-granddaughter
SCHNEIDER, JOHN ALLEN	8th great-grandson
SCHNEIDER, STACY LYNN	8th great-granddaughter
SCHWAIGER, DANIEL	7th great-grandson
SCHWAIGER, EUGENE CARL	Husband of the 6th great-granddaughter
SCHWAIGER, JACOB DANIEL	8th great-grandson
SCHWAIGER, KATILYN	8th great-granddaughter
SCHWAIGER, LINDA	7th great-granddaughter
SEILER, MARGARET	Wife of the 8th great-grandson
SELBY, ANDREW	Husband of the 2nd great-granddaughter
SELLERS, JOHN	Husband of the 3rd great-granddaughter
SHAFER, HERBERT EUGENE	6th great-grandson
SHAFER, JAMES EDWARD	6th great-grandson
SHAFER, JENNIFER	8th great-granddaughter
SHAFER, JOSEPH DAVID	6th great-grandson
SHAFER, JOSEPH DAVID	7th great-grandson
SHAFER, JUSTIN	8th great-grandson
SHAFER, RICHARD E.	7th great-grandson
SHAFER, RUTH	6th great-granddaughter
SHAFER, WILLIAM HENRY	Husband of the 5th great-granddaughter
SHANNON, CHRISTOPHER ADAM	8th great-grandson
SHANNON, NICHOLAS EDWARD	8th great-grandson
SHANNON, RICHARD SCOTT	8th great-grandson
SHANNON, RICKEY SCOTT	Husband of the 7th great-granddaughter
SHAPPIE, HENRY	Husband of the 6th great-granddaughter
SHARP, CYNTHIS	8th great-granddaughter
SHARP, MARY ALICE	Wife of the 7th great-grandson
SHARP, MAX	Husband of the 7th great-granddaughter
SHARP, RICKLIN	8th great-grandchild
SHARP, SUSAN DEE	8th great-granddaughter
SHAUM, CASSIDY LYN RUBLE	9th great-granddaughter
SHAUM, CYNTHIA JANE	8th great-granddaughter
SHAUM, ERNEST DUANE	8th great-grandson
SHAUM, GARY LOWELL	7th great-grandson

SHAUM, LEWIS DEAN	7th great-grandson
SHAUM, LOWELL	Husband of the 6th great-granddaughter
SHAUM, MICHAEL GARY	8th great-grandson
SHAUM, SARAH JANE	8th great-granddaughter
SHAUM, SHELLY DENISE	8th great-granddaughter
SHAW, JAMES	Husband of the 2nd great-granddaughter
SHAW, SHARON	Wife of the 8th great-grandson
SHEARER, AMANDA	Wife of the 4th great-grandson
SHELL, ELIZABETH	Wife of the great-grandson
SHELLABARGER, BONNIE	8th great-granddaughter
SHELLABARGER, LOUIS	Husband of the 7th great-granddaughter
SHELLABARGER, RANDALL	8th great-grandson
SHELLABARGER, ROGER	8th great-grandson
SHELLHAUS, CONNIE KAY	8th great-granddaughter
SHELLHAUS, DEBBIE	8th great-granddaughter
SHELLHAUS, KENNETH	Husband of the 7th great-granddaughter
SHELLHAUS, LEE ALAN	8th great-grandson
SHERRY, DANIEL BOONE	4th great-grandson
SHERRY, DAVID	Husband of the 3rd great-granddaughter
SHERRY, JOHN W.	4th great-grandson
SHERRY, MELISSA	4th great-granddaughter
SHERRY, SARAH LILLIS	4th great-granddaughter
SHERRY, WILLIAM PERRY	4th great-grandson
SHILLINGER, ADAM	Husband of the great-granddaughter
SHILLINGER, ELIZABETH	2nd great-granddaughter
SHILLINGER, JOHN GEORGE	2nd great-grandson
SHILLINGER, REBECCA	2nd great-granddaughter
SHOCKLEY, MR.	Husband of the 4th great-granddaughter
SHOENLEBEN, BETH ANN	9th great-granddaughter
SHOENLEBEN, BROOKE MARIE	9th great-granddaughter
SHOENLEBEN, STEVEN M.	Husband of the 8th great-granddaughter
SHONKWILLER, PEARL BLANCHE	Wife of the 5th great-grandson
SHORT, ABRAHAM	5th great-grandson
SHORT, ALLISON	5th great-granddaughter
SHORT, ALLISON	6th great-granddaughter
SHORT, ALSON	Husband of the 4th great-granddaughter
SHORT, CHARLES	5th great-grandson
SHORT, CORY	5th great-grandson
SHORT, IDA	5th great-granddaughter
SHORT, IVY DELL	5th great-granddaughter

SHORT, JASON	5th great-grandson
SHORT, LEONA	5th great-granddaughter
SHORT, MARTHA	6th great-grandchild
SHORT, MARTHA	5th great-granddaughter
SHORT, THOMAS	6th great-grandson
SHORT, THOMAS	5th great-grandson
SHORT, VIRGIL	5th great-grandson
SHORT, WILLIAM	Husband of the 4th great-granddaughter
SHORT, WILLIAM J.	5th great-grandson
SHOULTV, ABBIE M.	Wife of the 5th great-grandson
SHROVER, JACOB	Husband of the 2nd great-granddaughter
SHUFF, AUDRA	Wife of the 5th great-grandson
SIMMERMAN, HAROLD	Husband of the 8th great-granddaughter
SIMMERMAN, JEFFERY	9th great-grandson
SIMMONS, MR.	Husband of the 5th great-granddaughter
SIMONTON, PRISCILLA	Wife of the 2nd great-grandson
SINEV, SUE	Wife of the 8th great-grandson
SKILLEN, WILLIAM	Husband of the 2nd great-granddaughter
SMEDING, WILIMINA	Wife of the 4th great-grandson
SMITH, AUDREY	8th great-granddaughter
SMITH, CHRISTINE MARIE	8th great-granddaughter
SMITH, DONNA JEANNE	7th great-granddaughter
SMITH, ELIZABETH ANNE	9th great-granddaughter
SMITH, GARY LYNN	7th great-grandson
SMITH, GEORGE JACOB	Husband of the 6th great-granddaughter
SMITH, HENRY	Husband of the 3rd great-granddaughter
SMITH, HOMER	Husband of the 6th great-granddaughter
SMITH, JAKOB PAUL	9th great-grandson
SMITH, JAMES ALLAN	8th great-grandson
SMITH, JAMES BRADLY	8th great-grandson
SMITH, JAMES TRENTON	9th great-grandson
SMITH, JESSICA LYNN	9th great-granddaughter
SMITH, JODY LYNN	8th great-grandson
SMITH, JULIE NAN SMITH	9th great-granddaughter
SMITH, KENNETH LEE	8th great-grandson
SMITH, KENNETH LEO	7th great-grandson
SMITH, KENNETH WARD	7th great-grandson
SMITH, KIMBERLV LYNN	9th great-granddaughter
SMITH, KRYSENTHIA AUTUMN	9th great-granddaughter
SMITH, LESTER	Husband of the 6th great-granddaughter
SMITH, LORALEE GRACE	9th great-granddaughter
SMITH, MARK	Husband of the 8th great-granddaughter

SMITH, MICHAEL RAY	8th great-grandson
SMITH, NICHOLAS JACOB	8th great-grandson
SMITH, PHILLIP	Husband of the 7th great-granddaughter
SMITH, RUBY ELLEN	7th great-granddaughter
SMITH, RUSSELL	Husband of the 7th great-granddaughter
SMITH, STEPHANIE LEIGH	8th great-granddaughter
SMITH, TELCIE JO	9th great-granddaughter
SMITH, TRACY RENEE	8th great-grandson
SNOW, FLORENCE	Wife of the 6th great-grandson
SNYDER, DAVID OWEN	Husband of the 4th great-granddaughter
SNYDER, MARTHA BELL	5th great-granddaughter
SOVIS, ANTHONY DAVID	9th great-grandson
SOVIS, DAVID ANTHONY	Husband of the 8th great-granddaughter
SOVIS, STEPHEN JOSEPH	9th great-grandson
SPADE, MARY CATHERINE	Wife of the 4th great-grandson
SPAHR, RACHAEL	Wife of the 2nd great-grandson
SPARKS, ELLEN	Wife of the 2nd great-grandson
SPICER, JERRY ALAN	Husband of the 7th great-granddaughter
SPICER, KRISTIN SUZANNE	8th great-granddaughter
STACY	Wife of the 8th great-grandson
STANTZ, ALICE	Wife of the 7th great-grandson
STEPHENS, JAMES	Husband of the great-granddaughter
STEPHENS, JANE	Wife of the 7th great-grandson
STEPHENS, RICHARD JAY	8th great-grandson
STEPHENS, RONALD	Husband of the 7th great-granddaughter
STEPHENSON, ELIZABETH	Wife of the 3rd great-grandson
STEPHENSON, ISABELLA	Wife of the 3rd great-grandson
STEPHENSON, JANE	Wife of the 3rd great-grandson
STEPHENSON, LUCY	Wife of the 2nd great-grandson
STEWART, ELLEN	Wife of the 8th great-grandson
STICKLEY, CLAYTON SCOTT	9th great-grandson
STICKLEY, ROBERT SCOTT	Husband of the 8th great-granddaughter
STILES, ESTELLA ETHEL	Wife of the 5th great-grandson
STOCKER (FACHE), ENID LAREE	Wife of the 6th great-grandson
STOKER, MR.	Husband of the 5th great-granddaughter
STOKER, OLIVE	Wife of the 2nd great-grandson
STROBEL, AMY ELIZABETH	8th great-granddaughter
STROBEL, BRENT ALAN	8th great-grandson
STROBEL, BRIAN RICHARD	8th great-grandson

STROBEL, BRUCE CHARLES	8th great-grandson
STROBEL, CARL RICHARD	7th great-grandson
STROBEL, CARLA ANN	8th great-granddaughter
STROBEL, FLORENCE	7th great-granddaughter
STROBEL, KRISTEN HEATHER	9th great-granddaughter
STROBEL, LEE ANN MARIE	8th great-granddaughter
STROBEL, LEWIS	7th great-grandson
STROBEL, LOUIS HERMAN	Husband of the 6th great-granddaughter
STROBEL, LUTHER	7th great-grandson
STROBEL, MARY LOUISE	7th great-granddaughter
STROBEL, MATTHEW MICHAEL	9th great-grandson
STROBEL, MEGAN ELIZABETH	9th great-granddaughter
STROBEL, MICHAEL	8th great-grandson
STROBEL, NICHOLLE DAWN	9th great-granddaughter
STROBEL, STEVEN	8th great-grandson
STROHMEYER, HARRY J.	Husband of the 6th great-granddaughter
STRUKEL, ALBERT	Husband of the 6th great-granddaughter
STRUKEL, MICHAEL	7th great-grandson
STRUKEL, SANDRA	7th great-granddaughter
STUBBLES, HARRY	Husband of the 7th great-granddaughter
STUBBLES, SHARREN	8th great-granddaughter
STUBBS, ALAZANNAH	Wife of the 4th great-grandson
STUMP, DELBART	Husband of the 7th great-granddaughter
STUMP, KARLA KAY	Wife of the 7th great-grandson
STURM, MARY	Wife of the 6th great-grandson
SUSAN	Wife of the 4th great-grandson
SUTHERLAND, W.D.	Husband of the 4th great-granddaughter
SUTTON, RHONA	Wife of the 8th great-grandson
SWAILS, MALINDA	Wife of the 2nd great-grandson
SWANK, LINDA	Wife of the 7th great-grandson
SWEINHAGAN, AMBER NICOLE	8th great-granddaughter
SWEINHAGAN, JOHN ALEXANDER	Husband of the 7th great-granddaughter
SWEINHAGAN, THOMAS ALEXANDER	8th great-grandson
SWERKING, WILLARD	Husband of the 6th great-granddaughter
SWINGER, ELIZABETH	Wife of the 5th great-grandson
SWINNEY, MALINDA	Wife of the 2nd great-grandson
SWINNEY, SARAH	2nd Wife of the 2nd great-grandson
SWOB, GEORGE FRANKLIN	Husband of the 5th great-granddaughter
SWOB, JOHN	Husband of the 5th great-granddaughter
TAYLOR, BENJAMIN	Husband of the 2nd great-granddaughter
TEVIS, MR.	Husband of the 3rd great-granddaughter

THAYER, CHAD DALE	9th great-grandson
THAYER, CLAUDE	Husband of the 8th great-granddaughter
THAYER, JEREMY MATTHEW	9th great-grandson
THAYER, KIMBERLY JO	9th great-granddaughter
THIEBEAU, CHRISTINA MARIE	8th great-granddaughter
THIEBEAU, JANE ANN	8th great-granddaughter
THIEBEAU, JENNIFER	9th great-granddaughter
THIEBEAU, JERRY NICHOLAS	8th great-grandson
THIEBEAU, JOHN PAUL	Husband of the 7th great-granddaughter
THIEBEAU, JOHN PAUL WILLIAM	8th great-grandson
THIEBEAU, KATHERINE LOUISE	8th great-granddaughter
THIEBEAU, NICOLAS	9th great-grandson
THOMAS, DARINDA	Wife of the 2nd great-grandson
THOMPSON, ALBERT	Husband of the 6th great-granddaughter
THOMPSON, ALBERT JOSEPH	8th great-grandson
THOMPSON, BETTY LOU	7th great-granddaughter
THOMPSON, DALE EVERETT	7th great-grandson
THOMPSON, DELMAR LEROY	7th great-grandson
THOMPSON, DELOUISE KAY	8th great-granddaughter
THOMPSON, DOROTHY	Wife of the 7th great-grandson
THOMPSON, ESTHER ARLENE	7th great-granddaughter
THOMPSON, EVA	5th great-granddaughter
THOMPSON, HEATHER MARIE	10th great-granddaughter
THOMPSON, JAMES DALE	9th great-grandson
THOMPSON, JAMES JUDSON	10th great-grandson
THOMPSON, JONATHON	Husband of the 8th great-granddaughter
THOMPSON, JOSEPHINE	Wife of the 4th great-grandson
THOMPSON, MARGARET LOUISE	8th great-granddaughter
THOMPSON, MARILEE ANN	8th great-granddaughter
THOMPSON, MARRKUS JAY	9th great-grandson
THOMPSON, MICHAEL A.	Husband of the 9th great-granddaughter
THOMPSON, ROBERT LEE	7th great-grandson
THOMPSON, SANDRA LEE	8th great-granddaughter
THOMPSON, STEVEN JOSEPH	9th great-grandson
THOMPSON, TIMOTHY	8th great-grandson
THORNBURG, SHELDON	Husband of the 5th great-granddaughter
THORPE, MR.	Husband of the 7th great-granddaughter
TINGWALL, GEORGE T.	Husband of the 6th great-granddaughter
TISOR, C.C.	Husband of the 4th great-granddaughter

TODD, DAVID	Husband of the 8th great-granddaughter
TODD, JONATHON VINCENT	9th great-grandson
TODD, SARA MARIE	9th great-granddaughter
TOLBERT, BELLE (ISABELLE)	Wife of the 3rd great-grandson
TONEY, CYNTHIA MARIE	8th great-granddaughter
TONEY, ERIC	9th great-grandson
TONEY, HILTON A.	Husband of the 7th great-granddaughter
TONEY, RONALD HILTON	8th great-grandson
TONEY, SUSANNE CHRISTINE	8th great-granddaughter
TONEY, TARA	9th great-granddaughter
TOOMEY, JANICE	Wife of the 8th great-grandson
TOWER, PHYLLIS	Wife of the 8th great-grandson
TRICK, CHARLES EDWARD	Husband of the 5th great-granddaughter
TRICK, PERRY OTTO	6th great-grandson
TRICK, WELMA OPAL	6th great-granddaughter
TRIMBLE, DAVID	Husband of the 2nd great-granddaughter
TROST, NANCY	Wife of the 7th great-grandson
TROUTWINE, ETHEL LEOTA	6th great-granddaughter
TROUTWINE, IRA J.	6th great-grandson
TROUTWINE, OSCAR	Husband of the 5th great-granddaughter
TROWL, D.S.	Husband of the 5th great-granddaughter
TROWL, RUTH	6th great-granddaughter
TROWL, VARON E.	6th great-grandson
TRUEMAN, DOUG	Husband of the 8th great-granddaughter
TRUEMAN, TAMARA SUE	9th great-granddaughter
TRYDLE, BETTE	Wife of the 7th great-grandson
TUPICA, FREDERICK LEE	Husband of the 7th great-granddaughter
TUPICA, JOLE SUE	8th great-granddaughter
TUPICA, LYNN ANN	8th great-granddaughter
TUPICA, MICHAEL LEE	9th great-grandson
TUPICA, TONY LEE	8th great-grandson
TURNER, THOMAS P.	Husband of the 5th great-granddaughter
TYLER, MARTHA	Wife of the 3rd great-grandson
ULLERY, GLADYS GAIL	6th great-granddaughter
ULLERY, KESTON	6th great-grandson
ULLERY, MARY ELIZABETH	6th great-granddaughter
ULLERY, RISLEY O.	Husband of the 5th great-granddaughter
UNGER, ALLISON TAYLOR	9th great-granddaughter
UNGER, CRAIG DUANE	8th great-grandson
UNGER, KATHERINE JANELL	8th great-granddaughter
UNGER, KIMBERLY ANN	8th great-granddaughter

UNGER, LOWELL D.	Husband of the 7th great-granddaughter
UNKNOWN	Husband of the 3rd great-granddaughter
UNKNOWN	Husband of the great-granddaughter
VALENTINE, RUTH	Wife of the 6th great-grandson
VALERIE	Wife of the 7th great-grandson
VERARDI, ERIC	Husband of the 9th great-granddaughter
VICE, ASHLEY SUSANNE	9th great-granddaughter
VICE, BRANDON DAVID	9th great-grandson
VICE, DAVID	Husband of the 8th great-granddaughter
VOGEL, CHRISTY	9th great-granddaughter
VOGEL, GREG	Husband of the 8th great-granddaughter
VOGEL, RYAN	9th great-grandson
WAGNER, JEFFERY MICHAEL	Husband of the 7th great-granddaughter
WAGNER, JUSTIN HENRY	8th great-grandson
WAGNER, MEGAN LYNN	8th great-granddaughter
WAGNER, MICHAEL LEE	8th great-grandson
WALDREN, MARTIN	Husband of the 7th great-granddaughter
WALKER, BETTY	7th great-granddaughter
WALKER, CYNTHIA	Wife of the 2nd great-grandson
WALKER, DELORES	6th great-granddaughter
WALKER, EARL	6th great-grandson
WALKER, ELIZABETH MAE	6th great-granddaughter
WALKER, EVELYN	7th great-granddaughter
WALKER, HAROLD	6th great-grandson
WALKER, HAROLD GENE	7th great-granddaughter
WALKER, HOWARD	7th great-grandson
WALKER, JACK	7th great-grandson
WALKER, JAMES	7th great-grandson
WALKER, JUNE	7th great-granddaughter
WALKER, LARRY	7th great-grandson
WALKER, LARRY	7th great-grandson
WALKER, LINDA	7th great-granddaughter
WALKER, LOUISE	6th great-granddaughter
WALKER, MARGARET	6th great-granddaughter
WALKER, MARGARET	7th great-granddaughter
WALKER, MILLARD	6th great-grandson
WALKER, NORMA	7th great-granddaughter
WALKER, PHYLISS	7th great-granddaughter
WALKER, RAYMOND	6th great-grandson
WALKER, ROBERT	7th great-grandson
WALKER, RUTH	6th great-granddaughter
WALKER, SHIRLEY	7th great-granddaughter
WALKER, TERRY	8th great-grandson

WALKER, THOMAS	7th great-grandson
WALKER, TOILEY	6th great-granddaughter
WALKER, WARREN CLIFFORD	Husband of the 5th great-granddaughter
WALLACE, LOTTIE MAE	Wife of the 5th great-grandson
WALTER, CARL	Husband of the 5th great-granddaughter
WALTER, LUCILLE BERNICE	6th great-granddaughter
WARFEL, JOSIE	Wife of the 4th great-grandson
WARNER, BARBARA	8th great-granddaughter
WARNER, BRUCE	8th great-grandson
WARNER, CHARLES	Husband of the 6th great-granddaughter
WARNER, ELSIE	7th great-granddaughter
WARNER, GLENNA	7th great-granddaughter
WARNER, KAREN SUE	8th great-granddaughter
WARNER, LARRY ALLEN	8th great-grandson
WARNER, LAWRENCE RAYMOND	Husband of the 7th great-granddaughter
WARNER, MARK	8th great-grandson
WARNER, MARY	8th great-granddaughter
WARNER, NICKI	8th great-granddaughter
WARNER, RANDY	8th great-grandson
WARNER, RANDY	8th great-grandson
WARNER, RICHARD	7th great-grandson
WARNER, RICHARD	8th great-grandson
WARNER, ROBERT	7th great-grandson
WARNER, TODD PATRICK	9th great-grandson
WARNER, TRACY LYNN	9th great-granddaughter
WARREN, EVELYN	Wife of the 7th great-grandson
WATKINS, MARGARET	Wife of the 6th great-grandson
WATNE, TINA	Wife of the 8th great-grandson
WEATHERHEAD, BRUCE	Husband of the 7th great-granddaughter
WEAVER, CHARLOTTE	Wife of the 8th great-grandson
WEAVER, DAVID	8th great-grandson
WEAVER, JAMES	8th great-grandson
WEAVER, JULIA	8th great-granddaughter
WEAVER, MARY	Wife of the 4th great-grandson
WEAVER, RICHARD	Husband of the 7th great-granddaughter
WEBER, SHARON	Wife of the 8th great-grandson
WEHNER, DEBORAH	Wife of the 8th great-grandson
WEISENBERGER, HEIDI ANN	9th great-granddaughter
WEISENBERGER, KELLIE MARIE	9th great-granddaughter
WEISENBERGER, KENNETH R.	Husband of the 8th great-granddaughter

WEISEWNBERGER, MABEL	Wife of the 6th great-grandson
WELBAUM, BLUEFORD	6th great-grandson
WELBAUM, CARROL LESTER	6th great-grandson
WELBAUM, HAROLD W.	6th great-grandson
WELBAUM, IDA MAE	6th great-granddaughter
WELBAUM, INFANT	6th great-grandson
WELBAUM, JOHN	Husband of the 4th great-granddaughter
WELBAUM, LUCY	6th great-granddaughter
WELBAUM, MARTHA E.	5th great-granddaughter
WELBAUM, ORA FRANKLIN	6th great-grandson
WELBAUM, ORA HAROLD	7th great-grandson
WELBAUM, ORVILLE A.	5th great-grandson
WELBAUM, WASHINGTON TROY	5th great-grandson
WELBAUM, WILLIAM SHERIDAN	5th great-grandson
WELCH, SALLIE MUNDANIA	Wife of the 4th great-grandson
WERNER, RUTH	Wife of the 5th great-grandson
WESTFALL, LIBBIE	Wife of the 5th great-grandson
WHIPP, ANGELA	Wife of the 8th great-grandson
WHISLER, DAVID	7th great-grandson
WHISLER, HAROLD	Husband of the 6th great-granddaughter
WHITEAKER, CLAYTON LEON	Husband of the 7th great-granddaughter
WHITEAKER, KATHY	8th great-granddaughter
WHITEAKER, RICK	8th great-grandson
WHITEHEAD, SHIRLEY	Wife of the 7th great-grandson
WHITMARE, VIRGINIA	Wife of the 7th great-grandson
WICK, JOHN	Husband of the 4th great-granddaughter
WIFORD, MONA	Wife of the 7th great-grandson
WIGGINS, MARIAH	Wife of the 4th great-grandson
WILLAMS, BARBARA	Wife of the great-grandson
WILLIAMS, ABIGAIL CATHERINE	Wife of the 2nd great-grandson
WILLIAMS, FANNY	Wife of the great-grandson
WILLIAMS, TERRY JO	Wife of the 8th great-grandson
WILLS, AMY ELOISE	Wife of the 5th great-grandson
WILMOTH, LAURA	9th great-granddaughter
WILMOTH, RHONDA	9th great-granddaughter
WILMOTH, RICHARD	Husband of the 8th great-granddaughter
WILSON, LYDIA	Wife of the 2nd great-grandson
WINGLE, AMANDA JANE	9th great-granddaughter
WINGLE, CHRISTOPHER SCOTT	9th great-grandson
WINGLE, CRAIG	Husband of the 8th great-granddaughter

WINN, GOLDIE	Wife of the 5th great-grandson
WION, DOROTHY	Wife of the 6th great-grandson
WISEMAN, ELIZABETH	Wife of the 3rd great-grandson
WISEMAN, WILLIAM	Husband of the 3rd great-granddaughter
WOLF, MAX	Husband of the 7th great-granddaughter
WOLF, PHILLIP MAX	8th great-grandson
WOLFGRAM, SHARON M.	Wife of the 8th great-grandson
WOOLF, DAVID	Husband of the 8th great-granddaughter
WOOTEN, MARY ELLEN	Wife of the 4th great-grandson
WORTHINGTON, NINA	Wife of the 6th great-grandson
WRIGHT REED, LAVON	8th great-grandson
WRIGHT REED, REX	8th great-grandson
WRIGHT, ALICE JOSEPHINE	Wife of the 5th great-grandson
WRIGHT, ANDY	Husband of the 8th great-granddaughter
WRIGHT, JESSIE GRACE	Wife of the 5th great-grandson
WRIGHT, LAVON	Husband of the 7th great-granddaughter
YARIAN, DELORIS	Wife of the 8th great-grandson
YOUNCE, RUSSELL	Husband of the 6th great-granddaughter
YOUNG, ELIZABETH	Wife of the 2nd great-grandson
YOUNT, ALMA	5th great-granddaughter
YOUNT, ARLENE	6th great-granddaughter
YOUNT, DEWEY KENNETH	5th great-grandson
YOUNT, DOROTHY	6th great-granddaughter
YOUNT, DORSEY DOLPHUS	5th great-grandson
YOUNT, FLORIN E.	5th great-granddaughter
YOUNT, HENRY HALLICK	Husband of the 4th great-granddaughter
YOUNT, JAMES	6th great-grandson
YOUNT, JOHN	6th great-grandson
YOUNT, KEITH	6th great-grandson
YOUNT, KENNETH ELROY	6th great-grandson
YOUNT, LAURA	5th great-granddaughter
YOUNT, RUTH ANN	6th great-granddaughter
YOUNT, WILBUR METCALF	5th great-grandson

INDEX

1

DAVID 180, 210 RYAN MICHAEL 181,
210 SUSAN 181, 210 TOILA 122, 210
BURGESS, KAREN 197, 210
BURKETT, ESTHER 98, 210
BUSBAMKISH, VALERIE 195, 210
BUTT, BARBARY ANN 91, 210 CATHERINE
91, 99, 100, 210 CLEMENT 100, 210
EDWARD 101, 210 ELLEN 91, 210 FLORA
100, 210 GEORGE 91, 210 JACOB J.
91, 99, 100, 210 JOHN M. 91, 99,
101, 210 MARY JANE 91, 210 NATHAN
99, 210 RACHAEL 99, 100, 210
RACHAEL A. 91, 210 SARAH 91, 100,
210 THOMAS 91, 101, 210 WILLIAM
100, 210
CAIN, IONA P. 113, 210
CAINE, SAMUEL 104, 210
CAMPBELL, GEORGE M. 32, 210
CANAN, BRADLEY THOMAS 193, 210
RICHARD 193, 210
CANNON, MATILDA LAVINA 40, 210
CARLBERG, HELSHMAN 151, 211 IRVING
REINGHARD 133, 211 LEONARD R. 133,
151, 211 NANCY 133, 151, 152, 211
NORMAN 133, 211 SCOTT 151, 211
WILLIAM 151, 211
CARROLL RHONDA 177, 211
CASHMAN, ADA B. 109, 211
CASSADAY, DAVID 37, 211 JOHN 37,
211 ORA B. 37, 211 SARAH E. 37, 211
WILLIAM 37, 211
CHANEY, LEDA 169, 211
CHAPMAN, ROBERTA DIANE 151, 211
CHARPIOT, CLARA M. 112, 211
CHENOWITH ANGELA 148
CHOULYN, MARGARET 54
CHRISMAN, ROBERT 112, 211
CHRISTIAN, DOUG 42, 211
CHRISTINA (surname unknown) 150,
211
CLARK, CYNTHIA ANN 129, 130, 211
JEFFERY L. 186, 211 LUCY 108, 211
NANCY 35, 211 TERRY 185, 186, 211
VIRGIE 141, 211
CLAWSON, BEVERLY 147, 211 CECIL
ELSWORTH 113, 211 CHARLES EDWARD
113, 128, 211 CORA 101, 211 ELFA
MARCELLA 112, 211 ELIZA 97, 211

ELLA (EMMA ELLEN) 100, 211 FRANK
SILVESTER 113, 211 FRANK WILLIAM
101, 113, 211 FREDERICK 147, 211
FREDERICK A. 100, 112, 211 GARY
147, 211 GERTRUDE E. 101, 211 HELEN
113, 211 JAMES ELLIS 100, 211
LUCILLE MAE 113, 211 LUCINDA 113,
211 MARY 96, 212 MAURICE F. 128,
147, 212 NATHAN 100, 212 OPAL
FRANCES 113, 212 PEARL MARIE 112,
212 RACHEL ANN 113, 212 RALPH F.
113, 212 RICHARD 128, 147, 212
SARAH J. 92, 93, 212 SARAH JANE
101, 212 VERNISHES EMORY 113, 212
WALDO 113, 212 WILLIAM G. 100, 212
WILLIAM PETER 113, 212 WILMA IRENE
113, 212
CLAYTON, MR. 103, 212
CLYLOR, CHARLYNE RAE 193, 212
COATE, WILLIAM 106, 212
COLLIER, ADELAIDE 114, 212
COMPTON, PEGGY SUE 149, 212
COOK, CARL 143, 212 FRANK 110, 212
PHYLISS 143, 173, 212 SUSAN 96, 97,
212
COOPER, AUDREY ALBERTA 43, 212
DOROTHY 42, 43, 44, 212 EDWARD DODD
42, 43, 212 ELIZABETH BLUME 42, 212
HARRY 42, 212 MARY BELL 43, 212
MARY LOUISE 42, 43, 212 MARY
VIRGINIA 43, 212 RUTH LEY   43,
212 WILLIAM ANDREW 42, 212 WILLIAM
MOSS 42, 43, 212
COPPS, DEBORAH KAY 178, 212
COVAULT, JAMES 142, 212 SANDRA 142,
212
COVULT, CLARENCE CLYDE 145, 212
LOIS V.146, 212
CRAWFORD, CARL STEPHEN 148, 213
HELEN 163, 213
CREMEANS, CORA ADAMS 166, 213
CRENSHAW, JOHN ALLEN 42, 213
CRESS, BERT SAMUEL 108, 213 BLANCHE
108, 213 CAROLYN 121, 213 CHARLES
FORREST 107, 213 CLARA 108, 213
CLARENCE C. 108, 121, 213 DESSIE
MAE 108, 121, 213 DEWEY 108, 121,
213 EDNA R. 107, 120, 213 EDWIN

GRIFFITH, ROY 104, 219
GRIFFUS, CLAUDIA 183, 219
GRISE, ALMA 109, 219 CARL 124, 219
CORA 108, 219 CORDA ACHIE 108, 122,
219 CORDELIA 124, 219 EARL 109, 219
ELI C.109, 125, 219 ESTHER ANN 108,
122, 219 ETOILE 124, 143, 219 GAIL
143, 174, 219 GROVER 109, 124, 219
HARVEY DAVID 124, 143, 219 HELEN
IRENE 124, 143, 219 JENNIFER LYNN
174, 219 KERRI MARIE 174, 219 LAURA
JANE 108, 123, 219 LILLIE FLORENCE
108, 124, 219 LOVA CATHERINE 108,
123, 219 MARION 124, 219 MYRON 124,
219 NORMA 124, 219 PATRICK 143,
174, 219 PETER SANGLETON 108, 219
RICHARD 125, 143, 219 ROBERT 124,
219 RUBEN 109, 124, 219 SAMANTHA
108, 121, 122, 219 SANDRA 144, 174,
220 SHERYL 143, 174, 220
GROFF, JUDY 165, 220
HAFER, SHARON 154, 220
HAGAN, GREGORY ALAN 155, 220
JEFFREY 155, 220 KASEY 155, 220
MELODY LYNN 155, 220
HALE, MICHAEL 18, 220
HALL, REUBEN 28, 220
HALSTEAD, EMILY A. 19, 220 JOHN 17,
220 RHODA 19, 220 SARAH 18, 220
HAM, BRICE W. 37, 220 CARRIE 37,
220 CHLOE 37, 220 JAMES L. 37, 220
JESSIE B. 37, 220
HAMILTON, ANDREW LEE 189, 220 ANNA
LOUISE 64, 189, 220 AUSTIN TYLER
189, 220 BRYCE JACOB 189, 220
CLAIRE MACKENZIE 189, 220 DUANE
164, 189, 220 ELDEAN 164, 220
HANCOCK, MR. 103, 220
HANKINS, RICHARD LEWIS 182, 220
SHERRI 182, 220
HARLACHER, ELMER 105, 106, 220
LETHA 106, 220
HARSHBARGER, MINNIE C. 92, 220
CATHERINE 98, 220
HARTMAN, MARY 184, 220
HARVEY, HENRY 18, 220 LORENZO 18,
220 MILLIE 18, 220 MR. 17, 220

NANCY 18, 220 SARAH 22, 220 WILLIAM
102, 220
HATFIELD, ANDREW JR.57, 220 PENNY
176, 220
HAUGH, JOSEPH MICHAEL 196, 221
HAWYER, GEORGE W. 33, 221
HAZELBAKER, ANDREW 80, 221 ANDREW
JACKSON91, 221 DANIEL 80, 221
HECATHORN, OPAL 138, 221
HEISEL, FLORENCE M. 131, 134, 135,
221
HEISEY, ANNA 136, 221
HEITKAMP, ANDREW 190, 221 CHARLES
190, 221 KATHERYN MARIE 190, 221
HELEN (surname unknown) 118, 221
HELLER, HENRIETTA 110, 111, 221
HELMKE, LYNN ADELE 166, 221
HERMAN, ELIZABETH 54, 221 GEORGE
CHARLES 54, 221 MARIA ELIZABETH 26,
54, 221 PETER (HANCE) 54, 221
PHILIPPINA 54, 221
HERRON, NELLIE LOURIE116, 221
HESSE, IDA MARIA 36, 221
HESTER, MR. 104, 221
HETZLER, GEORGE 110, 221
HILE, THEDA 157, 221
HILL, CONIE EILEEN 162, 185, 221
EMILY 198, 221 GARY EUGENE 162, 221
GLENNA MAE138, 162, 221 KAREN LYNN
185, 198, 221 KENNETH 138, 162, 221
MEGAN SUE 198, 221 NANCY KAY 185,
221 NATHANIEL THOMAS 198, 221
THOMAS 138, 221 THOMAS JAMES 162,
184, 185, 221 THOMAS LOWELL 185,
198, 221
HINDS, SARAH JANE (JENNIE) 102, 221
HINGE, SHIRLEY 135, 221
HISSONG, HELEN 143, 221
HITE, CARL 118, 221
HOGG, MICHAEL 187, 222 WHITNEY NOEL
187, 222
HOLDREN, MARY ELIZABETH 175, 222
ROGER 152, 222 TOMMIE RAY 152, 222
HOLE, CORDELLA BELLE 126, 146, 222
HAZEL ESTHER 126, 145, 222 JOHN
LEWIS 126, 222 LARKEN 126, 222
HOLEBEK, GEORGEANNNA 160, 222
HONEYMAN, MARGARET 121, 222

HORNER, DAVID 166, 222 DONNA 139, 165, 222 H. DEAN 139, 165, 222 HARRY 139, 222 HERMAN 139, 166, 222 SCOTT 165, 190, 191, 222 SHERRY 165, 190, 222 THEODORE B. 96, 222 WILLIAM LEE 191, 222

HORTON, ISAAC HOMER 103, 222 TERRY 186, 222

HOUCHINS, JOHN 19, 222

HOUSE, MARY ANN 80, 222

HOUSER, MR. 137, 222

HOWELL, SUSAN 143, 222

HUBERT, AMY 184, 222

HUDELSON, ANGELA MARIE 189, 222 DENNIS 189, 222 MELISSA ANN 189, 222

HUGHES, GRETCHEN MARIE 161, 222 LUCINDA T. 97, 222

HUMPHREYS, MR. 157, 222 NANCY W. 21, 222

HUNT, CHARLES 41, 222 ELIZABETH 41, 222 JERRY 41, 222 JOHN E. 41, 222 JOSEPH 40, 41, 222 LENOX 41, 222 MINNIE 41, 222 WILLIAM 41, 222

HUNTER, GLADYS 114, 223

IMWALLE, HONDO LOUIS 193, 223

INDERRIEDEN, MR. 113, 223

IRVIN, RACHAEL 29, 223

IRWIN, (ERWINE), REBECCA JANE 93, 223

ISHMAEL, ARMILDA 38, 223 BENJAMIN L. 37, 38, 223 JOSEPHUS 38, 223 MILDRED 38, 223 OLIVER 38, 223

JANE (surname unknown) 110, 223

JEFFERS, LOUNIE SUE 147, 223

JENKINS, LYDIA 26, 223

JENNIFER (surname unknown) 172, 223

JENSEN, AARON 148, 223 ANDREW LOUIS 148, 223 KENNETH ANDREW 148, 223

JOHNS, RACHAEL ARENA 29, 223

JOHNSON, ANDREA S. 157, 223 CAROLL 157, 223 CHALMER EDWARD 136, 157, 223 CHARLES DALE 136, 156, 223 GARY 157, 223 JACK 136, 157, 223 JAMES L. 136, 223 JAY 136, 157, 223 JAYNIE 157, 223 JENA 156, 223 JOANN 156, 223 KELLIE H. 157, 223 KERI KAY 178, 223 MAC 136, 157, 223

PENNY 156, 223 PHYLLIS 136, 157, 158, 223 ROBERT 157, 178, 223 ROBERT JR. 178, 223 RONNIE 156, 223 RUBY 136, 223 STEPHANIE 157, 223 STEVE 157, 223 VALERIE D. 157, 223

JOHNSTON, ROSALYN MARIE 129, 224

JONES, BARBERRY 28, 224 CAROL 133, 152, 224 CHERRIE J. 154, 224 COURTNEY 178, 224 DIANA SUE 134, 224 DONALD R. 119, 133, 224 DOROTHY GLADYS 119, 134, 224 EDWARD 133, 224 ELIZABETH 27, 28, 224 ELSIE CORDA 136, 158, 224 ERNEST E. 119, 133, 224 EUGENE 122, 224 ICENA J. 154, 224 JACK 133, 224 JOHN E. 134, 154, 224 KATHIE 133, 224 KATHRYN 103, 224 LANCE DARREL 119, 134, 224 LAURA 122, 136, 224 LINDA KATHLEEN 133, 152, 224 LOMA IRENE 119, 133, 224 MARGORIE 133, 224 MARK RICHARD 153, 178, 224 PAUL E. 119, 134, 224 PERRY 122, 136, 224 RACHEL 136, 158, 224 ROBERT LANCE 153, 224 ROBIN 154, 224 RONALD 133, 224 RUTH ANN 134, 153, 224 SALLY ANN 133, 152, 224 SARA JANE 134, 153, 154, 224 STEPHEN D. 134, 153, 224 TOMMIE J. 154, 224 TRENTON 178, 224 WALTER 119, 224

KALSHIAN, ALICE 162, 224

KASPRAZAK, HARRY K. 152, 153, 224 HEATHER RENEE 154, 224 JASON TODD 154, 224

KEAGLE, THOMAS 118, 224

KEATON, JANE 19, 224 LUCY 19, 224

KELLER, BRANDON 176, 225 DARIN 176, 225 LYNN 145, 176, 225 MELVIN 145, 225

KELLY, DONALD 121, 225 DUANE 121, 225 EDITH 165, 225 JOSEPH 121, 225 MAX 121, 225

KENWORTHY, CELESTE MARIE 190, 225 JOSHUA DAVID 190, 225 SHANE 190, 225 SHANIA CARLENE 190, 225

KESSINGER, MARY 17, 225

KESSLER, CARL WILLIAM 146, 225
DOLLIE 121, 225 MICHAEL MADISON 98,
225 THOMAS 146, 225
KIDDER, ELIZABETH 153, 225
KIENITZ, ADAM TROY 161, 183, 225
ALAN JAY 161, 225 ALEXANDER STEVEN
183, 225 CAITLYN 183, 225 GAGE
TYLER 183, 225 GERALD 161, 225
JERRY TODD 161, 183, 225 KELLY LYNN
183, 225 KERSTIE ROSE 183, 225
LINDSEY ELAINE 183, 225 PATRICK
GERALD 161, 225 SALLY JO 161, 183,
225 STEVEN KENT 161, 183, 225
KING, DWIGHT 124, 225 MARY ELLEN
39, 225
KINNY, ROBERT 114, 225
KIRBY, ANN 159, 225
KISNER, ELIZABETH 125, 225
KITE, DAVID 58, 225
KNIGHT, ELLA 41, 225
KNOFF, ELIZABETH ANN 44, 225 GERALD
E. 44, 225 SARA LOUISE 44, 225
WILLIAM COOPER 44, 226
KNOUFF, ARTHUR BURDETTE 129, 226
KONZ, CHARLES 141, 171, 226 DEBRA
171, 226 DONALD 141, 226 MARVIN
141, 226 MICHAEL 171, 226 RICHARD
141, 226 RITA 141, 171, 226 TAMMIE
171, 226
KORRECKI, AMY 152, 226 BONNIE 152,
226 CINDY 152, 226 DIANE 152, 226
DON 151, 152, 226
KREMER, ANN 191, 226
KUHLMAN, MYRTLE P. 163, 226
KULP, DEBORAH 142, 226 DIANE 142,
226 MICHAEL 142, 226 PATRICK 142,
226
KURTZ, NANCY 194, 226
KUSSMAN, MARTHA 135, 226
LANE, WILLIAM CLYDE 168, 226
LARSON, GEORGE 174, 226 GEORGE
ROCHELLE 174, 226 MIRANDA 174, 226
LASHER, ELIZABETH ANN 186, 226
EMILY LOUISE 186, 226 JASON DAVID
186, 226 JOHN 186, 226
LAWSON, LINDA SUE 195, 226
LEIS, SOPHIA ADALINE 127, 226
LEMASTER, ANGELA KAY 168, 226

LEONARD, CORA ALICE 41, 226
LESHER, ROBERT RAY 110, 226
LEY, LILLIAN RUTH 43, 226
LIGHTNER, DONALD VINCENT 187, 226
ELIZABETH NICOLE 187, 226 MELISSA
MICHELLE 187, 226
LINDQUIST, MARY 114, 226
LINK, CHRISTINE 173, 227 GALE 173,
227 JACK 173, 227 MARVIN 173, 227
LINVILLE, EARL BERNARD 127, 227
LONG, CHARLES 18, 119, 227 LISA
191, 227 RICHARD 119, 227 SANDRA
173, 174, 227 VIRGIL 119, 227
LORING, KATHLEEN 178, 227
LOUNSBURG, CLIFFORD 116, 227 GERALD
116, 227 ROLAND 116, 227 VERNA 116,
227
LOVEJOY, SHEILA KAY 156, 227
MACHELAN, GEORGE W. 30, 227
MADDRY, WILLIAM 16, 227
MADDY, JACKSON 19, 227 JOHN C. 17,
227 MARY 17, 227
MAGATO, RHONDA 191, 227
MAGGIE (surname unknown) 118, 227
MAHAN, WILLIAM O. 102, 227
MANIX, TISH 166, 227
MANN, ABEL 98, 227 ABRAHAM L. 35,
102, 227 ADAM 16, 17, 18, 20, 22,
227 ADDISON 22, 227 ALBERT 21, 227
ALEXANDER 18, 227 ALICE MAE 116,
129, 227 ALLEN M. 35, 227 ALONZO
LEE 36, 227 AMANDA 20, 34, 228
AMELIA A. 31, 228 AMOS 28, 33, 34,
228 ANDREW 19, 228 ANDREW J. 93,
228 ANDREW JACKSON 36, 41, 228
ANGELINE 33, 228 ANN E. 35, 228
ANNA 96, 228 ANNA MARIA 12, 228
ANNIE 19, 22, 228 ANNIE H. 22, 228
ANNY 28, 228 ARCHIBALD 18, 228 ARLA
LOGAN 41, 228 ARMILDA 35, 36, 228
ARMILDA J. 35, 228 ARTHUR A. 39,
228 ASA A. 97, 228 AUSTIN 18, 31,
35, 228 BABY 41, 228 BABY BOY 39,
97, 102, 103, 113, 130, 228 BABY
GIRL 102, 228 BARBARA J. 33, 228
BENJAMIN F. 20, 22, 228 BERTHA
ALVILDA 96, 228 BERTHA JAUNITA 40,
228 BERTHA L. 102, 228 BETTY JEANNE

RIENDEAU, BRIAN 155, 244 CHRISTA
155, 244 D. J. 155, 244
RIFFE, CATHERINE 19, 244
RIFFELL, ALICE FAYE 138, 162, 244
AOUDA F. 138, 244 JANET 167, 244
RILEY, WILLARD 104, 244
RIPPEY, MATHEW R. 91, 244
RITTER, J.L. 114, 244 KARMEL L.
198, 244
RIVERA, ANGELA 178, 244
ROBBINS, DIANA 167, 168, 244
ROBERTS, EUGENE EARL 129, 244 KELLY
129, 244
ROBIN (surname unknown) 172, 244
ROBNETT, BILLIE 107, 244
ROGERS, ALLEN 168, 244 CHAD 156,
244 DURINDA 168, 193, 244 GENE 135,
155, 156, 244 JAIME 156, 244 MONTE
135, 244 MR. 135, 244 SHELLY KAY
168, 244
ROOT, ARTHUR 123, 244
ROSS, KATHERINE CLARINA 132, 244
KIMBERLY ELLEN 151, 244 LARRY
THOMAS 132, 151, 244 SUSAN 91, 244
WILLIAM ARTHUR 132, 244 WILLIAM T.
132, 244
ROSZEL, MR. 157, 244
ROWAN, GEORGE 39, 244
ROWE, DOUGLAS 150, 244 JEFFERY S.
150, 244 MR. 150, 244
SAMPSON, BRIAN ALLEN 197, 245
DANIEL LEE 179, 197, 245 DANIEL LEE
JR. 197, 245 DAVID BRYAN 180, 245
DEBRA SUE 180, 197, 245 JAMES ALLEN
158, 179, 180, 245 JEANETTE MARIE
159, 180, 245 JONATHON ROBERT 180,
245 JOSEPH PAUL 180, 245 LEO 158,
245 RANDY ALLEN 180, 197, 245
SHERRI LYNN 179, 245 STACI LYNN
197, 245 STEVEN LEE 159, 180, 245
THOMAS ALLEN 180, 245
SAMS, BECKY 169, 245 KATHY 169, 245
VICKY 169, 245 WILLIAM 169, 245
SARAH, (surname unknown) 38, 245
SARVER, ABIGAIL RAE 174, 245 JOSEPH
ELI 174, 245 KELSEY JANE 174, 245
THOMAS 174, 245

SCHEETS, JOHN R. 154, 245 JON 154,
245 JONATHON PATRICK 178, 245 JULIE
RENAE 178, 245 LORI 154, 245
PATRICK 154, 178, 245
SCHELL, DAVID 194, 245 ELIZABETH
65, 245 PAUL 194, 245 STEVEN 194,
245
SCHIERMEYER, ALICIA 179, 245
CHARLES ANTHONY 179, 245 CHRISTINE
179, 245 PATRICK 179, 246
SCHILLING, DOUG 188, 246 JOSHUA
CHRISTOPHER 188, 246 JUSTIN 188,
246 KENNETH 188, 246 BETTY 172, 246
SCHNEIDER, DAVID 149, 246 JOHN
ALLEN 149, 246 STACY LYNN 149, 246
SCHWAIGER, DANIEL 130, 150, 246
EUGENE CARL 130, 246 JACOB DANIEL
150, 246 KATILYN 150, 246 LINDA
130, 246
SEILER, MARGARET 187, 246
SELBY, ANDREW 79, 246
SELLERS, JOHN 80, 246
SHAFER, HERBERT EUGENE 125, 246
JAMES EDWARD 125, 246 JENNIFER 176,
246 JOSEPH DAVID 125, 144, 176, 246
JUSTIN 176, 246 RICHARD E. 144, 246
RUTH 125, 144, 246 WILLIAM HENRY
125, 246
SHANNON, CHRISTOPHER ADAM 149, 246
NICHOLAS EDWARD 149, 246 RICHARD
SCOTT 149, 246 RICKEY SCOTT 149,
246
SHAPPIE, HENRY 113, 246
SHARP, CYNTHIA 169, 246 MARY ALICE
163, 246 MAX 169, 246 RICKLIN 169,
246 SUSAN DEE 169, 246
SHAUM, CASSIDY LYN RUBLE 178, 246
CYNTHIA JANE 156, 246 ERNEST DUANE
156, 246 GARY LOWELL 136, 156, 246
LEWIS DEAN 136, 156, 247 LOWELL
136, 247 MICHAEL GARY 156, 178, 247
SARAH JANE 156, 247 SHELLY DENISE
156, 247
SHAW, JAMES 28, 247 SHARON 189, 247
SHEARER, AMANDA 108, 247
SHELL, ELIZABETH 65, 79, 247

www.ingramcontent.com/pod-product-compliance
Lightning Source LLC
Chambersburg PA
CBHW080233270326
41926CB00020B/4223